THE HUMAN BEING AS BODY AND SOUL

IN RELATION TO THE COSMOS

THE HUMAN BEING AS BODY AND SOUL IN RELATION TO THE COSMOS

HUMAN EVOLUTION AND THE SOUL AND SPIRIT OF THE UNIVERSE, PART I

Thirteen lectures given in Stuttgart, Bern and Dornach,
16 June to 17 July 1921

TRANSLATED AND INTRODUCED BY WILLIAM FORWARD

RUDOLF STEINER

RUDOLF STEINER PRESS

CW 205

Rudolf Steiner Press
Hillside House, The Square
Forest Row, RH18 5ES

www.rudolfsteinerpress.com

Published by Rudolf Steiner Press 2025

Originally published in German under the title *Der Mensch in Zusammenhang mit dem Kosmos 5: Menschenwerden, Weltenseele und Weltengeist—Erster Teil: Der Mensch als leiblich-seelische Wesenheit in seinem Verhältnis zur Welt* (volume 205 in the *Rudolf Steiner Gesamtausgabe* or Collected Works) by Rudolf Steiner Verlag, Dornach. Based on shorthand notes that were not reviewed or revised by the speaker. This authorized translation is based on the third German edition (2016), edited by Johann Waeger und Hendrik Knobel

Published by permission of the Rudolf Steiner Nachlassverwaltung, Dornach

© Rudolf Steiner Nachlassverwaltung, Dornach, Rudolf Steiner Verlag 2016

This translation © Rudolf Steiner Press 2025

A catalogue record for this book is available from the British Library

ISBN 978 1 85584 672 2

Cover by Morgan Creative
Typeset by Symbiosys Technologies, Visakhapatnam, India
Printed and bound by 4Edge Ltd., Essex

Contents

Lecture 1
Stuttgart, 16 June 1921

Our human soul and spirit in relation to the phenomena of the cosmos. Three levels of our soul life: hallucination as a delusion with no basis in reality; fantasy as the creative source of artistry; Imagination as the image of a spiritual reality. Our physical body as an image of our pre-birthly life in the spirit. Preparation in the second half of life for returning to a spiritual existence after death. Our soul as mediator. The power of our thought life as an echo of our pre-birth experience; developed to a higher stage it becomes Imagination; inappropriately applied, it produces hallucination. A hallmark of our time: the inclination towards untruth. Opposition to anthroposophy.

Lecture 2
Bern, 28 June 1921

The human being as a moral being in the cosmos. Successes and unjustified hypotheses of natural science. The dichotomy of thinking and feeling. Our chemical elements. The four elements in pre-Socratic Greek culture: earth, water, air and fire which encompass matter, life, soul and spirit. The power of abstraction, a spirit of unreality The bridge between the moral and the natural worlds. Einstein. Divine spiritual beings as the concrete foundations of the natural world around us. The risk we face of losing our eternal nature as a result of brain-bound thinking. The Christ spirit overcoming the ahrimanization of the earth.

Lecture 3
Dornach, 24 June 1921

Our dependence and independence of the world around us as human beings. The laws at work within the earthly world, the cosmos, the cosmic soul and the cosmic spirit. The worlds of minerals, plants, animals and human beings. Our surroundings within space and beyond space. The educated Greek and the living element of water. Today's natural science and its dead elements. Materialism as a necessary phase in human development towards freedom. Our journey back through Imagination to the element of water, through Inspiration to the element of air and through Intuition to the element of fire.

Pages 37-51

LECTURE 4
DORNACH, 26 JUNE 1921

The complete human being: composed of solid, fluid, aeriform elements and the element of warmth. The unconscious sleeping human being beyond the earth and the cosmos. The laws governing cosmic soul and cosmic spirit. Rhythm appears in space, but its origin lies beyond the world of the senses. The relationship of the airy element to time. Hexameter. The rhythms in our breathing and pulse. The consciously sleeping human being. Images arising outside our body out of which the forms of animals take shape in space. The logic of the outer forms of animals, spiritualized in the human being. The interplay of our thought activity and the experience of our senses. The essential, eternal human being in the element of warmth or fire. Overcoming time. Body-free consciousness delving into other beings. Pre-birthly existence and an egotistic attitude to immortality; knowledge imbued with morality and free of egotism.

Pages 52-62

LECTURE 5
DORNACH, 1 JULY 1921

The true nature of hallucination out of which we are born into this world as physical beings. How hallucination occurs normally between birth and death in the form of unconscious Imaginations whose forces build up and renew our organism each day. Its abnormal occurrence in the form of subjective soul experiences squeezed into consciousness out of our organs. Mystical poetry; Mechthild von Magdeburg; Saint Teresa. The forming of our organs. How our physical nature is connected with the cosmos. The chaos of living matter. The embryo, an earthly substance withdrawn from crystallizing forces and devoted to cosmic forces, giving form to our etheric and astral bodies in the ovum. The hen's egg as an imprint of the cosmos; the three dimensions of space. The power of our intellect as an image of our pre-birth existence in the spirit; today's culture of abstract images depends on it. Shutting out the sense impressions in our thinking while living in our image culture can lead us to Imagination; thoughts rising out of our body bringing hallucinations into our consciousness; thinking with our feelings, generating fantasy. The question of freedom.

Pages 63-75

LECTURE 6

DORNACH, 2 JULY 1921

The formative forces of our physical body metamorphose as they reach across from one life into the next. Spiritual beings at work behind the experiences of our senses. Contemplating the material substance within us. The surfaces of our organs as reflective instruments for our soul life, appearing in our consciousness as memories. Latent forces stored within our organs and working as formative forces in life between death and rebirth. How our liver, lungs, kidneys and heart work towards the formation of our head and its future capacities: memory, habit, temperament, pangs of conscience, moral strength. Premature manifestations: obsessive thoughts, visions, hallucinations, emotional disturbances, depression. Our mother determines the configuration of our astral and etheric bodies in the next incarnation, our father determines our physical body and I. The interrelationship of our organs and our surroundings. Illnesses, symptoms, diagnosis and therapy. Therapeutic insights by means of genuine mysticism. The law of conservation of energy contrasted with 'Heaven and earth shall pass away, but my word shall not pass away'.

LECTURE 7

DORNACH, 3 JULY 1921

Two riddles for everyday consciousness: the outer world hidden behind the veil of the senses and the inner world of our human organs. Normal and abnormal discontinuity of consciousness. Occult vision, free of memory. Our capacity for remembering and for loving between birth and death. Transformation of our thoughts into images after death. Growth of our soul from Imagination via Inspiration to Intuition. Then its return after the world Midnight Hour to Imagination saturated with will before rebirth. The activity of our will in the metabolic and limb system hidden from consciousness. Judgement and logical conclusions. Thinking, perceiving and remembering are all conscious. Our will and our disposition work their way up from the unconscious. Lucifer targets our will, Ahriman targets our thinking. Ahriman's goal: heaven and earth must not pass away! The fixed nature of materialistic thoughts. Atomism as an obsessive thought. Atrophy of the brain. Countermeasures: bringing abstract concepts into image form, individualizing our thoughts by means of our will. Cultural perspectives: having lost consciousness of the spirit, the awareness of our soul will also be lost. Future tendencies: raising children not by education but by the injection of equivalent substances. Edison's business practices. Anthroposophy as a cultivation of the whole human being.

and sense impressions. Our saturation with a sense of self during life after death. Hunger for non-existence prior to birth. Being born into Maya, into the world of phenomena as images. Possibility of freedom. Loss of sense of gravity. Risks to immortality. New education towards a sense of self. Exertion required to grasp weighty concepts from spiritual science. Imbuing ourselves with forces that can overcome death. Working towards the power of Christ.

LECTURE 11
DORNACH, 15 JULY 1921

Two poles in our soul life: the element of thinking and the element of willing. Thinking relates to the past, willing to the future. Origin of our thinking forces in our pre-birth life and its loss; development of our will forces and their transition into life after death. The reality of our senses and the illusion of atomism. The veil of the senses can be grasped by the logic of thinking because it originates in the past. Natural science. The present can be experienced as fluctuating images by means of Imaginations. Self-created images leading to higher Imagination. Insight into life before birth. Desire as the foundation of will, in contrast with 'satiation' as the foundation of thinking. Matter: spiritualized by Lucifer, hardened by Ahriman. Perception by means of the senses, reflection by means of thinking. Duality of good and evil, God and the devil as an error. An earlier view: Ormuzd and Ahriman. The Muspilli poem. Task of our time: recovery of the Trinity with Christ in the middle.

LECTURE 12
DORNACH, 16 JULY 1921

Polarity of the luciferic and ahrimanic principles; impulses within the development process in the cosmos. The bird kingdom within the cosmic order; the egg shape. Opposing forces inside and outside the egg. The calcareous shell, the coat of feathers. Mammals tied to the earth. The human being: luciferic and ahrimanic influences in our development and formation. The I in outer perception and movement of our limbs. Determination and freedom within the threefold human being; illness arising from wrong behaviour. Clouds of insects as an Imaginative picture of how our I experiences the world around us. The opposite: our I living within forms which it has created out of itself.

INTRODUCTION

Wᴴᴇɴ Rudolf Steiner gave this course of thirteen lectures in the summer of 1921 he was continuing his intensive work on cultural renewal, including the uphill battle for a threefold social order. This had started towards the end of the First World War when in March 1917 he gave a public lecture entitled 'The threefold nature of the human being' and later in the summer of that year wrote two documents titled *Memoranda* which spoke of the threefold nature of the social organism. The thrust of his argument was that if our social order was to be adequate for us it would have to reflect our threefold nature. This would translate as freedom in our cultural life, equality in our political life and fraternity in our economic relations. These three areas would be integrated, interdependent, but also organized independently.

Despite every effort being made, addressing leadership and grassroots representatives of society, the initiative did not succeed. However, it bore fruit in another initiative, namely the founding of the first Waldorf School in Stuttgart in the autumn of 1919. A century later, it has become the largest independent school movement in the world, with more than 1200 independent schools and nearly 2000 kindergartens in 75 countries, as well as more than 500 centres for special education in more than 40 countries. A salient characteristic of this educational impulse is its recognition of the whole human being, addressing head, heart and hands with equal emphasis. In the social context of each class and the school as a whole, each child is seen as a unique individual manifesting in body, soul and spirit; again each element cared for equally.

In these lectures, Rudolf Steiner speaks of humanity in the much larger context of the cosmos as a whole, encompassing aeons of time in the phases of our development, and space extending beyond our earth to the planets, the fixed stars and finally to realms of existence and development beyond even time and space. In the second lecture Steiner asks us to imagine a dialogue between an educated person of our own time and a representative of pre-Socratic Greece. Their worldviews are contrasted: the modern person speaking of 70+ elements (now over a hundred) and the Greek speaking of the four elements. It transpires that the Greek sees the four elements not just as constituent parts of the world around us but as four different stages of consciousness. The earth relates to dead matter which is, it seems to the Greek, all that our modern consciousness is prepared to take seriously. Water, however, as the element of life, relates to Imaginative consciousness and extends well beyond the earth out into the cosmos. The element of air takes us beyond the cosmos we are familiar with into the world of rhythm and the consciousness of Inspiration, the world into which we pass when going to sleep. Finally, the element of fire or warmth is the uniting element which also encompasses our spiritual essence in the highest stage of consciousness described in Steiner's *Knowledge of the Higher Worlds* as Intuition. Air and fire relate to our experience of soul and spirit, which disappear without trace each night as we fall asleep and return to us on awakening. Neither can be located anywhere in the known cosmos.

This exposes the limitations of modern natural-scientific methods which focus exclusively on physical phenomena in our bodies and in the world around us and seek the manifestations we describe as soul and spirit in electric-chemical phenomena in our brains. Steiner goes on to suggest in lecture 7 that—having lost our conscious awareness of each human being having a unique individual spirit following the Ecumenical Council of Constantinople in 869 AD, deciding that we are not beings of body, soul and spirit but consist of body and a soul with certain spiritual qualities—we are now entering a period in our development where even the notion that we have a soul as such will be denied in favour of the equivalent sentient qualities being attributed to the activity of our brains. However, whilst there are frequent criticisms of contemporary natural science in these lectures, and in particular its tendency to rely, even insist, on abstract thinking, the main thrust of each lecture is to encourage us to make the considerable effort of will necessary to see ourselves within this holistic organism of threefoldness in body (head, heart and hands) soul (thinking, feeling and willing) and spirit (waking, dreaming and sleeping).

We are also challenged to bring greater attentiveness to our daily experiences of breathing and pulse rate (in a ratio of roughly 4:1), falling asleep and awakening, concurrent states of consciousness in our waking state (clear, rational thinking, dreamy subconscious undercurrents, and unconscious impulses) and then to see them in the much wider context of cosmic rhythms (25,920 breaths in the average day, days in the average life, years in the sun's passage from the vernal equinox in one sign of the zodiac and through the entire zodiac back to the same place). Similarly the daily process of coming into bodily awareness and leaving it as part of the unfolding of each human life can be seen in the wider context of a series of earth lives, or incarnations as part of a longer term evolutionary journey, both for the individual and for humanity as a whole.

Far from speculative theories based on hypothetical questions such as: 'What would happen to time if a clock were to travel at the speed of light?', Steiner's spiritual science invites us to examine the boundaries of our everyday consciousness in the experience of our senses on the one hand and the experience of our memory and inner life on the other. We are shown opposing tendencies in what we might call the extrusion of calcareous matter to form the hen's egg, isolated from its surroundings, and the 'intrusion' of its coat of feathers, very closely connected to its outer environment. The same tendencies are at work as polar opposites in our own lives at all three levels mentioned above (away from the earth, or luciferic, and bound permanently to the earth, or ahrimanic). The challenge is always to see the intermediary, or balancing force in each context as the Christ being, transforming the problematic effects of polarity.

At the beginning and the end of the series of lectures, Steiner is at pains to highlight the now particularly acute dangers of untruthfulness in developing our own view of the world and our relation to the wider context in which we live, encapsulated in the title of the broader series: 'Human development, Cosmic soul and Cosmic spirit'.

William Forward

LECTURE 1

I FELT, despite my stay in Stuttgart being devoted to other matters, that I needed to speak to you this evening on an anthroposophical topic. Today I want to tell you something about the relationship of human beings to their context in the world, to the extent that this plays into their nature. I would like to frame this topic in such a way that its content can be particularly relevant to the decline of civilization in our time.

If we take stock of various aspects of the human being that we have come to know over the years from anthroposophical spiritual science, a great deal of it can be summarized under the heading of the threefold nature of man as spirit, soul and body; a concept that we have frequently dwelt on. Looking at what is increasingly evident in today's intellectual culture from the point of view of spiritual science, it becomes clear that the development of humanity has gradually reached the point where the focus is only on our physical aspect. This study of our physical nature has, it is true, resulted in a comprehensive body of knowledge. Moreover, it aims to know more of how this physical body relates to the other phenomena of the world. We have, however, reached a point now, where we must look more in the direction of our soul and our spirit. Precisely because the physical body is being as carefully studied as it is today, we ought really to devote more attention to the nature of our soul and spirit.

I would like to start with phenomena which cannot be understood today because only their physical aspect is taken into account. They nevertheless pose great questions for humanity. Looking at the physical body of the human being, we see that it is integrated into the whole natural order. Our contemporary way of thinking has gradually attempted to piece together the whole natural order out of indissolubly connected causes and effects. The underlying thought is that the physical human being is integrated into this chain of causes and effects and so can be explained by them. Generally speaking, it is down to the materialistic approach of our present-day thinking that we only refer to natural causes and effects and the way our physical body emerges from them as if by a kind of mechanical necessity.

If we are limited to explanations based purely on cause and effect we are suddenly confronted by phenomena which admittedly seem to be abnormal and yet stand there as great riddles, like a question mark. We see how human physicality unfolds. The natural scientist comes along and looks for the same laws at work in the human body that apply to the rest of the natural world. Sure enough, we then see certain laws at work, which give rise, admittedly in an abnormal way, to phenomena which cannot possibly be attributed to the natural course of events. The materialist thinker tries—so far unsuccessfully, but nevertheless as an ideal to strive towards—to explain our common expressions of will-impulses, feelings and thinking as the effects of physical processes, in the way that flames can be explained as the result of the combustion of fuel. But what then, for example, would be our approach to human thinking, if this concept were correct in every detail?

In the course of life we distinguish between thoughts which we accept, because we can identify them as right and those which we reject because we consider them to be wrong. We say they are mistaken. But according to the laws of nature surely everything can only follow from causes and be the appropriate effect of these causes. So according to the natural order we can say: error and illusion derive just as much from natural causes as do correct, justified thoughts. This then presents us with a riddle: why then do the phenomena of nature which are all supposed to be the product of necessity, produce in us on the one hand what is true, and on the other what is false?

It is even more of a riddle if we see illusory visions arising in the human being, or what we might call hallucinations, which we know conjure up appearances which have no connection to reality. What enables us to say then that something is an unfounded hallucination, when everything that goes on in a human being is a necessary consequence of the laws of nature, to which we are also subject? We would have to say that hallucinations are just as entitled to be considered as true impressions, true thoughts. And yet (we may feel and sense this) we are quite rightly convinced that hallucinations as such must be rejected. Why must they be rejected? Why are they not allowed to be recognized as a justifiable content of human consciousness? And how can we even recognize them as hallucinations?

We will only be able to solve these riddles when we turn our attention to something else, which might at first remind us of hallucinations, but which we feel is not to be rejected to the same extent as hallucinations, namely the products of our imagination. These products of our imagination arise from the unfathomable depths of the human soul life, take shape as images which appear magically before the human soul and are the source of much that gives beauty to life, that is uplifting. All forms of art would be inconceivable without these products of our imagination. Nevertheless, we are still conscious that they are not firmly based in reality, that we would have to see them as illusory if we wanted to attribute reality to them in the usual sense of the word. Then we come to something else.

We are familiar through our spiritual science with the first stage of spiritual knowledge. We are talking about Imagination, about imaginative cognition, and have shown how the soul can by means of certain exercises attain a pictorial content in its contemplation which the spiritual researcher identifies, despite its appearing as an image, not as a dream but as something that relates to a reality, that represents a reality.

So we can say that we have three stages of our soul life before us: hallucinations, which we recognize to be complete delusions; the products of our imagination, which we know we have somehow drawn up from reality, even though in the form in which they appear to us they are not directly connected to reality, and thirdly Imaginations, which also appear before our soul as images, and which we do relate to reality. The spiritual researcher is able in the course of life to relate this Imagination to reality just as he could relate a sure perception of a colour or a sound to reality. One could object that a real Imagination cannot be shown to be real; it could after all just be an illusion. Then someone who has experience in these aspects of soul life would have to reply: 'Similarly you cannot know that a piece of hot steel really is a piece of hot steel and not an imaginary one, a mere mental construct. It cannot be proved by thinking about it, but it certainly can by direct experience in real life.' The way in which we come into contact with external physical reality enables everyone to tell the difference between an imaginary hot iron that does not burn and a real one. In the same way in the course of life the spiritual researcher is able to distinguish, through the contact with the spiritual world which the Imagination enables him to have, between the purely imaginary spiritual world and a real phenomenon of the spiritual world to which the Imagination points.

Now one can only understand this threefold system of hallucination, imaginative picture and Imagination if one is able to penetrate into our relationship with our entire world context by means of spiritual science. We really are differentiated into body, soul and spirit. When we look at human beings initially in the way they present between birth, or let's say conception, and death, what appears to us most directly is their physical body. This physical aspect of the human being is very little understood, even by contemporary science. It is very, very complicated. The more one is able to delve into its details, the more it appears as a wonderful structure. But the answer to the question: 'How are we to understand this physical nature?' must come from a different quarter and can only come from the source that spiritual science offers, when it directs our attention to the spirit.

If you take stock of much that has been said over the years, you will be in a position to say: 'Just as between the birth and death of a human individual we are faced with a physical manifestation, so in the life that the individual spends between death and a new birth we are dealing with spirituality, a spiritual manifestation. And if we look at this in the way that I did in the lecture cycle I gave in Vienna in the Spring of 1914 on our life between death and a new birth, we shall be looking at the growth and development of the human spirit just as we are looking at the growth and development of the human body if we follow the human being between birth and death.[1] When we focus our attention on the newly born child and then follow its development, emerging from childhood, becoming ever more mature, then passing into decline and eventually death, we are doing this with our bodily senses, and combining our outer impressions with our understanding and thus following our human body in its process of development. Similarly we are following the human spirit in its development when we contemplate its growth and maturing and come to what in my *Occult Science* I described as the 'Midnight Hour' of existence between death and a new birth, the beginning of our approach to physical life; having looked at the spirit, which appears to us in its primal form between death and a new birth, we must turn to how it relates to what appears to us here in the physical world as its body and its development in that context.

Thus spiritual science has led us to the significant fact that what we experience as body here, is actually an image, an outer image, a faithful image of what we observe as spirit between death and a new birth. Likewise what we observe in the spirit as just described is a template for what we can observe as our body here in physical life. We must think quite concretely about the relationship of spirit to matter in this way. If you know nothing about life between death and a new birth, you actually know nothing about the human spirit.

When we now contemplate the human being, manifesting itself physically between birth and death and then carry into our awareness the thought that it is an image of the spirit pre-birth, we can ask ourselves: What mediates between the spiritual template and the earthly image? What brings it about that the template (which after all precedes the image), then reveals itself in the image? We might perhaps do without the idea of a mediator if the human being were to appear before us quite complete, so that its spiritual template immediately appeared as a complete human being and no longer needed to grow and develop into perfection. Then we could say: 'The human spirit is in a world of the spirit. Its physical image is here in the physical world.' But it isn't like that, as we know. In fact we enter the world of the senses as an incomplete creature and only gradually, slowly, come to resemble our spiritual counterpart. The spirit on the other hand can only work through to the moment of conception, or a little beyond that into the life of the embryo, let's say until birth, and then in a sense leaves us. There must therefore be some kind of mediator at work which for example at the age of twenty is still perfecting the being which until then did not fully correspond to its spiritual archetype. This mediator, forming the physical after its spiritual archetype, is the soul.

That is how we find ourselves as human beings in our whole context. We can then follow our spiritual existence between death and a new birth, our physical existence between birth and death and our soul nature can be viewed as the part of us that works the archetype step by step into our physical body, its physical counterpart. Then comes the midpoint so to speak of our earthly development, around the thirty-fifth year. That is when the process of decline begins. Our physical nature then becomes increasingly hardened. What has been at work forming it, now prepares to dissolve into its purely spiritual nature, so that we can then in turn live on in our spiritual form between death and our next birth. What is at work there, preparing our physical body step by step, so that it can become spiritual in death? Once more it is the soul. Thus our soul shapes us into an image of our spirit in the first half of our life. In the second half it prepares us to become spirit again. That is how we come to the trinity of spirit, soul and body in our human nature. And we can also form a concrete picture of the relationship between spirit, soul and body. In addition, we then have a conception of our physical body that is perfectly clear in itself, which holds no contradictions in terms of its role. For if our physical body is to be a true image of our spirit, then every spiritual attainment must be reflected in its physical counterpart. It must be possible to trace everything that is of a spiritual nature in our physical body. No wonder then that materialism has appeared in more recent times, claiming that our physical body is the source of our spirit. If we only take into account what happens in us between birth and death, and in particular what develops as mental pictures, we shall find everything that lives in these mental pictures contained in the images of our physical body. Our spiritual individuality can be traced in our physical body right down into the mental pictures it forms. We can thus come to the illusion of the materialistic point of view, because we are in fact bound to discover those fine ramifications which appear in our thinking process, in the forming of mental pictures.

That is how one can become a materialist. One can do so because the physical body is a true image of the spiritual. And if one has no idea about the spirit, one can content oneself with the physical, confine oneself to the physical body, and so believe that the whole human being is contained in it. However, this physical body comes into being in the life of the embryo and dissolves after death. What is physical is transient and everything that we develop in the way of mental pictures, bound to this physicality, is transient. Nevertheless, it remains a true image of the spirit. This physical body is indeed a true copy of the spirit if we look at how it works. An activity takes place in the fine ramifications of our nerve-sense system, and this fine activity is a genuine copy of a spiritual activity that took place in us between death and a new birth.

So when we look at this fine activity and, as I have suggested, see it as mediated by our soul, we must conclude that this physical manifestation is an image, a copy, and its spiritual archetype can only be found in the spiritual world. Here in the physical world, to the extent that we human beings inhabit it, the human being is indeed material and this materiality is organized so as to be a faithful copy of its spiritual archetype. What happens is that the soul is a medium for what works its way into the body right into the life of the embryo and which transforms into what we then mutate into after death: the spirit. Thus spirit, soul and body belong together.

Now if we can really grasp that—try to really grasp what I have set before you—then we must conclude: when we as human beings exercise our power of thinking, an echo of what preceded it even before life in the embryo must play into it, mediated by the soul. In other words, when I have my thoughts a certain power is at work in my thinking life which does not emerge purely from my body; my body is only its replica. This power echoes on, as it were; it is a resonance of the life I lived between death and my reappearance in the embryo. That is what plays into my experience of the present. When we as ordinary human beings of the present-day think, then in fact an echo, a resonance of our pre-birth life lives on in our thinking.

Now how do we human beings know we exist? We do so because we have the unconscious experience: 'When I think, it is my pre-birth existence that lives on in me, that resonates in me, and my body is a replica of this pre-birth existence.' If one were to reproduce this activity oneself, which should normally only take place as a result of the resonance from a pre-birth existence, what would happen? Then our physical body, a replica as described above, would be carrying out something similar to thinking in an inappropriate way. And this can indeed happen. When in ordinary life we think and have our ideas, our pre-birth existence echoes on in us. Since we are three-fold in nature, the nerve-sense aspect can be disconnected and any other part of us can begin to imitate this activity on a purely physical basis, though it should normally echo on from our pre-birth exis-tence. If the rhythmical human being or the metabolic/limb human being begins to do this on its own, which it normally should not do, then hallucination results. If you look at this from a spiritual-scientific perspective you can quite clearly distinguish an appropriate thought from a hallucination. The former is a living proof of pre-birth life the moment it is recognized as an appropriate thought, the latter, though a half-baked imitation from out of our purely physical nature, also proves the appropriateness of the original by virtue of the fact that it is an only an imitation of its spiritual origin. Our body in its physical existence is not justified in imitating the thought pro-cesses which should emerge from the spiritual life of the pre-birth human being.

These are the kind of considerations one has to take into account if one wants to get beyond the silly concepts that are in use today to define hallucinations and the like. We really have to look into the whole framework of the human being to be able to distinguish hal-lucinations from real thoughts and ideas. And when this real life of ideas is developed to a higher level, when it is taken up consciously and progresses to the realization that in thinking one is not merely experiencing the echo of a pre-birth existence but is able to transform this echo and in doing so see through it to the underlying reality, then we have an Imagination.

In this way a real spiritual scientist is able to distinguish between a hallucination, which is something conjured up by the physical body, and an Imagination, which points to the spirit and retraces its steps back into the spirit. So we could say: someone hallucinating links up with the body, someone having an Imagination, who retraces the echo back into the world of pre-birth links up with the spirit; he stretches out his life beyond physical existence and allows the spirit to link up with him. The spirit makes a connection within him. There are those who, for reasons of prejudice or malice, as can happen these days, keep saying that the Imagination described by spiritual science could just as easily be a hallucination. They wilfully ignore the fact that the spiritual scientist is well able to distinguish clearly between the two, whereas what is said about hallucinations in conventional science today is completely unfounded and amounts to arbitrary definitions. The fact that contemporary science does not know what hallucinations are is demonstrated by its inability to distinguish what manifests as an Imagination from a hallucination.

The insinuations that are made in this area are of a nature, it has to be said, that suggests deliberate slander. It is only down to the laziness of our scientists in respect of spiritual-scientific research that such things are put about. If they were not too lazy to engage with spiritual science, they would see how clearly the distinctions between hallucinations and Imaginations are drawn.

If we wish in all honesty to stand up for our movement, we will have to be conscious that there is animosity among our contemporaries which stems from laziness, and we will have to expose this laziness that can lead to untruthfulness in the culture of our time, right into its most hidden corners. There is no other way for spiritual science. So we can say: it is the body that is involved in producing hallucinations and the spirit in producing Imaginations and that the human being feels completely drawn beyond life between birth and death when fully experiencing Imaginative life.

The soul is placed between the two. The soul is the mediator, as it were, the fluid spiritual substance that links the spiritual template with its bodily image. This must not be sharply contoured in any direction, but must have fluid outlines; one should not be able to say of it that it is or is not based in reality. One can say of hallucinations that they are not rooted in reality, since they are produced by the body, which can't actually produce anything real, since it has no access to the resonances of pre-birth life. Imaginations on the other hand and our thoughts, their abstract replicas, do.

The forms that emerge from the engagement of our soul, our imaginative capacities, have something blurry about them; they are both real and unreal. They are drawn from reality; the clear outlines of reality are damped down, made paler and more blurry. We feel lifted out of reality but at the same time we feel that there is nevertheless something there that means something for our inner life, for our whole life. We feel a middle ground between illusory hallucinations and real Imaginations in the intermediary fabric of our imagination or fantasy. We could say that our body is involved with hallucinations, our soul with the fabric of our imagination and our spirit with Imaginations, whose replicas are to be found in the abstractions of everyday life. Here you see the threefold nature of the human being at work and in its relation to the surrounding world. We can say that in the realm of the spirit, whether in the shadowy replicas of thoughts or in Imaginations, by means of which we can raise ourselves to higher levels of cognition, we are connected with reality; in the realm of the soul and its fabric of imagination and fantasy we are connected with something that hovers between reality and unreality; in the realm of the body, hallucinations are conjured up which in fact represent something unreal.

If you accept what I have now presented, you will agree: 'Yes, an unprejudiced view of the human being reveals this trinity of spirit, soul and body. Likewise we can see that what is active in it may also be distinguished in a threefold way as hallucination, the exercise of native imagination and Imagination and can then be related to body, soul and spirit.' You see, with anthroposophy one has to delve deeper and deeper into its being to see how it can support every detail out of its entirety.

We can start by setting out the differentiation of the human being into body, soul and spirit in a more abstract way and then fill out the picture with more and more concrete detail. By looking at something one has placed there like this and seeing how it relates to other things, more and more evidence emerges. This is necessary in anthroposophical life, to constantly delve deeper. People of today however, who consider themselves so clever, are reluctant to do this. They would prefer not to say for example: 'Now I have read an anthroposophical essay, or heard an anthroposophical lecture, and though it is not yet clear to me what it means, I'll wait and see what comes of it.' If they were prepared to wait, they would see the progression from one thing to another and that eventually everything holds together, one piece of evidence supporting the other. If anyone responded by saying: 'Well if one thing is the proof of another then the whole universe has no foundation, everything is supporting everything else.' One might then reply, 'In that case there is no basis for what astronomy has to say about the earth. There too we are told that one bit of the earth supports the other and there too the whole thing has no foundation.' Anyone wanting further proof of one thing supporting the other is ignoring the fact that when we are speaking of a totality that is its characteristic, that one thing supports another.

What is necessary in order to place an idea before our souls as we have today, is not merely to go on talking about the spirit (someone talking about the spirit could quite easily be fooling you) but rather to talk about the spirit in a spiritual way, inhabited by the spirit, and able to link one thing in the world to another so that the working of the spirit is revealed. A purely materialistic approach would be unable to distinguish hallucinations from Imaginations or from creative imagination if they were juxtaposed. But someone who can see the living spirit at work in presenting the three can make connections between one and the other. This person is filled with living spiritual content in contemplating the world; the spirit is speaking through the words used. Science should not merely speak about the spirit, but should allow the spirit to speak in spiritual science. Please reflect on this sentence, which is actually very important if the essence of spiritual science is to be understood: We should not simply talk about the spirit but rather in a spiritual way allow the spirit to speak in spiritual science. That is when we become free, for the spirit gives us access in freedom and allows us to express its being through our own. Speaking about the spirit has to be done in a spiritual way, that is with fluid thinking, not with the hardened thoughts of our materialistic science.

Taking this up can lead to the core of the most essential task of our time which alone can deliver us from the decay that is such a strong tendency in the whole of our present-day civilization. We could say: 'If we feel able to live into the process of acquiring knowledge of the world today, without prejudice and with genuine devotion, then as if by a universal act of grace pouring out over us, we shall be enabled to think spiritually about the world.'

This capacity only entered the stream of earthly evolution at the end of the nineteenth century. Anyone who is able to follow the development of humanity with an open mind will see that before the last third of the nineteenth century we had a different goal. Now, however, the doors to the spiritual world have opened and it is our task, since the materialistic view of nature has achieved such triumphs, to look at the world spiritually again. The evolving of the human being is also a process of rhythmical movement, in which the individual takes part through repeated earth lives. Our life is rhythmical. In rhythmical succession, we live through phases of spiritual striving such as the one that culminated in the middle of the nineteenth century, with our attention directed only at what is material and what can be explained in material terms, and now in our own time we are in a phase in which we need to return to a spiritual perspective. If we can open our minds and allow them to be filled by what is coming towards us from the world, we shall feel the urge to see the world from a spiritual perspective.

That is the secret of the time we are living in. Anyone who has a sense for the spirit today must feel: the gate between the supersensible world and the world of the senses is open. Just as the world we can experience with our senses speaks to us through colours and sounds, so in our time the spiritual world is also speaking quite clearly to us. But people are still used to being spoken to in the language of the old, purely representational material world, and so have opened hostilities in every form against the spiritual way of looking at the world that is streaming in. This battle appears in the materialistic worldview of natural science; it appears in the terrible materialistic wars that shook us at the beginning of the twentieth century. But just as in a former epoch of human evolution, people reached up too high towards the spirit and fell prey to illusions and raptures which tried to find expression in their bodies, so now anyone who takes up arms against the spirit (like the majority of civilization today), will be trapped in the clutches of the power that seeks to oppose the descent of the spirit into the physical world.[2] That is why we have seen the emergence of what must necessarily appear in the souls of those who seek to oppose the influx of the spirit, which is the lie. This was horribly apparent during the World War. It had indeed already been prepared in advance and we are now living in a time when the world not only opposes knowledge but is even in a horrible way developing the inclination to tell untruth. Essentially most of what is spoken by its opponents against anthroposophy and everything that has to do with anthroposophy is just that. What profound insincerity there is in just those who pride themselves in being the bearers of truth, who call themselves the proclaimers of truth!

Here is an example—I always use topical examples, much as it pains me to do so: a paper is published in Stuttgart which styles itself *Stuttgarter Evangelisches Sonntagsblatt* [the Stuttgart Evangelical Sunday paper, SES]. In Number 19 on page 149 it published a few sentences which among other things contained what follows. An urban pastor by the name of Jehle wrote something about the opponents of the Church in our time. There was a good deal of valuable material on understanding monism and free thinkers and then this town pastor Jehle set out the deeper reasons for the bitter war waged by A. Drews against the historical tradition of Jesus, following which he focused on Christian Science, which in stark contrast to the materialistic worldview declared everything material to be unreal, finally stating: 'the Theosophy of Rudolf Steiner which by way of thanks to pastor Rittelmeyer for his discipleship, declares him to be the reincarnation of Bernard of Clairvaux'.[3]

Now my dear friends, one of our friends tried to get this corrected. It then came to the attention of pastor Rittelmeyer who wrote the following letter to those who publish this kind of thing:

> In No.19 of the *Stuttgarter Evangelisches Sonntagsblatt* dated the 8th May I have just read a report of the AGM of the Association of Evangelical Churches at which pastor Jehle stated in his lecture on contemporary movements hostile to the church that Dr Steiner 'by way of thanks to pastor Rittelmeyer for his discipleship, declares him to be the reincarnation of Bernard of Clairvaux'. This sentence is completely untrue in every detail. Dr Steiner has neither directly nor by implication declared me to be the reincarnation of Bernard of Clairvaux or anything like that—neither to me nor quite certainly to anyone else—neither have I myself said or thought anything like that. I request that in accordance with press protocol you publish this correction in full. Please permit me also to express my dismay at the low-point in church polemics that is evidenced here again. Any foolish gossip is welcome so long as it puts down an assumed opponent. Not even the common decency of prior checking of content is observed. I sincerely hope you can see what a base character is imputed to Dr Steiner and to me and how a message such as this appeals to the most primitive instincts of both listeners and readers, simply on the basis of gossip that can easily be disproved.

Now these last few words about the base character etc. were not quoted in the paper at all, but only the first words, to which were added: 'In response to this declaration [which was only partially reproduced!] we can only comment: The speaker's personal comments (which then also reached the ears of the person being referred to) and his tried and tested character which is well known and appreciated among so many of our readers, completely rule out even the slightest doubt that he quoted this remark to the best of his knowledge and belief.'

So the editors hear that the person quoted above says first of all that the whole thing is a lie, and secondly that it comes from base motives. Then they wriggle out of the whole thing, adding: 'Further to your wording and representation of the report in our paper which was made without the knowledge or consent of the speaker and without a final proofing by our editor in chief who has meanwhile gone on holiday'—so the speaker did in fact say this, but the report is excused on the grounds that the speaker was not informed of the report, and the person who published it is excused from the resultant criticism on the grounds that he was on holiday—'the reporter, the speaker and the editor regret that without any intention on our part'—so they do not regret that they published a lie, but rather the following—'that without any intention on our part, various readers (as we are informed by Dr Rittelmeyer) could have misunderstood them to be imputing to him vanity that would have given him pleasure at such a claim and to Dr Steiner the idea that he was counting on this'.

So they do not admit to publishing a lie, but rather that readers may have understood Dr Steiner to be counting on vanity. And it goes on:

> Much as for objective reasons we regret the promotion of Dr Steiner's views by a representative of the church, we had no thought of discrediting him personally.
>
> Equally we are in no doubt that Dr Rittelmeyer will have been surprised and embarrassed by such a claim.

Thus the impression is created that Dr Rittelmeyer is surprised and embarrassed by my statement, whereas he expressly states that he was shocked and embarrassed that such a lie could be spread abroad by the SES.

> Moreover, our regular readers know us too well to believe that we would deliberately engage in personal defamation or slander. They also know that we have plenty of better and more beautiful work to do. I shall leave it to the readers of the SES to decide on the merits of that statement.

This is how people work today, who profess to be the representatives of the truth, the official representatives of the truth and who many people believe have a duty to represent the truth. One only has to point out things like this to make people aware of the tendency towards untruth today. But too few people are sufficiently disgusted, and the disgust is not yet strong enough in the face of such immorality, such anti-religion as calls itself Christian Sunday service.

One need only point out one such symptom, of which there are hundreds to be found, to show how everywhere today—and it will get much worse, for these are the times we are living in—there are such phenomena which coalesce to produce vulgar displays like the one which we witnessed at our latest eurythmy performances in Frankfurt and Baden-Baden. The very same eurythmy performance which we saw here last Sunday, and which engaged people so much, was met in Frankfurt and Baden-Baden with jingling keys and other such implements, booed and whistled at, not for any objective reason but simply because two factors had coincided. The first originates from the widespread battle being fought for reasons you have heard from me today and often before, against the impact of the spiritual forces streaming into our physical world. It is linked with the tendency towards untruth. This is not yet widely recognized but it must be exposed right into its furthest nooks and crannies. The other factor is incompetence, which is linked with laziness and complacency. When a respectable journal from these parts, which I have already mentioned before, condescends to produce an authoritative statement, it turns to one of the contemporary authorities on the subject, for example Professor Traub from Tübingen; and in one of these articles, as I have mentioned, you could read some really peculiar things.[4] This university professor, who is still regarded as fit to prepare young people for professional life, simply writes: 'In Rudolf Steiner's worldview spiritual things, spiritual beings move here and there like tables and chairs in the physical world!' Now has anyone who is sober seen tables and chairs moving about in the physical world? But Professor Traub in Tübingen writes that I speak in my works of tables and chairs moving about in the spiritual world in the way they do here in the physical world. Since I doubt that Professor Traub would admit to being a spiritualist, I shall out of courtesy not suggest that he was writing this article in that other state of mind in which one sees tables and chairs moving about.

But these are the authorities to whom people turn when they want an opinion on today's spiritual science. These matters are just not often enough presented with sufficient clarity and above all they are not thought and felt with sufficient clarity by many of our friends.

Again and again we find that when someone speaks out against us and we expose the full nature of this person's character, the person is not blamed for being a liar, but we are blamed for calling him a liar. This is something we have frequently encountered lately both here and elsewhere.

We are perfectly entitled to speak of incompetence when stuff is written such as what Professor Traub wrote in Tübingen, who in the same essay wrote: 'Esoteric Science cannot be considered science because the terms Esoteric and Science are mutually exclusive; anything that is secret cannot be scientific.' Now I ask you, if someone wrote a scientific book and someone else decided on a whim to keep it secret for a hundred years, would it be less scientific for the reason that it was kept secret? It is not the fact of being kept secret or made public that makes something scientific, but its scientific character. One must have lost touch with all the basics of sound thinking to be able to write down something like that.

One more thing I would like to mention, since we are among friends and since there are too few other people prepared to say things like this. For many years now we have been working at developing alongside eurythmy an art of recitation or declamation, which in turn goes back to good and demonstrably sound artistic principles. It reminds us of what is truly artistic in poetry: rhythm, beat, musicality, imagery, in contrast to the prosaic recitation prevalent in our inartistic times. People tend to recite prosaically, literally, without going to the foundations of poetry in rhythm and beat. Now, since as we accompany the art of eurythmy we are seeking for what Goethe intended when he held rehearsals with his actors and rehearsed his iambic verses with a baton like a conductor or a choirmaster, namely the really artistic element of poetry; since we are making a return from the inartistic to a truly artistic expression, the patrons and even the people themselves, while pretending to recite poetry come up with all kinds of prosaic croaking and bleating. They rise up in their incompetence and vilify those who are devoting themselves to manifesting recitation as a real art.

I am sorry that I have to say this myself, but what is the use; if these things are not voiced by others, they simply have to be voiced by me. And I can't help thinking that this is simply a battle against another form of incompetence. Just as it can be shown that Traub was thoughtless, this is a battle against the incompetence of the bleaters who try to oppose what is striving to become true recitation. One can understand that the incompetents can only bleat, or have their patrons bleat, but we have a duty to protect our spiritual treasure and even if it causes offence, use strong language to point to the fundamental ills of our time.

I have spoken to you today on a topic from spiritual science and (while it was already past the time we had allotted), as a kind of addendum I had to allow my reflections to run on into current affairs which are closely associated with the main spiritual-scientific topic. I regret that I had to dwell on such controversial matters but we don't live in cloud cuckoo land and have to deal with the world as it is. If we have sufficient enthusiasm and feel it our sacred duty to stand for the cause of anthroposophical knowledge and its impact in our time, we must be clear about where the opposition is at work and in sharing our understanding of these things, must develop the strength of will to see off this opposition. It is only by doing this that we can join forces with what in the face of decadence will lead to resurgence, with the impulses that when confronted with the battle against spirit and soul wish to affirm spirit and soul in earthly life. We must come to an understanding of all that is ranged against spirit and soul if we are to join forces in the right way with the strong power that can and will affirm spirit and soul.

It was not my intention to bemoan or curse the opposition, but rather to speak with you about what it will take to enable souls to work together in harmony for the spirit and the soul. More of this when next we meet.

Lecture 2

Bern, 28 June 1921

TODAY we shall take as our starting point what I suggested when I spoke to you here last time.[5] There is a question which arises for people today as a kind of riddle of our time, and which is at the same time a deep riddle for the whole of humanity, namely: how do the phenomena of nature, to which we are subject as physical human beings, relate to those of the moral, or ethical world which we somehow have to acknowledge if we wish to retain our human dignity? People can be as materialistic as they like in respect of science, but if they have even the faintest notion of their human dignity, they will acknowledge the difference between good and evil, morality and immorality. However materialistic they are, they will nevertheless, somehow look up, however reluctantly, perhaps with questions, with doubts, to a kind of spiritual world, a spiritual world order which pervades the natural world and to which we belong with our physical, sense-oriented bodies. But when we look at what comes towards us from contemporary culture as guidance on the nature of the world, our human thinking, human feeling and all our human impulses are faced with a dichotomy which cannot easily be resolved. On the one hand we have the results of natural-scientific research, which has proved so impressively successful and which from observation of outer phenomena can rightly or wrongly go on to make hypothetical statements about the beginning and the end of the world, and on the other we have the challenges of the ethical, moral world. But how is one to resolve this dichotomy when one hears on the basis of quite consequent natural-scientific considerations: there was once a kind of world nebula; from this our world took shape, initially as a kind of mineral wave-form? Then gradually the world of plants emerged, followed by the animals. The human being appeared last of all. Then if we extend this way of thinking, this same system of laws, to the evolution of the earth itself we will conclude that in time this earth will return to being a kind of mineral nebula and will no longer be the stage on which to live out our lives, will no longer sustain living beings and will in other words become a big cemetery in which lies buried everything that was once alive, ensouled and home to the spirit.

So we stand midway between one mineral world and another, are fashioned out of this mineral world with all our organs, which are in fact just structures in which the materials which constitute the outer world appear in a more complicated form; and now the human being who has emerged in this way from the hypothetical world posited by natural science faces the challenge to be moral, to be good. Ideas and ideals will be held and the question will arise: What will happen to these requirements of a moral world, these ideals and ideas when one day all that we can grasp with our natural science, including the human being, will fall into decay in that great, final cemetery?

Of course one can argue that this is taking the natural-scientific way of thinking to its hypothetical extreme and one is not obliged to do so. But then at least the question should arise: Where then are we to turn? Where can we obtain any clarity about the position of the human being in the universe as a moral being, a being that can have ideas and ideals ? These questions have to be faced unless we simply leave it to natural science to develop hypotheses about the beginning and the end of the world.

However, from all that can be offered by currently accepted scientific sources, based largely on the achievements of natural science, nothing can be determined about the role of the human being in the universe. I'd like to explain what we experience as a dichotomy at present, one which is closely connected with all the forces of decline which are so terribly evident in our time, by asking you to imagine one of our contemporaries. This person will have absorbed all that counts as enlightenment, education and scientific knowledge today, in other words someone who feels really well-educated. This person will be compared to one from a Greek cultural background, someone who lived in pre-Socratic times, roughly in the era of which we know so little today apart from a few sayings of the great philosophers Heraclitus, Anaxagoras and so on. I would like to juxtapose a Greek from that period with an intelligent person of today. By this I don't mean a Greek in his current incarnation, who would after all, if he were in a human body, be a very clever contemporary of ours, but rather a Greek as he would have been in that bygone era. So someone in their incarnation as a Greek is what I would like to juxtapose with a clever person of our own time.

Such a person from ancient Greece would say: 'Well you modern people no longer know anything about the human being because you basically don't know anything about the world either.' 'What do you mean?' the intelligent modern person would say. He would add: 'We have identified roughly 70 elements [there are now 118], hydrogen, oxygen, nitrogen, sulphur and so on.[6] Moreover we have now reached the point where it seems that all these elements can be traced back to one source, but we have not yet quite got there. These 72 elements which combine with each other and separate, we recognize as what is basically responsible for everything that goes on in the physical world.'

Then the Greek would reply: It's all very well that you now have so many elements, but this will in no way enable you to come to an understanding of what the human being is. There is no question about that because the beginning of all understanding,' the Greek would say, 'relies not on the 72 or 76 elements you might mention (hydrogen, oxygen, nitrogen, etc.) but rather on the idea that everything that belongs to the outer world of the senses is composed of earth, water, air and fire.'

Our clever contemporary would say: 'Yes that used to be the case, in the childlike times when people did not know as much as we do today. They would talk about earth, water, air, and fire, but we have progressed far beyond those childlike views. People then assumed there were only four elements but now we know there are 76 elements. That was a childlike way of looking at the world. We know that H_2O is not an element. We also know that air cannot be referred to as an element.

We know that warmth or fire is not an element at all; we are immensely knowledgeable. You simply had a childish view of the world.'

Now the Greek might reply:

> I have given some thought to your 70-odd elements and the way in which you look at them. What matters is how you look at things, and these roughly 70 elements all belong (according to our way of thinking) to earth, but not in any way to water, air or fire, simply to earth. It was very good that you were able to distinguish and to differentiate and specify the components of the earth into 72 or 76 different elements, absolutely fine; we had not yet identified all these interesting details but grouped them all together under the concept earth. On the other hand you have absolutely no idea of what we mean by water, air and fire and for that very reason can have no understanding of what the human being is.

You see,' the Greek of that era would say, 'there are two kinds of human beings. On the one hand the kind that wanders the earth between birth and death as a child at first, then as an adult and on the other there is the human being who is laid out as a corpse for a few days and subsequently buried. We are only speaking of the physical human being', the Greek would say:

> and thus there is only this twofold figure: the person who wanders about between birth and death and the one who lies in the grave. What you have come to know with your 72 or 76 elements that combine and separate refers only to the human corpse lying in the grave. Your chemistry and physics can tell us about what is to be found in the corpse, but can tell us nothing of the living person who wanders the earth between birth and death. You have a science that focuses only on observing the dead human being. You understand nothing of the live human being. You have been quite happy to develop your science into a science of the dead human being, but with no concern for the living one.
>
> If, however, you want a science of the living human being you will first have to turn your attention to the comprehensive, universal living and weaving of what we call 'water'. Moreover we don't only refer to water as the crude fluid element that flows in the brook but what we call water contains everything in the world that flows together and is cold and fluid.

That is what the Greek would say. And the moment we wish to develop a living concept of what flows together as coldness and wetness in all its forms we face the necessity of thinking in pictures rather than in mere concepts, mere ideas, abstractions. The Greek would go on to say:

> If one can perceive moisture together with any sensation of cold, when that in turn blends with another form of moisture shaped by the watery element or manifesting in another sensation of cold then one can have weaving, living images in moisture and coldness. One can then begin to achieve an understanding of the nature of plants and see the weaving together of moisture and coldness in such a way that it is not merely crude, material water but rather the interweaving of moisture and cold. The plant world manifests in images as it tears itself away from the ground. By means of the moisture within it, it tears itself away from the cold, for the earth is dry and cold. In the way in which the plant world takes shape through spring, summer and autumn one can see different aspects of the weaving of the watery element and all at once the mighty Imagination of this outer weaving and living of wateriness grows within us. Contained within it is the entire plant world in all its forms.

The Greek would go on to say:

> What matters to us is not what belongs to the senses, but rather the supersensible interweaving of coldness and moisture. That is what matters to us. We can apprehend the weaving and living of the plant world within the fluid, watery element. If we begin to understand this, not by means of abstract concepts but by means of these images which attune us to inner movement, then we need only look into ourselves to become aware of how all that we can follow in the passage of the seasons through spring, summer, autumn and winter in the burgeoning plant world, the overcoming of the cold by warmth, in all that goes on as we pass from autumn to winter, how in all this we can sense something like a miniature image form within us. When we fall asleep, something happens inside us that is very similar to the spring and as we go on sleeping it becomes more like the sprouting, blossoming of summer, and as we begin to wake up again we are heading towards winter. We can see in miniature form what is going on in the outer world in terms of vegetative processes within our etheric bodies.

The Greek would have said:

> In your 72 or 76 elements you can only learn about the human corpse
> but this human corpse is imbued with something that can only be
> grasped in picture form, the kind of pictures that arise when one
> thinks of vegetative processes as infused with the watery element.
> That is when we can see how the etheric body within us brings into
> movement what you have recognized as the element of death with
> your 70-odd elements. Thus unless you raise your awareness to the
> level of the watery element you will never be able to understand the
> human being as a living entity.

But now something else comes into the picture. The earth represents what is dead in the human being. The moment a person
dies, the corpse is received by the earth and taken over by the
70-odd elements and from then on the laws that pertain to the
earth, the laws of the earthly element, will take charge. What happens to the laws that belong to the watery element? 'These do not
extend to the earth but their realm is out in the cosmos' the Greek
would go on to say:

> and if you wish to know what brings forth this element of coldness
> and moisture welling up through spring, summer, autumn and winter
> you will have to look into the nature of the cosmos. First of all to the
> planets then to the constellations, and out into the widths of the cos-
> mos. Your earthly element is only relevant to the human being when
> lying in the grave. The person who is walking about on the earth with
> his etheric body within him, is subject at every moment to the laws
> of the cosmos. These are the laws that work down into us from the
> weaving of the planets or the forces of the fixed stars.

For the Greek of the era I am referring to, the watery element was so
significant that he would have said: 'In all that constitutes the watery
element that surrounds the earth, swathes it in mists or discharges
itself in thunderstorms; wherever the watery element is at work, the
cosmos itself works into the earth with all its forces. There is no point
in trying to find out about the watery element in the element of earth
or in anything that is earth. Instead we should direct our attention to
the cosmos and then we can raise ourselves up into the nature of the
cosmos simply by virtue of the active etheric body within us which

wrests the elements free from the destiny, or shall we say the chemistry, at work in our bodies between birth and death.'

Moreover in saying this we have by no means uncovered the whole truth of the human being. We have only grasped what is infusing our physical body with life, what enables it to grow, what enables digestive processes, and what accompanies us in the way of life forces between birth and death. A third force is at work in us, and the Greek from the period I am referring to would mention this too. A third force makes itself felt within us for the whole time between birth and death in a way that differs from the ordinary life forces. This is the force that is embedded within our rhythmic system, our breathing, our blood circulation and so on. In everything that involves rhythm and rhythmic activity you will be able to sense a certain connection between your soul life and the process of breathing, as opposed to merely living. Consider the following phenomenon, that we will all be familiar with. You will all at some time have woken up with a peculiar feeling of anxiety. You emerge into consciousness from a feeling of anxiety and you notice something is not right with your breathing. It is true that the connection between our breathing and our soul life is a mysterious one, but at the most basic level it can be perceived when our breathing is irregular. There is a connection between our soul life, between all the sensations and feelings surging through us, the feelings of anxiety and fear, of joy and delight, and the rhythm of our breathing and of our blood circulation. This rhythmic system is something altogether different from our simple life processes. Our rhythmic system is connected with our soul. It is after all the air we breathe which activates the whole rhythmic system and in days of old, people spoke of the element of air and of its relationship to the human being, for instance when in the Mystery schools they studied the rhythms which govern our inner activity, the same rhythms which belong to the metre used by Homer: the hexameter. If you look at the average rate at which we breathe, and our pulse rate, you will observe the following: we draw breath roughly 18 times per minute and our pulse rate is four times that. The rhythm of blood circulation and breathing is four to one. Now take the hexameter: long, short short,—long, short

short,—long, short short. There are three feet, with the caesura as the fourth element. Similarly there are the four heartbeats to each half of the breath; after the caesura: dactyl, dactyl and once more the caesura. The inner structure of Homeric verse, and indeed of all ancient verse, is drawn from the human rhythmic system.

People who took the airy element seriously, the element that unites with us and is released by us, felt that in drawing breath we were drawing something into ourselves that has to do with the forces governing our soul life. And as the Greek began to speak of the airy element, he began to speak of the most beautiful and also the ordinary aspects of human soul life and he could call to mind that during the course of a 24-hour day the human being draws breath 25,920 times and that the sun takes 25,920 years to complete its cycle through the entire vault of the heavens from one spring equinox and back to the same place. He saw the harmony between the rhythm of the world and our own daily rhythm. He pointed out the connection between the soul of the world and the soul of the human being and he said that what is expressed in the human etheric body is related to the life that passes between birth and death and which in its 24-hour cycle represents in miniature form spring, summer, autumn and winter.

What regulates the watery element that is spread out in the cosmos, cold and moist, and which is subject to the cosmic laws at work in the seasons, the changing weather patterns, and in the movements of the planets: all this is also expressed in the human etheric body. When we come to the rhythmic system, we must turn to the element of air. We must turn to what in times of old, when people understood it better, gave rise to the soul quality that was expressed in the metre of poetry, because one could sense the connection between the human soul and the soul of the world. When we look at life processes we are still in the realm of space, albeit by extending our consciousness into cosmic space. When we come out of space we turn our attention to the rhythmic system and perceive what is sent into space from the realm of time in the form of rhythm.

You see, in the rhythmic element, the element of air, the Greek could still perceive something which he described as follows: the human soul has its roots in the cosmic soul and it is the cosmic soul itself which living in its rhythms sends miniature images of them into our lives. Out in the cosmos the world soul brings it about that the spring rising point moves forward a little every year and over 25,920 years will have completed the entire circuit of the sun through the zodiac. Similarly in the 25,920 breaths we draw each day there is a miniature image of this vast world rhythm. Within 24 hours we replicate in miniature the 25,920 years it takes the sun to complete its course through the cosmic year. We thus have our roots in the cosmic soul within which our own souls have their existence.

If we now rise to the level of the element of fire, we are concerned not just with our soul life but with the spirit that penetrates us with our sense of I and then we are also concerned with what finds its physical expression in our blood. Just as the airy element enables us to perceive the relationship between our own soul and the cosmic soul, so the element of warmth or fire brings to our consciousness the relationship between the human spirit, or I and the spirit of the cosmos. In earlier times human beings were led up into spiritual realms when they heard of the very elements which are considered the product of a childlike consciousness by the clever people of our times. It is now up to us to find our way back to this way of thinking, the difference being that we have to attain it in fully awake consciousness rather than instinctively, as was the case in those earlier times.

So once we penetrate into the watery element we experience the world itself as a great living being, for we are led out into the cosmos with all its sources of life; we experience the world as something living. When we reach the rhythmical element we experience the world as ensouled, and once we break through into the element of warmth we experience the world as essentially spiritual.

However, we cannot develop an understanding of the watery element with our abstract concepts: all the concepts that we acquire going through primary and secondary school and on into further education; none of these concepts will enable us to grasp the watery element. This will only reveal itself in picture form. It has to be grasped through Imaginations. To do that we have somehow to transform our abstract way of thinking into a concrete one, into one that is artistic in its approach. Then of course the modern philosopher will retort: 'There is no such thing as seeing the world in pictures; there is no such thing as an artistic approach to science. I am constructing a theory of knowledge. The laws of nature must be encompassed by logic. Everything you might wish to know about the world must be capable of expression in abstract concepts, in abstract laws.' This may be a requirement we human beings set ourselves, and such theories of knowledge may be developed, but if Nature herself works in an artistic way then she cannot be encompassed by that kind of epistemology; her laws have to be grasped in the form of images. It is not up to us to prescribe how Nature is to be understood. We should listen to her instead, if we want to know how she wishes to be understood. In the watery element of the plant world she will only reveal herself through the medium of Imagination. In the rhythms of her life right out into their connection with cosmic rhythms she can only be understood by means of Inspiration, by following the rhythms of life or by living our way into the rhythms of our breathing.

When you have a nightmare, the rhythm of the world comes over you so strongly that you can't bear it. However if, having done certain exercises, you can creep into this airy element yourself and move within its rhythms yourself, then you will find yourself within the world of Inspiration. Then you will be outside your body just as the air itself which we breathe in and out is outside your body, then you can move with the air into and out of your body. Only then you can begin to grasp what the human being truly is, as opposed to what lies in the grave, which is all that modern science can grasp.

To do this one has to let go of abstract concepts, of purely logical images, and acquire the capacity to experience Imagination, Inspiration and Intuition. In our time however, abstraction has been developed to a very high degree. It is indeed intelligent. So one can develop the following thought construct. I have perhaps already mentioned it here but it is important to continue to refer back to such things.

Let us suppose that we drive past two places at a given speed. At one place a cannon is fired and at another place which one passes through later, a second cannon is also fired, but later. Then we would of course hear the sound of the cannon that was fired later but only after hearing the sound of the first. Now it is quite possible to think as follows: if you continue to accelerate you will eventually reach the speed of sound, and if you move at the speed of sound, then when you reach the second place you will hear the first sound at the same time as the second, or if you travel faster than the speed of sound you will hear the second report before the first because you have left it behind, having travelled faster than the speed of sound.

Many such speculative thought constructs are devised today. One thinks: 'How would two cannons sound to me if I were moving faster than the speed of sound? I'm moving ahead of sound, aren't I, and so I am bound to hear the second sound before the first, which I will have left behind.' You see it is quite possible to think something out quite logically but in a way that does not correspond to reality. For if you were to move at the speed of sound you would be a sound yourself and give off sound yourself. You would begin to sound. You would blend with the sound itself. It is completely impossible for anyone who thinks realistically to come up with speculation of this kind, but such speculations are rife today. They are referred to as Einstein's theories. Einstein goes to America; the newspapers spread the word that he has achieved enormous results but he himself said in London that no one in America had understood him. Thus his successes had been achieved among the very people who had not understood him. Perhaps so. In London, however, there was a huge kerfuffle, with people portraying these abstractions coming from a very abstract mode of thought as the greatest and most significant world events, and even the elderly Lord Haldane felt moved to high-light what had actually happened. Fundamentally all that happened in reality was that one person took the power of abstraction to its pinnacle, the spirit of unreality, the preoccupation with concepts and ideas that are completely removed from any kind of reality and have even less content than the logic that is based on corpses in their graves. For with Einstein's concepts one can no longer grasp even a corpse but only the extract of one. There is, however, essentially no countermeasure available to deal with what is spreading throughout humanity. The only remedy is to be found in anthroposophical science which is seeking a path to concepts based in reality. It is these realistic concepts that will lead us out again into those worlds for instance that still appear to us as spatial. There before us we have the world as one great living being, the one Goethe spoke of out of a powerful intuition in his prose hymn '*Die Natur*'.

But then, rising up from this world we come to the world's soul, to cosmic rhythm, to what essentially was once referred to as the harmony of the spheres. We come to cosmic rhythms when we develop the faculties that I tried to describe in my *Occult Science* and can experience Imaginations, and rhythms of the kind I portrayed there and from these cosmic rhythms can then be perceived the creative forces of the epochs of Saturn, Sun, Moon, Earth and in future those of Jupiter, Venus and Vulcan. These things are the emerging creation of a world developing out of the cosmic rhythms themselves. But look at the way in which these rhythms are spoken of, which flow and come to fruition in sequence! First of all as human beings we belong within these rhythms. We do not arise from some whirling about of mineral or animal properties but from a spiritual, universal wholeness, and where there is a world we will also find a human being.

Then you will discover more: when you reach the world where we are interacting with rhythms, you cannot help speaking of divine spiritual beings, but do you think there is any point when describing the world that is portrayed in a modern chemistry or physics textbook in speaking of angels, archangels or archai? Of course it would be very inappropriate when discussing the particular combinations of carbon, the etheric compounds of carbon, alcohol, and so on! If we listed all these formulae with their carbon, oxygen, hydrogen, and so on and then added: that belongs to angels and that to archangels, it simply wouldn't do. But once we have reached the realm in which one inevitably sees the earth's emergence through Saturn, Sun and Moon evolutions, when one sees the fabric of life at work in the world, in the rhythms of the world, that play into the human soul through their inner rhythms, which one can follow right down into versification and at the same time can show how this verse is related to the rhythms of blood and breathing; when we reach the realms where Saturn, Sun and Moon etc. are depicted, then one is obliged to speak of beings and spiritual hierarchies. We come into a world in which there are real spiritual beings, unlike the world of vague pantheism to which some people who do not wish to be materialists aspire, and say that the world is full of spirits.

Well yes, the world is filled with spirit. Spiritual quality is to be found everywhere—it is as if someone says: 'A lion: you say it has a larynx through which it roars and an oesophagus, a windpipe, lungs and a stomach—I can't be bothered with that, I don't wish to talk about that. It is simply filled with lion-ness through and through.' The philosophical posturing of the pantheists, who like to think of nebulous spirituality dispersed everywhere, is equivalent to someone saying ' it is completely filled with lion-ness'.

If we really wish to speak about the spirit we will have to speak about individual spiritual beings. To do that we have to know how, once we have progressed from the element of water to the element of air, we can encounter the spiritual beings who are described in the hierarchies. Then once we enter the realm of the fire element we reach the highest hierarchy: Thrones, Cherubim, Seraphim, and only then to true spiritual forming of worlds where indeed we humans are unable to distinguish individual details. But before we enter what superficial pantheists would like to describe as the nebulous one-ness of all, we pass through the world in which individual, distinct spiritual beings live. Amidst these distinct spiritual beings we now recognize what also lives in Nature that surrounds us, for in doing so we encounter its foundations. We cannot have our being within this Nature as we study it with our chemistry and physics. We can only be united with Nature when we experience it as also containing the elements of water, air and fire.

The moment we enter the airy element we find the beings whom we describe as angels, archangels and archai. That is how we come into the world of concrete spiritual beings. We are then also in a world which we can grasp both physically and morally. Because our vision is obscured today we do not see for example that real morality sounds forth out of the same world as verse. It is true that we will not find the source of morality in the world of the 76 elements; nor will we find there what enlivens us; the world of morality is not even contained in the cosmic and spatial world that is the realm of the element of water. But the moment we enter the rhythmic element we simultaneously enter the world of morality. People of our time face the task of recognizing the world of morality as a real one and to recognize that the same material or the same substance which forms our astral body is to be found in moral ideas. The same substance from which our I is fashioned is to be found in religious ideas, in a religious ideal.

We have to find a way of bridging the gap between the contemplation of Nature and the contemplation of the spiritual world in which our moral intuitions have their origin. It was this interplay of the world of perceptions and the world of Intuitions that I wanted to point out in my *Philosophy of Spiritual Activity* in 1893. I wanted to show how concrete moral intuitions are drawn from a world that lies beyond the world of sense perceptions and can be integrated into our world.

This is after all the great task of our times: not to remain stuck in that aspect of the world which is actually only of any use to us when we're lying in the grave, but rather to rise up into the world which reveals itself to us when we live out our life of soul in the rhythms of the physical world, for it is precisely in the rhythms of the physical world that we learn to know rhythm in its essence.[7] Thus we can come to an understanding of the world rhythms and these world rhythms can only be understood once we understand the sources, the springs of the moral world. Then we can say to ourselves: Yes, I currently do have a natural science but it is only applicable to the human being as a corpse. Obviously it must itself originate in the corpse of the world and derive its being from all that is in decline in the world. It must relate to that aspect of the earth which will one day become its corpse. On the other hand what we engage with in terms of rhythm, what we might express in verse for example, in images, in a spiritual form of any kind so that it is alive in its rhythmic form of expression, and what we grasp intuitively in our moral ideals, in all this we create something that outlives the death of the earth in the same way that our individual soul lives beyond the death of our physical body. The earth will perish in accordance with the natural laws that we recognize today. These laws state that the earth will perish, but according to the laws which apply when we approach the spiritual world or act on moral Intuitions, on genuine religious Intuitions, human souls will evolve who will leave the earth when it falls away dead, and progress to a new future existence.

What we have today then is an officially recognized science. It teaches us about what is dead. It teaches us about what will perish with the earth and lie in the great grave of the world. What we need now is spiritual science which concerns itself in all seriousness with the words of Christ Jesus: 'Heaven and earth shall pass away but my words shall not pass away.' We need a spiritual science which seeks the true substance of these words spoken by Christ, for these words relate to rhythm, relate to morality, relate to the divine and to what will pass on to new forms of existence when the earth and the cosmos fall apart and become corpses. We must have an awareness that we need to leave behind a science that only speaks of what is dead and move on to a science which raises itself up to what is alive and thus to what belongs to the soul and the spirit.

A science of the mysteries did in fact still exist until the year 333 AD, roughly up to the first half of the fourth century AD. It was actually not until the sixth century that the last of the Greek sages were fully driven away. Now what were the intentions of this Mystery Science? This Mystery Science wanted to help humanity pass the great danger of physical life. In those days it was still relatively easy to help people avoid the great danger of physical life because people still retained some of the cohesive power of group souls. This relationship to their group souls was still very strong until the fourth century AD. This changed, however, when the great migrations started and the tendency to relate to group souls was broken up by the particular element that came from the Germanic peoples. The leaders of these mysteries, however, only drew certain individuals towards them whom they regarded as having special capacities. They then helped develop them within the mysteries to particular levels of attainment. In doing so, however, they not only did something for the individual involved but also, given the group spirits still at work there, at the same time did something for all the people in that area. Going back to ancient Egyptian times there were only a few initiates but they were also the intellectual leaders in all fields, leaders of the entire Egyptian people, and because the group soul was still active their influence extended to the others who were not initiated. Thus at that time there was no need for more than a few initiates.

What was the motive for this initiation? The intention was nothing less than to enable the people to avert the danger of their souls becoming mortal. They had a different view of immortality in Egypt to the one that prevails today. Today we tend to think of immortality as something that belongs to us as a matter of course, something we cannot lose. In the mysteries of Samothrace, however, the teaching was this: there are four Cabiri and three of these always kill the fourth. What they meant was that the human being has a physical body, an etheric, an astral and an I. First the physical body succumbed to death as a physical corpse, then the etheric body dispersed into the cosmos, the astral body also dissolved in a certain way as I have shown in my *Theosophy*. If the I does not sustain its self-consciousness by engaging with the spirit the other three will also kill the fourth and drag it down into mortality. The task of the mysteries was to save human beings from losing their immortality. People did not think that one could attain immortality by prayer; they did not imagine that one could have a purely passive relationship to immortality, but they understood that those who were initiates would be able by the particular transformation of their soul-being as a result of an inner awakening, by the awakening of their I, to avert the danger of not being able to grasp their own spirituality and thus of having to go the way of their physical body. Moreover, since some initiates had this power of retaining thinking beyond the physical body they could pass it on to the others by virtue of the group soul/spirit. Today this group soul quality is no more; a condition that has been in gradual preparation since the first third of the fifteenth century. Today we are called on to acquire freedom as individuals. Today we have essentially reached the point where we face the opposite danger.

Whilst people were in danger of not being able to grasp their own spirituality until the fourth century AD so that one had to bring about an inner awakening into this spiritual experience, today's human being is now capable of thought by virtue of the particular way in which his physical body has developed, the way matter has evolved, and we live extremely strongly in our thinking. Those who believe they are living in reality are precisely those who live in their thoughts. People today are terribly given to abstractions; they instantly fall for anything that is abstract, because they have an affinity for abstractions. Moreover these are not simply wrongly understood when it is said that they are dependent on our brains; they are indeed dependent on our brains, because our brains imitate the processes that we have gone through in the spiritual world before our birth or conception. Our brains mimic what our souls experienced before they descended. Because this thinking which has now been developed to a particular state of perfection is purely brain-bound, materialism is correct. It has to be continually emphasized that materialism is quite right in regard to the thinking that applies today, for it is just an imitation of true, living thinking, and that is why we must attain the capacity to grasp freedom in our thinking and thus to save ourselves. In practice this means not simply letting our brains think, but rather to take hold of our thinking in such a way that we become aware that we are free beings. That is why I have attached such importance to pure thinking, to free thinking, which can simultaneously apprehend itself as will, so that we can think and at the same time will, so that thinking and willing are substantially one activity which can apprehend itself in pure freedom as I have set out in my *Philosophy of Spiritual Activity*. This is intended to show people: you are only free when you can grasp what is immortal within you, with which you can rescue yourself, preserve yourself from the death of the four Cabiri.

Admittedly, we have now reached a point where we are about to step onto thin ice, which people today are reluctant to approach because we would much rather that our immortality were guaranteed in some way by some outer agency so that we are not obliged to contribute in any way to awakening in ourselves what otherwise would fall asleep and which would then follow the human body as it goes through death. As people of our time increasingly make our thinking resemble the processes going on in our brain, we not only risk no longer understanding anything about immortality but we run the risk of losing immortality altogether. This is indeed the primary aim of Ahriman: to destroy our individuality, no longer allowing anyone to be individual, but instead to take the forces we have, our power of thinking, into the forces of the earth, so that when one day the earth is one great corpse, it will be woven through with all the powers that human beings have embodied in it by means of our logic. Thus we would have one great earth spider in which 70-odd elements would exist in a completely pulverized form. Within that, like gigantic spiders tangling each other up, would be woven our purely abstract thinking. That is the ideal towards which Ahriman is striving: to destroy the individuality of human beings in order, with the power of human thinking, to transform the earth into a web of gigantic thought spiders, but real spiders. That is the ahrimanic goal from which we must escape by really imbuing ourselves with the spirit word: 'Not I, but the Christ in me'.[8] This will enable the true I to come alive within us, the immortal I which can understand the words, 'Heaven and earth shall pass away, but my words shall not pass away'.[9] That wisdom cannot pass away, the wisdom that is reality, that embraces reality within it and by means of which when the earth is a corpse the whole essence of the human being can reproduce itself in a new form of existence. The New Jerusalem spoken of in the apocalypse refers to such a form of existence. The greatest hindrance to this is of course every kind of Einstein-like thinking, everything which is spreading through the world as the great and terrible addiction to abstraction, which is increasingly capable of developing forces of decline. Humanity can only be helped by resorting to powers of regeneration, real powers within body, soul and spirit. That is what I wanted to say to you this evening.

LECTURE 3

DORNACH 24 JUNE 1921

FOLLOWING the historical considerations that we have taken into account, we shall devote our attention today to the human being of the present time, which will then give us the opportunity to look more closely over the next few days at how we are situated in time as a whole. We must be clear that the person before us as a being of spirit, soul and body is integrated into the world in three different ways. That is already obvious when, let's say, we look at a person purely from the outside. From the perspective of the spirit, the person can move about independently of outer phenomena; from the perspective of the soul one is not so independent. We need only look at certain connections which are evident in the course of life and it will become apparent how what belongs primarily to our soul life is also connected with the outer world. One can be downcast or cheerful. Try to remember how you may often have felt oppressed in a dream and have found on awakening that this is related to an irregularity in the rhythm of your breathing. One might object that this is a crude observation, but there is nevertheless always a similar connection between the rhythms at work in our breathing, our blood circulation and the outer rhythms and the outer rhythmic life of the whole cosmos. All that goes on in our souls is connected with the rhythm of the world. Thus while on the one hand as spiritual beings we feel to a large extent independent of our surroundings, we cannot feel the same in respect of our soul life, for that is always embedded within the general rhythm of the world.

We are even more embedded in the phenomena of the world as physical beings. To begin with, we can start from basic phenomena: as a physical body one is heavy, one has a certain weight. Other purely mineral objects also have their weight. Minerals, plants, animals and also humans to the extent that we are physical beings are all subject to general gravity and in a certain sense we all have to lift ourselves out of this general gravity if we wish to make our body the physical instrument of our spiritual life. We have often mentioned that if it were purely a matter of the physical weight of our brain, it would be so big—1200 to 1500 grams—that it would flatten all the veins beneath it. But this brain is subject to the Archimedean principle in the sense that it is floating in cerebral fluid. So much of its weight is lost by virtue of it floating in cerebral fluid, that it in fact only weighs 20 grams and so only presses down on the veins in the cranial cavity with 20 grams weight. You can see from this that our brain is reaching up far more than pressing down. It resists gravity. It tears itself free from the general gravitational force. In doing so, however, it is no different from any other body you might place in water and which loses as much of its weight as that of the water it displaces.

This is one example of the whole interplay between our physical body and the outer world. Moreover in this case we are not incorporated in a rhythm, as we are with the weaving of our soul life, but instead are standing fully within this outer physical life. Whenever we are standing in a particular place on the earth, we are pressing down on that place. When we go to another place we press down on that. Thus with our physical bodies we are no different from physical beings in the other kingdoms of Nature.

To summarize: in our spiritual nature we are in a certain sense independent of our surroundings, in our soul nature we are incorporated in the rhythm of the world, and in our physical nature we are incorporated into the whole surrounding world as if we did not also have a soul or a spirit. We have to make this distinction. We will be unable to understand our higher being unless we take account of this threefold orientation of our body towards all that surrounds us. Let's now look at these surroundings. Initially we have what is determined by the laws of Nature. (Here I am summarizing various things that we have looked at over the last few months, only from different points of view.) Imagine the universe, governed by the laws of Nature, the whole visible or otherwise sense-perceptible world, harnessed by the laws of Nature. Let's first take a look at this aspect of our surroundings.

A simple reflection will tell us that we are now dealing with the purely earthly world. Only thoughtless and unfounded hypotheses by physicists could suggest that the laws of Nature which we observe around us here on earth would also apply in the cosmos beyond us. I have often mentioned to you how surprised physicists would be if they could reach up to the place where the sun is. Physicists after all view the sun as something like a big gas oven, albeit without walls: roughly speaking as burning gas. They would not find this burning gas if they reached the place in the cosmos where the sun is. They would find something very unlike what they imagined. If this [drawing begins] encompassed the space we imagine to be taken up by the sun, we would find not only none of the materials that are present on the earth but not even what we call empty space. Start by imagining the space filled; after all as we live here on earth we are always surrounded by space that is filled. If it is not filled with dense or fluid substances then it will at least be filled with air or warmth or light and so forth. In short we are always dealing with space that is filled. But you also know that one can create an empty space, at least approximately, by pumping the air out of a cylinder with an air pump.

Now imagine any given filled space; we will give it the letter A with a plus sign in front of it: + A. Now we can empty the space more and more and the space A will become smaller and smaller; but the space is filled and so we will keep the plus sign in front of it. Although in reality it is not possible in our conditions here on earth, because we can only approximately empty the space, we can nevertheless imagine that it would be possible to completely empty an airtight space. Then in the part of the space that has been emptied, there will remain only space. I shall give it the symbol O. It has zero content. In principle we can do the same with this space as you can with your purse. When your purse is full, you can take more and more out of it; finally there will be nothing left in it. Zero. If you want to continue to spend money you can no longer take money out of the purse because there is nothing in it, but you can run up a debt. Thus you can imagine both the space and the purse as being not only empty but, as it were, sucking—with less than nothing left in it.—A. We now have to think of the sun as occupying the space of the sucking chamber which is not only empty but has a content which is the opposite of being filled with matter. So the sun is sucking in rather than pressing out as it would be if it were gas. It is filled with negative materiality.

saugend = sucking

I only wish to bring this as an example, so that you can see that one cannot simply transfer earthly laws into extraterrestrial conditions in the cosmos. We have to think of these as quite different from what we are familiar with in our surroundings on earth. Thus when we are speaking of certain laws at work we have to say: there are laws at work within our earthly surroundings, including the world of matter which is immediately accessible to us. Now imagine this world of our earthly existence: you need only observe the processes that are going on in the mineral world and what you have initially, to the extent that you can see it, is completely subject to the laws of earthly existence. We could say that the mineral world is an enclosed system. However, something else is also enclosed. When we walk around, or are carried around, if I may put it so crudely; when we only behave like objects in this physical world, we are subject to the same system of laws. In terms of earthly laws it makes no difference whether a cobble is being carried around, or a human being. In terms of the laws governing the earth there is no difference. You have only to think it through. In terms of earthly laws what matters is only our change of place, which we could also of course bring about ourselves. (That is connected with other things.) But if we are only studying earthly laws it doesn't matter what is going on inside the skin of a person or what is going on in the person's soul. All that matters is the change of place in earthly space.

The second point then, apart from the mineral world, is the moving human being, moving as seen from the outside. [See table on page 45.] We can see no other relationship of this outer world to the human being, in so far as it is earthly and perceptible to our senses, than that it is concerned with the externally moving person. If we want to see the human being from a different perspective, we shall have to look elsewhere. That is when we come to our extraterrestrial surroundings and if for example we were studying the environment of the moon we would be looking at what emanates from the moon. Something of the effect of the moon on the earth can still be detected, at least many people think so. It is widely held that there are such influences of the moon on the earth, for example in the case of the link between the movements of the moon and rainfall. Educated people today consider that to be a superstition. Now I have told at least some of you about a charming event that took place in Leipzig. The interesting natural philosopher and aesthete Gustav Theodor Fechner went so far as to write a book about the effect of the moon on weather conditions.[10] He was a university colleague of the well-known botanist and researcher Schleiden. Schleiden of course, as a modern materialist, was deeply convinced that any idea such as his colleague was promulgating about the influence of the phases of the moon on weather conditions must be based on superstition. Now it happened that as well as the two learned men, their two wives were also in Leipzig, and in those days conditions there were so simple that people collected rainwater for their washing. The women maintained that in certain phases of the moon one could collect more rainwater for washing than in others. Moreover Frau Professor Fechner said that she believed what her husband had published about the influence on the moon's phases on weather conditions; for that reason she wanted to reach an agreement with Frau Professor Schleiden, who did not believe this, that the latter would put out her rainwater barrel, according to Professor Schleiden's directions. She would then certainly collect just as much rainwater as Prof. Fechner's wife would collect on the good advice of her husband. Sure enough, although Prof. Schleiden regarded Prof. Fechner's view as extremely superstitious, Frau Professor Schleiden refused to do this deal and wanted to put out her barrels at the same time as Frau Prof. Fechner.

Well now, our modern scientific consciousness is at present less able to see the influence of the forces exerted by other planetary bodies. But if for example we were to focus our attention more exactly on the line taken by the leaves on the stem of a plant, as will be done in our Institute for Science and Physiology in Stuttgart, then we would see how every single line is linked with the movements of the planets, how these lines are somehow miniature images of the planetary movements. And we would find that there are a number of things on the earth's surface which can only be understood when one is familiar with extraterrestrial phenomena and does not simply identify them with terrestrial ones; in other words when one starts from the premise that laws apply in the cosmos that are not telluric.

So we can say that there is a second system of laws that work within the cosmos and only once we begin to study these cosmic influences—it will be quite possible to do so empirically—will we have a genuine science of botany. Our world of plants growing on the earth does not grow out of the earth in the way that materialistic botany imagines, but is drawn up out of the earth by cosmic forces. And the plant growth drawn out by the cosmic forces is infused with mineral forces which in a way infuse the plant's cosmic skeleton so that it can be perceived by our senses. So we can say: firstly, that the world of plants is encompassed by the working of these cosmic laws and secondly, that everything that is involved with our inner movement, certainly physical, but inner movement, is likewise governed by these cosmic laws. This is admittedly not so easy to observe as it is in the plant world because these movements have acquired a certain independence and do not rely on the rhythms of outer processes to the same extent, but inwardly imitate them. In the first place earthly laws encompass our outer movements; but if we turn our attention to our digestion, to the movement of nutrients in our digestive organs, and go on to look at the flow of blood through our blood vessels—there is a great deal more that moves within us—we will have an image of what is moving in us, regardless of whether we are walking or standing still. This cannot be so easily integrated into the first system of laws but it has to be integrated within cosmic rules just like the forms and movements of the plants; the only difference is that with human beings this process takes place more slowly. So we can say: secondly, the movements that take place within the human being are included there.

So you can imagine the cosmos somehow exerting its influence from indeterminate distances down into the life that is unfolding on the surface of the earth. However, if there were only these two sets of laws that work in the way I have just suggested, then nothing but the mineral world and the plant world could be present on the earth. We ourselves could not be there. If human beings were there, they would be able to move and inner movements could happen, but of course it takes more than that for a human being to be present. Animals would likewise be excluded; in practice only minerals and plants could exist on earth. For animals and humans to be present, cosmic laws and cosmic content would have to be imbued and interwoven with something which we can no longer attribute to space, where space is no longer something we can refer to.

Naturally everything that belongs in categories one and two can be thought of as belonging to space but now we have to conceive of something where there is no space but which is nevertheless subject to all the laws of the cosmos. You have only to think of how all our movements, our inner movements, are linked to the rhythms at work in us. Initially we can think of the nutrients within us moving about in the blood circulation. But our blood circulation is not just the coursing of nutritious fluid through our veins.

The movement of our blood is rhythmical, and what is more, this rhythm has a particular relationship with the rhythm of our breathing in which oxygen is consumed for our blood formation. We have this dual rhythm within us. I have pointed out how there is an inner law in the four to one relationship between our breathing rhythm and our pulse that is also the inner, soul foundation for the rhythms of metre and verse.

Thus there is a relationship between the movement that goes on inside us and rhythm. We went on to say that rhythm also has a relationship with our soul life. Similarly we must find the relationship between what we observe in the movements of the stars and the cosmic soul, so that as a third point we can refer to the laws at work in the cosmic soul. [See table on page 45.] This will include firstly the animal kingdom and secondly all the rhythmical movements that take place in our physical human nature. These rhythms are connected to all the rhythms in the cosmos as a whole. We have mentioned this before, but will consider it further in the coming days.

You will be aware that we take roughly 18 breaths per minute. If you multiply that by 60, you get the number of breaths taken per hour. Multiply that by 24 and you will have the total number of breaths taken in a day. The normal person will take roughly 25,920 breaths during the course of a day. This number of breaths is our daily rhythm, day and night. We know that the vernal equinox moves on a little every year. One could say that the sun moves its spring rising point forward in the vault of the heavens. The time it takes for the vernal equinox to move through the twelve signs of the zodiac is 25,920 years. We can take that as the rhythm of our cosmos, and the rhythm of our breathing over a 24-hour period is a miniature image of it. Our own rhythm is woven into the rhythm of the cosmos through our souls and thus into the laws of the cosmic soul.

The fourth point that we can take into consideration is the system of laws governing the whole cosmos. As in all three previous sets of laws, this is a law within which we feel ourselves embedded when we become aware of ourselves as spiritual beings. To begin with we cannot understand this or that about the world since there is very little that can be understood with our present-day intellectuality, which is the commonly accepted approach to thought; so with our spirit in this particular phase of human development there is little that we are able to understand to begin with. However, once we do become aware of ourselves as spiritual beings it is in the nature of how the spirit sees its own role to say to itself: if I develop myself, no limits can be set to my understanding. The human spirit has by its nature to develop into the cosmos in thinking, feeling and willing. And so because we bear our spirit within us we have to relate to a fourth law which is at work within the cosmic spirit [see table below].

Only now do we come to what this means in terms of real being, for of course we ourselves could not be present at all in the other sets of laws. Only now do we find our own essence, but in particular the aspect of ourselves which resides in the nerve-sense system, all that is basically the bearer of our spiritual life, the processes at work in our nerves and our senses. When considering the human being we first of all look at ourselves as a whole with our head as the principal bearer of our nerve-sense system, and then at the head itself. We are human beings you could say by virtue of our heads and our most common, our most recognizably human feature is our head.

1. The laws at work within earthly existence

    including: 1) the mineral world   2) the human being brought
                                              into motion from outside.

2. The laws at work within cosmic existence

    including: 1) the plant world   2) what is moving within us.

3. The laws at work within the cosmic soul

    including: 1) the animal kingdom   2) rhythmic processes.

4. The laws at work within the cosmic spirit

    including: 1) the human being   2) nerve-sense processes.

We thus have two approaches to our own nature as human beings. If we take this as a summary of what we have been considering in the last few weeks, we are left with an image of our connection with our surroundings, but our surroundings extending beyond the purely spatial, since only items one and two in the table refer to the world of space.[11] Items 3 and 4 refer to what is non-spatial. It is particularly difficult for people of the present day to think of anything not being in space, or to recognize that it makes no sense to talk of space when we are dealing with realities. Without doing that, however, we can't raise ourselves to the level of a science that takes account of the spirit. Anyone who wants to remain in the world of space will be unable to raise their awareness towards spiritual entities.

The last time I was here I spoke to you about the worldview of the Greeks in order to demonstrate that people saw things differently in other times. The image that I have just presented to you is what can be understood by a person of the present day: all that is required is an unprejudiced attitude to the world, unhindered by the rubbish produced by today's science.

I must now add something to what I told you about the Greek view of the world, so that we can find a connection to what I meant by this table. If someone today is well educated, he will see: the world of space consists of roughly 70 elements which have different atomic weights and so on. These elements combine, and one can analyse them. What goes on in the world is based on chemical combinations and chemical releases among these 70-odd elements. At the moment we will be less concerned with ways in which they can be traced back to something more fundamental.

If an ancient Greek were to drop into our times, (not someone in their current incarnation, who would then naturally think like our contemporaries, if he were well-educated) he would say: 'These 70-odd elements are all very well but they will not get you very far, since they do not really tell you anything about the world as a whole. We thought about the world in very different terms. We thought of the world as made up of fire, air, water and earth.'

The present-day person would reply: 'That is a childlike way of thinking. We progressed beyond that a long time ago. We consider them to be aggregate states of matter. The aeriform we would consider a gaseous aggregate state, the watery, a liquid aggregate state of matter and the earthly a solid aggregate state of matter. But warmth no longer has any validity for us in the terms you are speaking of. We have simply progressed beyond these childlike concepts. What constitutes the world for us is contained within our 70-odd elements.'

The Greek would then reply: 'That is fine but fire or warmth, air, water and earth are quite different in our view from what you consider them to be. You have no understanding at all of what this meant to us.' The educated person of our time would at first be strangely affected by this reply and would think that he was talking with someone from a more childlike level of cultural development. The Greek however—who would at once see what was passing through the mind of the modern educated person—would certainly not hold back but would go on: 'Yes, you see, what you call your 72 elements all belong to what we think of as the earth; it is fine that you differentiate, that you specify in more detail, but the qualities that you recognize in your 72 elements all belong to the earth as far as we are concerned. You have no understanding of water, air or fire. You know nothing about them.'

The Greek would go on: (you see, I have not chosen a remote cultural epoch in the Far East, but a knowledgeable Greek)

What you say about your 72 elements with their syntheses and analyses is all very well, but what do you imagine they relate to? They all relate to us physical human beings once we are dead and buried. That is where our material substances, our whole physical body would undergo the processes you would learn about in your physics and chemistry. What you can learn about the structural relationships within your 72-odd elements has no connection with our nature as living human beings. You know nothing about living human beings because you know nothing about water, air and fire. Only when you know something about these can you understand anything about us as living human beings. What you can comprehend with your chemistry only tells you about what happens to a person who is dead and buried, about the processes that a corpse goes through. That is all you will find out about with your 70-odd elements.

Well this would not get him very far with the modern educated person but the Greek would perhaps try to explain a little further as follows. He would say:

> Look, what you consider your 72 elements, we consider as belonging entirely to the earth. It's true we looked at things in general terms; but when you go into the specifics it is only a more exact form of knowing and this exact form of knowing will not let you reach any depth of understanding. If on the other hand you know what it is that we call water, you would have an element which is no longer governed purely by earthly conditions, but which, the moment it comes to expression in its weaving and living nature, is subject in its whole activity to the conditions prevailing in the cosmos.

What the Greek meant by water was not physical water but rather all the forming principles that play into the earth from the cosmos which include the movements found in water. The plant world is also included in these movements; it is in its nature to do so. Distinguishing it from all that belongs to the earthly element, the Greek saw the living and weaving characteristics of the element of water and within these the principles of vegetable life that are bound up with it. If we drew a diagram we could place this watery element anywhere on earth and in any way but always determined by the cosmos. Then we could imagine the mineral element sprouting up from below upwards, in all kinds of ways, the purely earthly element, which then infuses the plants, as if injecting the plants with the earthly element. Now the Greek's conception of the watery element was of something substantially new which he saw in a very positive light. He did not think of it in terms of concepts but in images and in Imaginations. We would have to go back in time to Plato—since this way of seeing the world was destroyed by Aristotle—back to pre-Platonic times and would then find out how the truly knowing Greek would use his faculty of Imagination to see what lived in the watery element and what actually sustained vegetation whilst being closely related to the cosmos.

Then he would go on to say: 'You see, what is left lying in the grave when a person dies and which is governed by the laws of your 70-odd elements, is bound up with the life of the etheric, the etheric life streaming towards us from the cosmos between birth or conception, let's say, and death. That is what one is imbued with as a living human being, and that is what you have no idea of unless you think of water as a special element, and unless you see the plant world as bound up with this watery element, and can see these images as Imaginations'.

'We Greeks,' he would say:

> did indeed speak of a human etheric body, but this was not something we made up. We described it as follows: what appears before our inner eyes when we see the world of plants sprouting and greening around us in the spring, when we see how this gradually takes on all kinds of colours, then how it bears fruit in the summer and the leaves wither in the autumn, what can appear to us when we follow the course of the year in the vegetation around us, and when we have an inner understanding of it, we can relate to in the same way in which we relate to the mineral world when we eat our bread and meat. Just as we relate to the mineral world through our bread and meat, we can relate to what we can see in the world of plants in the course of the year. If we now immerse ourselves in the view of the world that sees everything that takes place within us in the 24-hour day as a miniature image which then repeats itself throughout our whole lives, we can see that we contain within us a miniature image of what is going on out there in the watery, etheric element and which constitutes our surroundings from out of the cosmos. If we can understand the outer world in this way, we can then say: 'What is outside there lives within us.' Just as we say: 'The spinach is growing out there, I'll pick it, eat it and then have it in my stomach, i.e. in my physical body', we can also say: 'The cycle of the year in my surroundings lives and weaves as an etheric life and I have this within me too.'

It was not physical water the Greek was thinking of. What he grasped in these Imaginations and related to the human being in such a living way was fundamental to his view of the world. Then he would go on to say to his speaking partner: 'You are studying the corpse lying in the grave because you only study the earth, and your 70-odd elements are themselves earth. We studied the living human being. In our time we also studied the person who has not yet died but who grows and moves out of inner activity. We cannot do this unless we raise our consciousness to the other elements.'

That is how it was for the ancient Greeks and if we went further back, the elements of air and fire or warmth would also appear
before us in full clarity. We shall later investigate this too; but today
I wish first of all to point out how the fact that we cannot see the
right interrelationship of forces within us is because we cannot work
out how these forces interrelate in the world outside, because we
choose to ignore them. This is characteristic of our cultural development since the first third of the fifteenth century: the fact that we
have simply lost our understanding for the interrelationship of the
elements and with it our capacity for understanding the living human
being. The science we recognize studies what is dead. Now we have
often heard that this phase in the history of human development had
to come about and had to do so for other reasons, namely to enable
humanity to go through the phase of developing the capacity for
freedom. But a certain capacity for understanding our relationship
with Nature has been lost to us since the first third of the fifteenth

century. Since then our understanding has been focused entirely on this one element, the earth. We must now find our way back. We must find our way back to understanding the element of water through the power of Imagination, the element of air through Inspiration and the element of fire through Intuition. Fundamentally, our progress to higher knowledge from our customary, concrete way of thinking through Imagination, Inspiration and Intuition is a progression through the elements. We will speak more about this the day after tomorrow.

Lecture 4

T HE day before yesterday we spoke of what a Greek from the period when there was still a more inward approach to knowledge would have thought of today's view of the world, the scientific perspective. I then tried to set out how from the perspective of Imaginative knowledge such a Greek would have described what we tend to refer to as the human etheric body in relation to the element of water. I said: Imaginative understanding would see a certain connection between the whole working of water, the waving and weaving of the element of water, its reaching out to the widths, its sinking towards the depths of the earth, and how these forces are connected with the individual manifestations of the life of plants. We are led in this way to a concrete example of what we find in the Imaginative world, or at least a part of the Imaginative world. It is a form of knowledge we can only attain in practice by going through a process of development such as I have described in my book *Knowledge of the Higher Worlds*, with the aim of acquiring Imaginative knowledge.

Even this form of knowledge, however, would leave us in the dark with respect to what is described as the element of air in the earlier view of the world. As the ancients saw it, this element of air can only be fully understood by a so-called Inspired consciousness. You will get an idea of Inspired consciousness, this experience of the element of air, if you try to imagine the following: I have often mentioned how today's view of the human being is based quite strongly on outer appearances. We need only remind ourselves of how today's images of human anatomy or physiology are composed; they are made to look as if there are clear contours to the internal organs: heart, liver and lungs etc. These clear contours are of course to some extent justified. The problem is that in using them we portray our bodies as if they were solid bodies, which they are not, of course. The very least part of our anatomy is composed of solid mineral substance. At the very most we could reckon with 8% of the human body being solid; 92% of the human body is a column of liquid. It is not solid. The solid elements are merely deposits within us. Little attention is drawn to this among today's students of physiology, anatomy and so on. We do not develop any understanding of the watery human being, of our fluid nature, if we represent it with clearly contoured organs. We are on the contrary in a process of constant flow and our organism is in a state of constant movement. Our airy organism is integrated into this fluid system. Air streams in, combines with substances within us and whisks them up, so to speak.

It is only by virtue of this airy element within us that we are fully at one with the world outside us. The air that is now inside me was not there a moment ago; it was outside. The air that is now inside me will soon be outside again. Looking at our nature from the perspective of this third element, the element of air, we cannot really say that we are enclosed within our skin and we are even less so with regard to the element of warmth, or fire. It cannot truly be said that we are entirely self-contained.

Let us now compare what we see as the complete human being, one who is not just organized as a solid body but whose organization includes the elements of water, air and warmth, with someone who is asleep. The warmth is integrated, and in constant intermingling movement, with the same person who is asleep, with both soul and spirit absent from the etheric and physical bodies lying there. The soul and spirit with which we are imbued when we are awake are not there between us falling asleep and waking up. They are in another world, which has its own rules, and we must ask ourselves, 'What are the rules that apply in the world we inhabit between falling asleep and waking up?' Yesterday we laid out four different sets of laws: firstly the laws governing the earthly world, secondly the laws that apply within the world of the cosmos, thirdly the laws within the cosmic soul and fourthly the laws governing the cosmic spirit. We ask ourselves: 'Where are we with our soul and spirit, or with our soul life and I, between falling asleep and waking up?' Now on reflection and comparison with what we have said before, it becomes clear that the astral body and the I are here between the time of falling asleep and waking in the region of the cosmic soul and of the cosmic spirit:

1. the laws that apply within the earthly world;
2. the laws that apply within the cosmos;
3. the laws that apply to the cosmic soul
4. the laws that apply to the cosmic spirit　} astral body, I

We must treat what was said yesterday very seriously, namely that the two first worlds, the earthly and the cosmic, are all that there is in the realm of space. So when entering these other two realms, we have already left the realm of space. We have to sharpen our awareness of this continually. Every time we sleep, as has often been said, we are led not only beyond our physical bodies but also beyond the whole realm of normal space. We are led into a world which may not in any way be confused with the world which we can perceive with our senses. This world is governed by all the laws which apply to our rhythmic nature, that imbues our watery element and our airy element with rhythm. This rhythm appears in space, but the source of the rhythm, the principles at work in what produces the rhythm, all spring forth at every point in space from depths that lie beyond space. It is governed by a real world that lies beyond sense-perceptible space. When we contemplate the wonderful interaction within us of our breathing rhythm and the beat of our pulse we can perceive, coming into the world we inhabit as physical human beings, a quality in this rhythm that springs from an order prevailing beyond space and which is founded in the spirit. We can have no understanding of the airy element until we achieve a concrete grasp of what expresses itself in the rhythmic processes at work in us within this airy element.

When we are using our powers of imagination to grasp what I described to you yesterday, the weaving of the world of plants and the parallel weaving of the watery element in our own body, we are still within the world we normally inhabit; what we have to do is to think of ourselves as transported away from the earth, poured out, as it were, into the whole cosmos. But if we take the step into the element of air, we have to project ourselves beyond space, we have to be able to recognize that we are in a world which no longer has a spatial dimension, but exists only in time, a world in which only time has a meaning. In the days when people could have a living experience of this, they were able to see the properties of such a world as including the work of the spirit playing into human activity indirectly via rhythm. I drew attention to how the Greek of ancient times formed the hexameter: three beats of our pulse together with the caesura corresponding to one breath, and a further three heartbeats with a caesura or the end of the verse, completing the hexameter: two breaths and their corresponding eight heartbeats. This harmony of breathing and pulse was artistically integrated into the recitation of Greek hexameter.

The way in which we are permeated by our supersensible nature, trickling into our blood circulation, our pulse beat, and synthesizing itself into four rhythmic pulse beats to one breath is replicated in the speech formation of the hexameter. From the very beginning, all efforts to compose verse have been drawn from this rhythmic organization within us.

$$— \cup\cup \ — \cup\cup \ — \cup\cup \mid — \cup\cup \ — \cup\cup \ — \cup\cup \mid$$

We ourselves can only experience the world from which this rhythmic activity originates when we become conscious in our sleeping state. The activity in which we are asleep, but conscious, plays into our own rhythm. We are oblivious to what is going on there in our normal everyday consciousness, let alone in the scientific consciousness of today. If we do attain this consciousness, then not only do we become aware of what I described yesterday: the surging, weaving, waving world of the plants, but now also a phenomenon which goes beyond the images common to the animal world, which would after all be spatial: a clear consciousness (which can only occur outside our body not inside it) which contains the concrete pictures from which the forms of animals as they appear in space are drawn. Just as our human rhythms bubble into us from a realm beyond space, the forms in which the various animals are organized also bubble into them from the world that lies beyond space.

The first thing we notice when we consciously experience how we normally are between falling asleep and waking, when we dive into the world which is the source of our rhythm, is that we understand the animal world in all its forms. This cannot be explained on the basis of outer physical forces. If zoologists, or morphologists believe they can explain the form of a lion, a tiger, a butterfly, or a beetle on the basis of anything that can be found in physical space, they are deluded. Nothing in our physical world here is capable of explaining the forms of the animal world. We only encounter it in the way I have described when we enter into the third of the guiding principles, the guiding principle of the cosmic soul.

Now I'd like once more to go back to the Greek whom we heard in conversation yesterday with the modern educated person who knows everything; well, this person occasionally admits to not knowing everything, but does nevertheless claim that everything must be capable of explanation in his way. The Greek would say, 'Nothing at all can be explained in your way, because I have heard that you have something like a form of logic. This involves listing all kinds of abstract concepts in categories such as to be, to become and to have etc. This logic is governed by what are supposed to be the principles of concepts and ideas.' If I think back to a Greek from the pre-Socratic era when the philosophies of Thales, Heraclitus and Anaxagoras were developed, which are now only partially extant, he would say that what we now call logic was made by a person who no longer had much knowledge of the secrets of the world. It was developed by Aristotle after he had applied his philistine view of the world to Platonism. Aristotle was of course a great man but also a great philistine who totally corrupted real logic. He converted real logic into a fabric which relates to reality in the same way that something finely woven and insubstantial relates to something solid and real. The Greek from this era who would have been a scientist in his own way would say: 'Real logic includes the forms which become outwardly visible in the animal world and to which we can have access only when we become conscious in the state we are in between sleeping and waking. That is what real logic is, the real content of logical consciousness.'

The animal world contains nothing different from what is in the human world; but in the human world it is spiritualized. So we can think the logical forms that project into the outer world and become animals.[12] Just as when we contemplate our etheric nature and observe the world of plants, thinking of it as embedded in the element of water, we can understand our soul nature, (we might call it the astral world) when we immerse ourselves in this living weaving which belongs to the consciousness we have between sleeping and waking, as reflected in the outer shaping and forming of the animal world. We have to think of our own forming processes in the world of ideas as woven into the rhythms of the airy element.

Much of what I have indicated to you about our human nature can be conceptualized quite concretely. To take such a concrete example: you breathe in, and the air goes into you through the lungs in the normal way, but once you have drawn this breath, the air enters the space occupied by the bone marrow and its surrounding fluid; within the arachnoidal cavity the fluid that surrounds the bone marrow is thrown rhythmically against the brain. The cerebral fluid comes into motion. The activity generated in the cerebral fluid is the activity of thinking. In reality, thought comes in waves on the in-breath which are conveyed to the cerebral fluid, and the cerebral fluid which keeps the brain afloat conveys its rhythmic pulse to the brain itself. Our sense impressions, from our eyes, ears and other nerve-sense activity live in the brain. The rhythm of our breathing collides with these sense impressions and an interplay develops between our sense impressions and the activity of thought. This is the formal thought activity which is outwardly expressed in the forms of the animal world. It is brought about by the breathing rhythm as it encounters our cerebral fluid in the arachnoidal cavity and then plays on the sense impressions living within our brain. This now contains all that rhythm has brought to life in us out of the world of ideas.

The important thing is that you try gradually to penetrate the way the spirit plays into the physical world of the senses. The great damage done to culture in our time lies in the fact that we have a science that only reaches the spirit in abstract forms, in purely intellectualized forms, whereas the spirit has to be grasped in its creative element, failing which the material world remains outside it like something hard and untamed. We must gain an insight into how the third and fourth sets of principles we mentioned play a practical role in all that we do.

It is the most wonderful thing when we become aware of, and learn to know the true inner reason for what can take place within us with every breath we draw; *can* take place rather than *does* take place when the in-breath has its effect on our cerebral fluid. Now comes the reverse: the cerebral fluid is pressed back again through the arachnoidal cavity and the out-breath follows. This is an act of devotion to the world, emerging into the world. The essence of what comes to expression in the rhythm of breathing is just this: becoming an I, merging with the world, becoming an I, merging with the world.

This is what we are referring to when we speak of the reality of the element of air, whereas the element of earth can only deal with what is contained in our 70-odd chemical elements. There you see it: what eventually turns into a corpse is subject to the set of principles governing the 72 elements. On the other hand what brings activity into this collection of elements comes streaming in from the cosmos, so that it can grow and digest. It is an element from beyond space that enables it not only to grow, to digest but to manifest itself in continual rhythmic activity in the rhythm of our pulse and the rhythm of pulse and breath. We study this extra-spatial world in the element of air, for that is where it manifests itself, just as we study the cosmic world, (not the earthly) in the element of water. That is where it is revealed. What is revealed to today's chemist or physicist is only based on the differentiated aspects of the element of earth.

We can also find the crossing point into the element of warmth or fire but that is only possible in practice when one has developed the faculty not only of consciously leaving one's body, but also merging this consciousness with other beings. There is a clear difference. It is perfectly possible to have the faculty of leaving one's body (even with a remnant of egotism in regard to the world) so that one can grasp all that I have spoken of so far, but one cannot really merge with this outer world, one cannot surrender to it. Once the elements of a capacity for genuine supersensible love are acquired, an immersion in the world in which we live between sleeping and waking, only then do we acquire a practical knowledge of the element of warmth or fire. Only then do we really know our own true nature. What we see with our senses from the outside is initially only an illusory image of the person, the person from the other side, the sense-perceptible side.

If we raise our consciousness to the level of the element of water it is at first the etheric being of the person that flows out before us. It becomes a miniature image of winter, summer, autumn and so on. Once we reach the element of air we become aware of a rhythmical movement. Our essential humanity, eternal in nature, can only be known through the element of warmth. This is where everything comes together, the moving and weaving of the water element and the rhythms and pulses of the element of air. They bring each other into balance, move in and out of harmony with each other in the element of warmth or fire, and that is where our own true essence can be known. Only then are we in the active principle of the cosmic spirit.

When we are told today of how earlier science viewed earth, water, air and fire, we should not think: our modern-day science has made great advances, we should rather think: there was once a totally different understanding of the human being as rooted in supersensible depths. At that time they also knew about the different ways in which the element of earth related to the supersensible sphere. The element of water is already a little closer to it; the watery element is actually closer to the world of the spheres, spread out in the widths of the cosmos than to the earth itself. However, when we seek the source of the rhythms of the air within us, in other words our air organization, we leave the world of space completely. This is where we create rhythms and dissolve rhythms. Finally we come to the universality beyond space which even overcomes time when we enter the element of fire, of warmth. Only then do we encounter the wholeness of our own nature. It may actually be found, albeit in a corrupted form, in literature going back before the fifteenth century once it has been rediscovered, and it is indeed necessary that it is rediscovered today.

A couple of years ago a piece of research was published by a Swedish academic on the topic of alchemy.[13] This Swedish academic reads a process as described by an alchemist and says: 'If you examine this process today it turns out to be pure nonsense, you can make nothing of it.' It is quite easy to understand how a modern chemist, even the Swede, who is somewhat less prejudiced than the Middle-European ones, could take what is expressed in the form in which it appears in the corrupted literature of times gone by, replicate it and then say that one can make nothing of it! I looked up the procedure in the literature that the good Swede could make nothing of, and found that the process described is actually related to a part of embryonic development, human embryonic development! That became evident very quickly. One just had to be able to read what was written! The modern chemist reads something like this and applies the terminology he has learned in his studies of chemistry. Then he sets up his retorts and replicates the process. Nonsense! What he had been reading was in fact part of a process that takes place in the development of the embryo in the mother's womb. You see, that illustrates the chasm that has opened up between what the modern academic can read and what was understood in earlier times.

What was described then was based on concepts such as those we are rediscovering in more recent spiritual science. There is no way of reading these ancient writings until these concepts are rediscovered; they were accessible then but by very different methods to those we are familiar with today. They were instinctive or atavistic, it is true, but they were accessible, and humanity has regressed from them to an understanding which is confined to the element of earth. It is now up to us to develop an understanding of the elements that goes beyond the mere corpse towards a full understanding of the whole living human being. That will, however, require of our modern civilization that we open our minds in all seriousness to the question of pre-existence.

When the concept of pre-existence was rejected in the course of Western cultural development, selfless research went with it. Today's sermons of whatever faith essentially appeal to human egotism. We know that people are afraid or uncomfortable about the thought of life ending. Of course it doesn't end. But these sermons don't appeal to our powers of understanding, they appeal to our fear of death, to the desire to continue living on after the death of our body. In other words they appeal to our egotism. This can't happen if we take pre-existence into account. As far as this egotism is concerned it is actually a matter of complete indifference to people of our time whether or not they were alive before birth or before conception. They are alive now; they know that. That is why they are not particularly concerned with the question of pre-existence. It is the post-existence they are concerned about. They may be alive now, but don't know whether they will live on after death. This is all based on egotism. Given that they are alive now (and unless they have worked on their self-knowledge) they will say instinctively or unconsciously: 'Well, I am alive now and whether or not I was alive before my birth or conception doesn't matter. The main thing is that I have now started to live and don't stop again!'

This is essentially the mood out of which people's feelings today can be enthused for immortality. In most familiar languages there is therefore the word 'immortality' to denote eternity after the end of life, but most major languages do not have a word for 'unbornness' This is something we must struggle to acquire over time. It would be better suited to a path of knowledge, a non-egotistic search for the source of our being. That is what is needed in our time. Knowledge in general must increasingly be infused with morality, with an ethical awareness. The development of our culture can only take an upward course once the laboratory table has become an altar, once synthesis and analysis have become a kind of spiritual art form and when there is an awareness that any given action has an impact on the world's development. We shall inevitably fall into a terrible decline unless there is a more widespread understanding that our striving for knowledge must be free of egotism, that our knowledge must be fully imbued with morality and must overcome the scientific methods of our time which cannot deal with the higher worlds. We have to reach a new understanding of the rhythm that so profoundly affects our lives and also of what is at work in our interactions with warmth. It is morality that works into us through warmth. Whilst there are simple variations in warmth, nuances of warmth, in reality they consist of all-permeating waves of morality within which we can develop our humanity. We must gradually become more aware of this. It is not simply an idealistic whim that challenges us to read the signs of our time but rather the signs of our time themselves which urge us towards a deepening of our understanding of the supersensible world.

LECTURE 5

DORNACH, 1 JULY 1921

TODAY I would like to make a kind of excursion from the remarks I made eight days ago or more, and then lead on into the continuation of our studies. In our experience of the world we can see much in ourselves and in the world itself that appears abnormal or pathological and from a certain point of view rightly so; but the moment we see the world as abnormal or pathological in an absolute sense, we have not yet understood it. Indeed we often bar the way to an understanding of the world if we simply stick to evaluations such as healthy and ill, right, wrong, true, false, good, bad and so on. What from one point of view can appear abnormal or pathological can from another point of view seem fully justified in the wider context of the whole world. I will now give you a concrete example and you will see what I mean.

The incidence of so-called hallucinations or even visions is rightly considered pathological. Hallucinations, or figures that appear in human consciousness and which on closer, critical examination do not correspond to any equivalent reality are pathological when viewed from the perspective of life as we know it between conception and death. However, in determining that hallucinations are abnormal, and that they certainly do not belong in the course of normal life between birth and death we have by no means grasped the essence of their nature.

Let us set aside any such judgement about hallucinations. Let us look instead at how they appear to the person who is hallucinating. They occur in the form of images which are more intensely connected to the person's subjective experience, to their inner life, than the usual outer sense impressions. A hallucination is inwardly experienced more intensely than a sense impression. Moreover a sense impression can be subjected to clear critical thinking; the person having a hallucination will avoid subjecting the hallucination to clear, critical scrutiny, preferring to live in the hovering, weaving imagery.

What is this experience the person is living through? It cannot be understood if one is only familiar with what appears to ordinary human consciousness between birth and death. The content of a hallucination will invariably appear unjustified to such a consciousness. A hallucination must be seen from a completely different point of view and can then reveal its true nature. This point of view is attained when in the course of inner development towards knowledge of the higher worlds, one is able to understand one's own living and weaving passage between death and a new birth and in particular when one's own being is decades away from approaching conception and birth.

When we have acquired the faculty of feeling our way into what we all normally go through on approaching birth or conception, we are feeling our way into the true nature of what is experienced as abnormal, as a hallucination, in life between birth and death.

Just as here in our life between birth and death we are surrounded by the world of colour, where we can sense every breath of air and so on, in other words what we consider normal experience between birth and death, in passing between death and birth the experience of our being of soul and spirit would be in an element that is completely identical with what we would consider a hallucination. We are born out of the element of hallucination and particularly so in respect of our physicality. What occurs in a hallucination is, as it were, wafting through the world that underlies our own soul and we emerge from this element at the moment of birth, an element that can seem abnormal in our soul life thereafter.

So what is a hallucination in ordinary consciousness? Now when we have gone through life between death and the new birth and have entered physical existence through conception and birth, certain spiritual beings from those higher hierarchies we have become familiar with will have had an Intuition and our physical body is the result of this Intuition. In short: certain beings have Intuitions; the result of these Intuitions is the human physical body which can only come into existence by means of the soul permeating it on emerging from the element of hallucinations.

What happens when hallucinations are experienced pathologically in normal consciousness? I can really only represent this to you in the form of an image; but this is natural, since hallucinations are after all images. It is therefore obvious that one will not get very far with abstract concepts. One has to resort to representing hallucinations in picture form.

Now try to imagine the following: our physical bodies, as I recently pointed out, consist only minimally of clearly defined contours; they are mostly watery, partly airy and so on. This physical body has a certain consistency, a certain density. When this natural density is rendered unnatural, when its natural consistency is interrupted—try to imagine it symbolically as being compressed in its elasticity—then the original hallucinatory ele-

ment out of which it was born is squeezed out, like water out of a sponge. The origin of a hallucinatory experience is nothing other than the original element of the physical body, out of which it was born and shaped, being squeezed out of it. The pathology that comes to expression in hallucinatory experiences in consciousness always indicates ill health in the physical body, that spiritually squeezes itself out, as it were.

This fact shows us that in one sense our thinking really is what materialism says it is. Our physical body really is a copy of what pre-existed us in the spiritual worlds before our birth or conception. It is a copy. The thinking that appears to us in everyday consciousness, on which we pride ourselves more than anything, is indeed completely bound to our physical body, as materialists point out with some justification. The fact is that the thinking faculty that we have been using since the origins of modern scientific thinking in the fifteenth century, ceases to function when the physical body does. What you will often find in the Catholic philosophy commonly accepted today (though not what people believed in previous centuries) is the idea that the abstract, intellectual working of the soul continues after death. This is wrong; it is simply not true. The type of thinking that characterizes the cultural life of our times is indeed bound to the physical body. The quality of thinking that survives the death of the physical body will only be found in the next, higher stages of inner development: in Imagination, in Imaginative thought processes.

You might then think that anyone who does not have these is deprived of immortality! The issue has to be viewed in a different way. To say one has no Imaginative thought processes is meaningless. You could say: 'I have no Imaginative thought processes in my everyday consciousness. I cannot introduce them into the way I think every day,' but we are constantly forming Imaginative pictures within us. Imaginations are constantly taking shape in us but are then utilized in organic life processes; they turn into the forces which we use to renew our bodily organism. Our materialistic philosophy and our materialistic natural science take the view that our depleted organs are revitalized in some way when we are asleep but do not take much trouble to determine exactly how that happens. What actually happens is that it is precisely in our day-waking consciousness that we are constantly developing Imaginations, even when we are working with our everyday intellectual consciousness, and these Imaginations are then in a sense digested in our soul life where they enable us to rebuild our bodies. It is because these Imaginations are rebuilding our bodies that we are not aware of them separately in our everyday consciousness. Developing higher faculties of knowledge relies on us partially withdrawing (from an external point of view) from this work of rebuilding our physical bodies and drawing up into consciousness what is otherwise bubbling and simmering below. That is the reason why spiritual science is necessary to attain higher knowledge, since this process is not sustainable for any length of time without undermining the health of our organism. So in ordinary life we do form Imaginations but these are then digested during our time between birth and death. We could go on to say that there is an unconscious process going on in ordinary life which is in fact hallucinating and would be recognized as such if we became conscious of it. Hallucinating is undoubtedly a primitive response in our existence; it should not, however, appear in our consciousness inappropriately. Hallucination as it normally manifests should really be confined to our subconsciousness. When the body, as it were, squeezes out its primal substance, it can happen that this primal substance becomes embodied in our normal consciousness and then hallucinations appear. Hallucination simply means that our body sends up into our conscious mind what it would normally use for digestion, growth and other such processes.

This in turn relates to what I have often explained in connection with the illusions people have about certain mystics. It is as if one were devaluing their essential character by pointing out the underlying phenomena. I said: Take for example the hallucinations that have a remarkably beautiful poetic character like those described by figures such as Mechthild von Magdeburg or Saint Teresa. They are certainly beautiful, but what are they in reality? Anyone who has a true understanding of these phenomena will find that they are hallucinations, squeezed out of the organs within the whole organism of the person having them. They are primal substance. A truthful description of them will on occasion include processes very similar to digestion in the cases of Mechthild von Magdeburg or Saint Teresa, however beautiful the mystic poetry may be that streams from their consciousness.

One need not actually say that some of the fruits of historical mysticism are thus deprived of their flavour. The sensual delight that some people experience when they turn their thoughts to mysticism, or when they wish to have mystical experiences themselves, can, however, be traced back to its true origin in this way. A great deal of mystical experience is in fact simply inner sensual delight which can appear in our consciousness as poetic beauty; the only thing that is destroyed by this consideration is prejudice or an illusion. If we are set on penetrating through to an understanding of the reality of our inner life we will have to be prepared to find not the wonderful descriptions of such mystics but the products of their liver, lungs and other organs out of the cosmos, the hallucinating of the cosmos. In essence it is not so much removing the flavour of mysticism as opening a doorway towards a higher understanding if we are able to show how liver is formed by the hallucinating of the cosmos, how it is in a way the transformed result of a condensation of the spirit, and its hallucinating. We can thus gain an insight into the nature of our physical body and into its relationship with the entire cosmos.

Whenever we try to explain the truth in detail, there will be very clever contemporaries who will raise their objections and one such might be: 'What are you saying! That the human form takes shape out of the cosmos? But we know human beings are born out of the mother's body. We know how they look in embryonic form and so on!' Now there is a fundamentally wrong idea at the root of such an objection which we shall have to deal with, despite the fact that we have done so before.

If we look at the variety of forms in the natural world around us we will find the greatest diversity. We might name them crystals. We will also find other forms emerging from any given inner configuration of let's say carbon, hydrogen, oxygen, nitrogen or sulphur. We know that when carbon and oxygen combine to form CO_2, a gas emerges that has a certain weight; when carbon combines with nitrogen the result is cyanide gas and so on. The materials arising can always be analysed by a chemist but do not always have an outer crystalline form. They do, however, have an inner configuration. This inner configuration has even been pointed out recently by means of structural formulae familiar to contemporary science.

This has, however, always been subject to certain preconditions, namely that the molecules, as they are termed, always become increasingly complex the further we progress from inorganic to organic matter. Moreover it is said that the organic molecule, the cell molecule, consists of carbon, nitrogen, hydrogen and sulphur. They combine in one form or another. It is further stated that the way they combine is very complex. It is regarded as an ideal within natural science to discover just how these individual atoms can combine in such complex organic molecules. Scientists admit that it will take a long time to find out how organic matter is built up, atom by atom into the living molecule. The secret, however, is this: the more an aggregation of matter is organic, the less its individual elements are combined by chemical processes, the more the constituent parts are whirled about chaotically; even an ordinary protein molecule, let us say in a nerve substance or in the substance of blood are essentially inwardly amorphous forms rather than complex molecules. On the contrary they are composed of inorganic matter that has been torn apart inwardly, that has rid itself of the forces of crystallization, the very forces that hold the molecules together, that connect one atom to another. This already holds true of any ordinary organic molecule and most of all of the molecules of the embryo, in the protein of the seed.

If I illustrate this schematically, with the organism here and the seed there, i.e. the beginnings of the embryo, then the seed is the most chaotic combination of material components imaginable. This seed has emancipated itself from any crystallizing force, any chemical force at work in the mineral world etc. An absolute chaos has appeared at one point, which can only be held together by the other organism. The fact that this chaotic protein appears here is what enables the entire cosmos to work on the protein so that in fact it receives the imprint of forces from the entire universe. The ovum meanwhile contains the forces which give form to the etheric body and the astral body, before fertilization has taken place. Once this has happened, it also embodies the physical form and the vessel or sheath for the I.

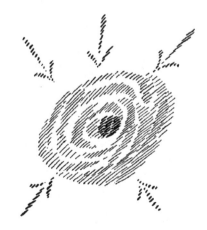

Here we have the situation before fertilization, and this is a purely cosmic image, an image from out of the cosmos because the protein emancipates itself from all earthly forces and thus can be determined by what lies beyond the earth. The earthly substance within the ovum truly is devoted to the forces of the cosmos. These create their own image within the ovum. Certain forms of egg in the animal kingdom, birds for example, enable us to see something very important. This is naturally not evident in higher animals, nor in human beings, but we can find a reflection of the cosmos in the shape of a hen's egg. An egg is in fact a genuine image of the cosmos. The cosmic forces work into the dedicated protein that has emancipated itself from its earthly origins.

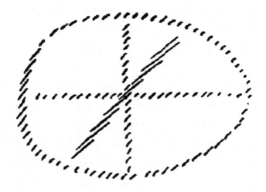

An egg really does bear the imprint of the cosmos and philosophers need not speculate about the three dimensions, since the riddles of the world are revealed openly everywhere if one knows where to look. The shape of a hen's egg is a proof of the fact that one axis of the world is longer than the two others and the outer contours of a hen's egg, the eggshell, are a true image of our space. As an aside to mathematicians—it will be necessary for our mathematicians to examine the relationship between Lobachevsky's geometry or Riemann's definition of space and the form of a hen's egg.[14] There is a great deal to be learned from this. Problems actually need to be addressed concretely.

You can see, when we contemplate the receptive and adaptable protein we are able to study how the cosmos works into it and can elucidate in detail how the cosmos has determined it. The caution does have to be added however, that we cannot yet go very far with this, since if people of our time were able to pursue this in detail, the resultant knowledge could be abused in the most appalling way, given the extraordinary moral low point that has been reached by the civilized population of the world.

We have now observed how our body produces these mental images: it squeezes out of itself the world of hallucination from which it originated. Apart from our physical bodies, we also carry a soul within us as part of our being. We will do best to leave this soul aside for the moment and focus on our spiritual aspect. Just as during our life between birth and death we can walk around and, seeing ourselves from outside, we can say: 'We wear our physical bodies like a garment', so in the life between death and a new life we can say that we have a spiritual existence. That corresponds to what we can observe inwardly and it means that there is no essential difference between what we can say about our bodies between birth and death on the one hand and our spiritual beings between death and rebirth on the other. We have grown accustomed here to speak of the spirit as the fundamental essence of everything. This is, however, an illusory way of putting it. We should rather speak of the spirit as what belongs to us between death and a new birth just as our bodies belong to us here between birth and death, in the sense that we are embodied here, so between death and the new birth we are spiritualized. Moreover this spiritual essence does not cease to be when we take on our bodies (which have emerged from the hallucinating of the cosmos) but continues to work on in us.

Imagine the moment of conception, or perhaps rather a moment between conception and birth. It is not so important to focus on this particular moment but imagine any point where we pass out of the spiritual world into the physical and you will say to yourself: From this moment on our physical existence integrates with our soul and spiritual dimensions. Soul and spirit undergo a metamorphosis into our physical nature. Now the powers that we had acquired between death and a new birth do not cease to work at this moment of stepping into physical existence, but continue to have their effect in a very particular way. I shall illustrate it schematically like this:

Tod = death; Geburt = birth; Tod (rot) = death (red)

Now take the strength from your last death that works on in you in the spiritual world through to the moment—I shall call it birth— of your birth in your current life. The forces of your physical and etheric bodies will continue their work there. Then there would be a new death [red, darkly shaded]. But this power which belongs to us leading up to the new birth continues to work on in us and yet in another sense does not; its true being has been poured into our bodily nature, filling it with spirit. What remains of this power and continues on, as it were, in the same direction are only images, a picture of existence. Between birth and death then there lives on in us in the form of an image what we possessed between death and the new birth. This image is the power of our intellect. Our intellect has no reality between birth and death but is in fact an image of our existence between death and a new birth.

This perspective sheds light both on philosophical and cultural riddles. The whole configuration of our contemporary culture which is dependent on the intellect becomes clear to us when we know that it is a culture of images, a culture that has not been created out of any reality but is an image, an image it has to be said now of spiritual reality. Today's culture is an abstract one. Materialism is after all a culture of abstraction. One can think the finest thoughts once their origin is denied and one becomes a materialist. Material- istic thoughts were fundamentally quite penetrating, though they did follow an erroneous course. What is at work there is an image of a world, not a world in itself.

This concept is challenging; but do make the effort to grasp it. The only easy part will be to imagine images in space. When you are standing in front of a mirror you will not attribute any reality to the image that appears to you—it is you who are real, not the image. What is taking place here in space is also happening as a reality in our time. The mirror image is what we experience as our intellect, an image that reflects back in time to our previous existence. Our physical bodies contain a reflective surface which has the capacity to reflect back in time and the image that appears in the reflection is that of our pre-earthly existence. The complication arises when our experience of self (our sense impressions) is constantly thrown into this intellectual image. Sense impressions mingle with it. That is why we do not notice that it is in fact a reflection. We live in the present. If as a result of doing the exercises as described in my *Knowledge of the Higher Worlds* you reach the point where you can really throw out your sense impressions and live entirely in this image existence you will actually penetrate through into pre-birth existence, into life before birth. That is when you will experience pre-existence as a fact. The reflected image of pre-existence is after all within us; what we have to do is to see through it and then we will be able to see into pre-existence itself.

Everyone is capable of this in principle, unless they succumb to the other phenomenon which occurs when sense impressions are switched off, namely falling into a deep and healthy sleep. That is true for most people. We exclude all sense impressions but are then no longer capable of thinking. If, however, you really are able to shut out your sense impressions and retain a lively thinking capacity then you will find yourself no longer looking into space but back through the time you spent between your last death and rebirth. This is initially very indistinct, but you are aware that the world you are looking into is the world between your last death and most recent birth. The truth, a true perspective of all this, depends entirely on our ability not to fall asleep when sense impressions are suppressed and to keep our thinking as lively as it otherwise is with the help of our sense impressions when we are in possession of our senses.

Once we are able to see through our nature in this way and into our life before birth, continuing to do our inner exercises of course, then distinct contours will appear in our spiritual world; our spiritual surroundings will become apparent to us. That is when our situation turns into its opposite: here we live within the physical world, we do not squeeze its hallucinations out of our physical body but lift ourselves out of our bodies and transplant ourselves into our pre-birth existence and there fill ourselves with spiritual reality. We dive into the world which is awash with hallucinations and in perceiving our surroundings it is not hallucinations that we perceive but Imaginations. The moment we raise ourselves to spiritual awareness we perceive Imaginations.

It is of course loutish, lacking in common decency I would say, if someone claiming to be a scientist today constantly counters anthroposophy with the objection: 'That's all very well but what anthroposophy has to offer could itself simply be hallucination; there is no way of distinguishing it from hallucinations.' Such people should try really engaging with the research methods used in spiritual science and they would then find that it is just by following them that clear and precise distinctions can be drawn between hallucinations and Imagination.

And what is the distinction? Well I have pointed out that on the one hand we are clothed with a physical body between life and death and on the other with a spiritual body between death and a new birth. Our soul is the mediator between the two. Spiritual experience is drawn into our physical body through our life of soul; what we experience by means of our physical bodies is likewise carried by our soul through death and into the spiritual world. Our soul is the mediator between body and spirit.

When our physical body experiences awareness it produces hallucinations; in other words it brings hallucinations into our consciousness. When our spirit is consciously active as a spirit Imaginations are experienced, and when it is our soul experiencing as a soul and as the mediator between the two, then it neither experiences inappropriate hallucinations squeezed out of the body, nor does it progress directly to experience of spiritual realities but lives in a less clearly defined middle sphere: the realm of fantasy. The conclusion is that if our body is conscious (its task between birth and death is not normally to be conscious, but it nevertheless has a certain consciousness of its own) if it still breaks through to awareness, inappropriately, abnormally, then hallucinations result. If our spirit comes to full consciousness by genuinely releasing itself from our body and experiencing realities, then it has Imaginations. Our soul is the mediator between hallucinations and imaginations in the less clearly defined realm of fantasy.

When our body has a conscious experience as a body:	hallucinations;
when our soul has a conscious experience as a soul:	fantasy;
when our spirit has a conscious experience as a spirit:	Imaginations.

In describing processes such as these we are describing real processes. In our intellectual thinking we only have an image of our soul life in our pre-birthly existence i.e. the image of a life steeped in Imaginations, which emerges from a hallucinatory state. Our intellectual life is, however, not real. We ourselves are not real when we engage in thinking, but turn ourselves into an image when we think. We could not otherwise be free. Human freedom is founded on the fact that our thinking is not real when it becomes pure thinking. A mirror image cannot be a 'cause'. When you are facing any mirror image, something which is nothing more than an image, and you then act on it, it is not the image which determines the action. Once your thinking is a reality, there is no freedom. When your thinking is an image, your life between birth and death is a school of freedom because thinking itself cannot determine anything. A life lived in freedom must be a life without determination.

Living in the realm of fantasy on the other hand is not completely free; it is partly real as a form of living in one's thoughts. The free life that we bear within is not a real one in terms of our thinking activity. On the other hand when we can engage in pure thinking and can then develop the willpower to accomplish a free deed out of this pure thinking, we have made a start with experiencing reality. Where we are able to endow our pure thinking with reality out of our own substance, a free deed can take place. That is what I intended to explain purely philosophically in my book *The Philosophy of Spiritual Activity* in 1893 by way of preparation for later work.

LECTURE 6

DORNACH, 2 JULY 1921

Today it will be my task to develop further what I began with yesterday. Let me remind you of something that most of you will already have heard from me. When we go through death our physical body remains behind with the forces of the earth; our etheric body dissolves into the forces of the cosmos and we continue our passage, our existence, through the realms that lie between death and a new birth. I went on to add that one can trace back the effects of the formative forces reaching over in the physiognomy of each individual from one life to another. Now we know that we human beings are essentially threefold in nature, having three independent elements to our nature. I am referring to the formative forces at work in our physical organization to begin with. We have the nerve-sense organization which is of course spread out over our whole body but is chiefly concentrated in our head; we have the rhythmic organization, the breathing rhythm, the rhythm of our blood circulation and other rhythms; then we have the metabolic and limb system which we can consider as a single organism since movement is inwardly very closely associated with our metabolism.

Now you know that everyone's head has a different shape. We are not thinking of course of the physical substances involved but of the formative forces which give to each head its individual physiognomy, its phrenological expression. If we look at these forces we shall see how they have carried across from the metabolic/limb organization of the previous incarnation. The form of the head then is the result of the metamorphosis of the forces within the metabolic/limb human being in the previous incarnation. Similarly the forces at work in our metabolic/limb organization in this incarnation will undergo a transformation and give shape to our head in the next incarnation. Thus once we have understood the forces at work in shaping our human form we can gain an insight via the concept of metamorphosis through the manifestation of our head today into the metabolic/ limb system of the previous incarnation and likewise through the metabolic/limb organization of today get a glimpse into the head organization of the next incarnation.

This view of the world which plays a certain role in our spiritual science and in fact has done so throughout the ages contains the truths concerning repeated lives on earth. These are by no means idle theories but can be directly derived from a study of the constitution of the human being by anyone who has the appropriate knowledge. The problem is that the direction taken by natural science in our time could scarcely be further from the point of view required to undertake such a study of the human being. If external anatomy and physiology are the only permissible means of studying the human being there is of course no alternative to the blinkered view that liver and lung can be examined in exactly the same way. The liver is placed on the dissecting surface next to the lung and is considered a comparable organ, made up of cells and so on. There is absolutely nothing to be learned from these things with that approach and two such different organ systems as the lung and the liver simply can't be studied so superficially on the basis of the configuration of their cells, which is the method prescribed today.

In order to truly understand the relevant factors one would have to undertake to learn the methods necessary to gain access to these things. Once these faculties have been acquired in the appropriate way as described in my *Knowledge of the Higher Worlds* our ordinary access to knowledge which is externally through our senses and internally in our experience of thinking, feeling and willing is enhanced.[15] When we bring about this enhancement by means of the exercises I have often described, our perspective on the outer world changes and the first outcome is that we realize that it is complete nonsense to talk about atoms in the way that is prescribed by our current view of the world. It is not waves that underlie our sense impressions, our qualitative experience of yellow, red, the notes C or G but spiritual substance. The outer world becomes increasingly spiritual the more we develop our powers of cognition. We can then no longer take all the constructs of chemistry and other such ideas seriously. Any form of atomism is thoroughly eradicated from our consciousness once we have enhanced our means of perceiving the outer world. What lies behind the surface of the outer world is spirit. Once we apply this enhanced cognition to penetrate more deeply into what lies within, it is not confused mystical perception that appears (though it does admittedly have a justified transitional role which has to be explained in the way I did yesterday) but a psychic apprehension of our organs. We really learn to perceive and understand our internal organs. Outwardly our perception becomes increasingly spiritualized, inwardly it becomes increasingly material to begin with. Looking inwards it is not the nebulous mystic but the genuine spiritual researcher who will learn about the individual organ; one will be able to discern the differentiated human organism. The only way to reach the spiritual world is indirectly, via a contemplation of our inner materiality. Without acquiring an understanding of our liver, lungs etc. this indirect approach through our insides will not enable us to develop the kind of spiritual enthusiasm that can lead us out of the confusion of mere mysticism and into a concrete understanding of our internal organs.

One consequence of this is that one then learns more about the inner structure of the soul. We learn to let go of the presupposition that our soul life is connected only with the nervous system. It is the world of thoughts and ideas that is connected with the nervous system but not the world of feelings. These are directly connected with our rhythmic organization, and the world of our will impulses is connected with the metabolic/limb system. When I exercise my will to do something my metabolic/limb must go through a process. The nervous system only serves the purpose of becoming aware of what is going on in my will system. There are no nerves directly connected to the will, no motor nerves, as I have often pointed out; the classifying of nerves as sensory and motor nerves is nonsense. Nerves are all of a kind and the so-called motor nerves have no other purpose than to sense or perceive what is going on within us; they are also sensory nerves.

If we make a thorough study of this we will eventually come to a holistic view of how the human being is organized. If we take for example the liver organization or the lung organization and study them inwardly using our spiritual faculties, we will come to a certain picture of the surface of the individual organs. What is this surface? The surface of our organs is purely a device for reflecting the life of our soul. What we perceive and think about is reflected from the surface of all our internal organs and this reflection amounts to our recollections, our memory during life. Once we have perceived and processed something it is then reflected from the surface of our heart, our lungs, our spleen etc. and results in our memories. This involves the most diverse organs. If for example we are dealing with the memory of let us say very abstract thoughts, it is our lungs, the surface of our lungs that is very strongly involved. If our thoughts are more tinged with feeling, if they have a nuance of feeling about them, it is the surface of the liver that comes into play. As a result we can give a good description, and in some detail, of the involvement of our inner organs in this reflection which then appears as memory, as the faculty of recall. It is our soul life that we are considering. We cannot say: it is the nervous system alone which acts as its parallel organization; on the contrary it is the entire human organism which contains the parallel organization of our life of soul.

In this respect there is a great deal of knowledge that was once instinctive and has now been lost to us. It appears in certain words and expressions, but we no longer sense how much wisdom is contained within them. For example if someone has memories which always tend towards a depressive condition, this was described by the ancient Greeks as hypochondria: abdominal gristle, a calcifying process within the abdomen which results in a reflection arising in the individual, which leads to his memories becoming a source of hypochondria. The whole organism is always involved in these things. We have to take this into consideration.

Now when I spoke of the faculty of memory I mentioned the surfaces of our organs. In a way everything that we experience strikes the surface, is reflected, and that leads to our memories. But something of these impressions also penetrates through into the organism. In ordinary life this is processed; it goes through a metamorphosis with the result that the organ secretes something. The organs that carry out this process are usually glandular; they have an inner secretion and the forces that enter in this way are initially processed during the course of life. But not everything is processed in this way, in organic metabolism and so on, and the organs can absorb something which then becomes latent in them, generating an inner force. This is the case for example with all thoughts that we take in which have to do mainly with the way in which we view the outer world, so that these thoughts result in images of the outer objects: the forces which are developed in these thoughts are stored in our lungs, in the inner part of our lungs. Now you will know that the inner part of the lung is activated by the metabolism, by the movement of the limbs, and there these forces are transformed in such a way that our lungs become a kind of reservoir into which our metabolic/ limb organization is constantly playing during the course of life between birth and death. When we die these forces are stored up. Naturally the physical aspect falls away but these forces do not; they accompany us through death and through our life between death and a new birth. When we then embark on a new incarnation it is primarily the forces that were accumulated in our lungs which outwardly form our heads, which impose on us the physiognomy of our heads. The outer form of our heads as studied in phrenology is prefigured in the inside of our lungs in our previous incarnation.

That is how concretely one can trace the transformation of forces from one life to another. Then these things no longer constitute abstract truths but can be observed concretely, just as one observes physical objects in concrete detail. Spiritual science is only really valuable when one can go into concrete detail in this way. Talking in generalities about repeated earth lives and so on is just words. They only take on meaning when one can go into individual, concrete detail.

If one cannot control what is stored up in one's lungs in the right way, it gets squeezed out as I mentioned yesterday, rather in the way a sponge can be squeezed out, and then the forces which should really be forming our head in the next incarnation tend to produce abnormal phenomena, usually described as compulsive thoughts or some other form of illusion. It would be interesting to study at a higher level of physiology what peculiar ideas appear in patients with advanced lung disease. This is connected with what I have just outlined as the squeezing out of thoughts. Thoughts that are squeezed out in this way are compulsive because they already have formative forces within them. Thoughts that we have in our consciousness under normal conditions should be merely images; they should contain no formative forces and should not be compelling. Throughout the long process between death and a new birth they do compel us; they are causal and have a formative effect. Now, during everyday life, they should not overwhelm us; their power should be exercised only in the transition between one life and another. That is what needs to be considered.

If you now study the liver in the same way as I have set out for the lungs you will find: forces are concentrated within the liver which translate in the subsequent life as the inner disposition of the brain. The inner forces of the liver in the present life are transferred indirectly through the metabolic organism, this time not into the form of the head, as was the case with the lungs, but into the inner disposition of the brain. Whether or not someone is an acute thinker in the next incarnation depends on their behaviour in the present one. Certain forces manifest themselves indirectly through the metabolic processes of the liver; if, however, these forces are squeezed out in the present incarnation, they lead to hallucinations or strong visions.

What I indicated yesterday in a more abstract way you can now see concretely: as they are squeezed out of the organs, these things intrude into our consciousness, emerging from the general hallucinatory life that should play into one life from another, and then make their appearance in these ways.

Adopting the same approach to what is involved with the secretions of our kidneys, we will see how forces are concentrated there which influence the organization of our head in the following incarnation, this time more in the direction of our emotions. Kidneys, secretory organs, generally produce what has to do with one's temperamental disposition (in the broadest sense of the word) in the next incarnation, but indirectly through the head organization. If these things are squeezed out in the current incarnation they give rise to all kinds of nervous conditions, conditions which are connected with our excitability, emotional upsets, hypochondria, depression and so on, every condition that is particularly connected with that aspect of our metabolism. In fact everything that has to do with our memory and is of an emotional nature is connected with what is reflected from the kidneys. What is reflected from our lungs or liver tends to have more to do with memories, memories as such. If we look at the kidney organization we will find the basis of our enduring habits in this incarnation and the inner part of the kidneys prepares our disposition to one or another temperament in the next incarnation, but indirectly through the head organization.

Let us study the heart in the same way. Our heart is an exceptionally interesting organ, also from the perspective of spiritual-scientific research. You will know that our contemporary, trivial science takes a simplistic approach to understanding the heart as an organ. It is regarded as a pump that pumps blood around our bodies. Nothing could be further from the truth. The heart has nothing to do with any kind of pumping of blood. On the contrary, blood is activated by the responsive nature of our astral body and our I working together, and our heart moves as a reflex reaction to these movements. The movement of blood comes from within the blood itself and the heart then expresses what is caused by these forces in the movement of the blood. Our heart is in fact the organ which expresses the movement of our blood. Today's scientists are furious if one mentions this. I once explained it many years ago to a medical researcher. I think it was 1904 or 1905 on a journey to Stockholm, and he was almost beside himself at the notion that the heart should no longer be regarded as a pump but that it is the blood itself that moves out of its own vitality. Our heart is integrated in the general circulation of the blood and the heart accompanies it with its beat.

What is then reflected from the heart is no longer just a matter of memory or habit but life that has become spiritualized as it encounters the outer wall of our heart. It is our pangs of conscience that are reflected. We can look at this purely at a physical level: the pangs of conscience that radiate into our consciousness are what is reflected back from our heart as a result of our experiences. This is what is revealed by spiritual research on the heart. If on the other hand we look into the inside of the heart, we will find forces gathered there from the whole of the metabolic/limb system. It is because everything that has to do with the heart and the forces of the heart is spiritual, and what follows from our actions in outer life is also spiritualized as it enters the heart. Paradoxical as it might seem to someone who is well versed in the science of our time it is in fact the case that our karmic predispositions are formed in our heart. To speak of the heart as a mere pumping organ is foolish in the extreme for it is in fact the organ which through the medium of our metabolic/limb organization carries into the next life what we will there experience as karma.

You can see then that once we have become familiar with this organization, we can learn to differentiate it, and its connection with the whole of life extending beyond birth and death becomes apparent; one can then see into the whole structure of the human being. There was nothing to be said about the head in connection with metamorphosis since our head is simply shed; its forces have found their fulfilment in this incarnation, having been the transformed outcome of the previous incarnation. On the other hand what we have in the four main systems of lungs, kidneys, liver and heart passes over indirectly via the metabolic/limb system as forces that form and shape the head of our next incarnation with all its faculties. We must direct our attention to the forces in our present vital organs which will carry forward into our next incarnation what we are presently experiencing.

Our human metabolism is nothing like the bubbling and simmering in a retort that is portrayed in today's physiology. You have only to take one step and a metabolic process takes place. This metabolic process is not merely the chemical process that can be examined physiologically or chemically, but also has a moral quality, a moral nuance. This moral nuance is then stored up in your heart and is carried forward into the next incarnation as a karmic force. Thus a study of the whole human being means finding the forces at work in us that will extend beyond this life on earth. Our head is a sphere, which is only incomplete on account of the rest of the organism that is attached to it. Our head is formed in its entirety out of the cosmos. The elements of soul and spirit that remain with us after death must then adapt to the whole cosmos as the whole cosmos takes us into it. Then, leading up to the midpoint between two incarnations (in one of the Mystery Plays I referred to it as The Midnight Hour of existence) we are continually in a process of expanding into our surroundings. We gradually become identical with our surroundings. The part of us that reaches out into our surroundings in this way then becomes the configuration for the astral and etheric bodies of our next incarnation.

That is in essence what the cosmos determines in the mother. What determines the configuration of the physical body and the content of the I comes from the father in the fructification process. This I, as it has then become, passes over into a completely different world after the Midnight Hour. It goes into the world through which it can make its way through the fatherly nature. This is a particularly significant process. The fact is that the time leading up to the Midnight Hour and the time following it (both take place between death and a new birth) are actually very different from each other. In the cycle of lectures I gave in Vienna in 1914, I described these experiences from within.[16] Looking at them from the outside, we would have to say that the I becomes more cosmic in the first half, leading up to the Midnight Hour and there prepares what will pass indirectly through the mother into the next incarnation. Then from the Midnight Hour of existence until the next birth the I passes over into what used to be known in the old mysteries as the underworld and indirectly from there into fertilization. The two poles of the human being are thus brought together through the mother and the father: the higher world and the underworld.

What I have now said comes from an older, instinctive form of knowledge and as far as I know was a substantial part of the content of the Egyptian mysteries. The Egyptian mysteries were particularly concerned with leading humanity to an understanding of what were then called the higher and the lower gods, the higher and the lower worlds. In summary one can say that in the act of fertilization the polarity of the worlds of the higher and the lower gods is resolved and the I passes through the higher and then the lower of these worlds in its journey through life between death and a new birth. The curious nuance that many associate with the higher and the lower worlds today was by no means thought of in the same way by people of ancient times. People of our time always consider the higher world a good one and the lower the bad. Originally this nuance did not apply to them. They were considered to be simply the two polarities that had to play their part in the formation of the world as a whole. The higher world was directly experienced as the world of light and the lower world was the world of gravity: gravity and light as the two polarities viewed more externally. You can see from this how such things can be described quite concretely.

In relation to the other organs, I have told you that what flows out of them when squeezed can become hallucinatory life, particularly so in the case of the liver system. However, when the contents of the heart are squeezed out it involves the system of forces which call forth our particular inclination to live out our karma. Observing how each person's karma works itself out, it can only be described as a kind of hunger and satiation. That is how it should be understood. Let us start by looking at it from the point of view of everyday life and take a striking example: a woman meets a man and begins to love him. Well now that is the equivalent of cutting out a piece of the *Sistine Madonna*, a little finger of the baby Jesus for example, and studying it. You do of course have a piece of the *Sistine Madonna* but it tells you nothing. Similarly you are none the wiser when you take the phrase: a woman meets a man and begins to love him. It is simply not like that. One has to follow the sequence of events that led up to it. Before the woman met the man she went to other parts of the world and before that she was elsewhere and before that somewhere else again. One can find reasons everywhere why the woman went from one place to the other. This is of course hidden in the subconscious but there is some sense in it; it is somehow coherent and it is possible to follow the trail in this way right back into early childhood.

The woman concerned follows a trail from the very beginning that leads to the event in question. From the moment of birth we have a hunger to do what we do and do not stop until it is satisfied. The drive that leads us to the karmic event is the consequence of this kind of general spiritual feeling of hunger. We are driven by it. We are all like this. We have forces at work within us that lead us on to later events despite the freedom which is nevertheless present but operating in another sphere. We humans bear these forces within us.

Expressing themselves as a kind of hunger that leads to the ful-filment of karma, these forces are concentrated in our heart. When they are squeezed out and appear in our present consciousness (they remain located in our hearts but arise in our consciousness) they form pictures which in turn give rise to impulses which manifest as maniacal rage. This can be studied in real-life situations and is essen-tially the precocious experience in this incarnation of karmic forces destined for the next incarnation. We must get used to viewing world events quite differently once we have grasped these underlying con-nections. Of course if one is prone to outbursts of maniacal rage in the current incarnation one might be inclined to say (like the king who once ruled Spain): 'If God had left it to me to create the world, I would have done a better job of it.'[17] People do ask, 'Why did God create maniacal rage?' There are good reasons for outbursts of mani-acal rage but everything that is at work in the world can also appear at the wrong time and in the wrong place. This misplaced appearance in the present incarnation of karmic forces destined for the next incar-nation results in maniacal outbursts of rage. In this case it has been brought about by luciferic forces, like everything else that appears in the world before its due time. Thus we can literally study what is due to appear in subsequent lives in the abnormalities of the present one.

You can imagine what a huge difference there is between what lies in our hearts throughout the whole of our present incarnation and the condition it will be in once it has been through the long process of development between death and the new birth and then appears in the outer behaviour of the person concerned. Nevertheless, if you look into the depths of your heart you will get a fairly good idea (although it is still latent and not developed into a full picture) of what you will be up to in the next life. You can say then, not only in abstract terms and in general, that what is now being prepared in the current incarnation will work itself out karmically in the next. Not only that, you can even point out the coffer within which the karma of times to come lies resting. These are things which will have to be seen in quite concrete terms if we are to carry out genuine spiritual research.

You can see what huge importance these things will take on when they are studied and become part of our general education. What does modern medicine know about a possible illness of the liver or of the heart when it does not know the most important thing about them: what are they there for?! This remains unknown to modern medicine. It cannot even find a true connection between hallucinations due to overstimulation and let's say the kidney system, while the calm hallucinations that simply appear and are present as I explained a short while ago are liver hallucinations. Hallucinations that appear as if they were creeping around a person, that lead to the person involved wanting to scrape things off, come from the kidney system. These are hallucinations produced by stimuli which have to do with our emotions and temperaments. Symptoms like this can lead to much more secure diagnoses than the diagnostic tools so widely used today. Purely external diagnostic tools are very unreliable compared to what they could achieve if such things as these were studied.

They are all connected with the world around us. I pointed out that lungs as an internal organ or organ system contain in compressed form all the compulsive thoughts and everything that we take in as we perceive the outer world in concentrated form. Our liver relates to the outer world in a completely different way. The configuration of lungs is quite different on account of them preserving the substance of thoughts. It is more connected to the element of earth; our liver, which contains within it hallucination per se, calm hallucination that simply appears, is connected with our watery system, with the element of water, and the kidney system, paradoxical as it may sound, is connected with the element of air. One would think of course that it would relate to our lungs but they are connected with the element of the earth, although not exclusively so. It is the kidney system, however, which is connected with the element of air and the heart system is the organ connected with the elemental warmth; it is formed in its entirety out of the element of warmth. Now this element, which is the most spiritual, is also the one which absorbs the predisposition for our karma into its uncommonly fine warmth structures which we also have in our warmth organism.

Since the whole human being is related to the outer environment, we can say the following: our lungs will have a particular relationship with the element of earth in our surroundings, and the liver likewise with the watery element. If we now turn our attention to the earthly qualities of plants we will find within them (in the widest possible context,) the remedies for illnesses that originate in the lungs. If we go on to look at what is circulating within a plant, at the circulation of sap in plants, we will find there the remedy for everything that is connected with the liver organization. By studying the relationships of our organs with their environment you can find the basis for a rational therapy.

Our present-day therapy is a hotchpotch of empirical notes. A truly rational therapy can only be achieved by studying the inter-relationships of the world of the organs within us and the world around us. We would then, however, have to overcome within us the yearning for the delights of subjective mysticism. If one really has no intention of progressing beyond Meister Eckhart's well-known 'flickering flame of the Divine' etc., if one simply wishes to wallow in the delights within and their beautiful images, without penetrating through these to the concrete configuration of our internal organs, one will not break through to really significant therapeutic discoveries. These can be found on the path of genuine mysticism which penetrates into the inner human being. Just as we can penetrate into our inner core and thus indirectly learn about our passage from one incarnation to the next, when we turn our attention to the world outside us we can penetrate through the world of the senses, the veil of the senses, into the spirit. There we come into the world of the spiritual hierarchies which we will not have been able to reach indirectly via the inner path of mysticism but which is to be found by means of a deeper contemplation of the outer world. On this path we shall also find what at first can only be expressed in the form of analogies. These will not be just superficial analogies but will genuinely contain deeper relationships within them.

We breathe, don't we, and last time I worked out the number of breaths drawn in a 24-hour period. If we calculate on the basis of 18 breaths a minute, there will be 60 times 18 in an hour and over a 24-hour period of day and night there will thus be 25,920 breaths taken. We could look at another rhythm which we share, namely day and night. Every morning as you wake up, you draw your astral body and I back into your physical and etheric bodies. That is also a form of breathing. You breathe in in the morning, and out as you fall asleep in the evening; you breathe out your astral body and I again, amounting to one breath over a 24-hour period, so one breath per day. That amounts to 365 such breaths in a year and if you take the average life of a human being as 72 you arrive at roughly the same figure; if I had not taken 72 as the basis, but something below that I would have arrived at the same figure. That means that if you take the whole earthly lifespan of an individual and see the falling asleep and waking up as one breath, you will have the same number of breathings in and out of the astral body and the I as you will have taken breaths in a 24-hour period. During a life you will have had the same number of breathings in and out of your I and astral body. These rhythms are genuinely related to each other and they can show us how we are integrated into the wider world. Our life in a day from sunrise to sunset, i.e. the daily cycle, corresponds to an inner sunrise and sunset that lasts for the period between birth and death. You can see then that we are integrated into the whole cosmos and I would like to conclude today's reflections by drawing your attention to an idea which I would ask you to dwell on, to meditate on for a while. Contemporary science takes the view: this is the evolution of the world. During the course of this evolution at one point the earth arises. Then in turn, once entropy has taken its course, the earth will come to dissolution by heat. If we form a worldview today like the Copernican worldview or any kind of modified Copernicanism we only take into account the forces that have formed the primal nebula and so on, and the human being ends up as redundant. Geologists and astronomers take no account of human beings. It would not occur to them to look for the causes of a future world configuration within humanity in some way. We are present everywhere in the world process but are regarded as redundant. The world process plays out and we have nothing to do with it. Now imagine it differently: this whole world process comes to an end there, is lost in space. It comes to an end and as to what happens next, the cosmos will always be found within human beings; we will continue.

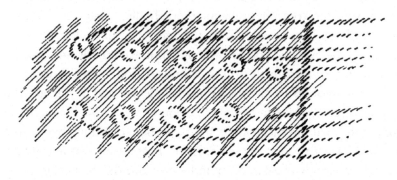

What we experience as the world today has its origins within our predecessors of earlier times. That is the reality. In the way that books of wisdom convey these things, Christ Jesus points to them as follows: 'Heaven and earth will pass away, but my words will not pass away.'[18] All that belongs to the material world will subside, but what emerges from the spirit and the soul and is uttered in words survives the decline of the world and lives on into the future. The causes of the future are not to be found outside us, they are not for geologists to study, but must be looked for within us, in the inwardly directed forces of our organization which will initially pass on into our next earthly life but then continue on into other metamorphoses. Thus if you are looking for the future of the world, you will have to look within the human being. Everything that is external will die away completely.

A barrier was erected against this understanding of the world in the nineteenth century and is referred to as the law of conservation of energy. This law sees the forces at work around us as continuing indefinitely. But they will pass away, disappear. It is what lies nascent within us that will shape the future. The law of conservation of energy is the most wrong-headed one could imagine. In reality it would translate into humanity being redundant in the evolutionary process of the world. The truth is to be found not in the law of conservation of energy, but in the words: 'Heaven and earth will pass away, but my words will not pass away.' That is the correct expression. Unfortunately these words stand in direct contrast to one another. The fact that there are certain followers of positive confessions today who wish to be true to the Bible and to theoretical physics only shows thoughtlessness on their part. It is nothing but dishonesty dressing itself up as culturally creative, but this dishonesty within the body of cultural creatives (which is in reality anti-creative) must be rooted out if we are to emerge from decline into resurgence.

LECTURE 7

DORNACH, 3 JULY 1921

FOLLOWING yesterday's considerations, we are now in a good position to address a fundamental fact of our living and being. It is just when we set about looking more exactly at the relationships between ourselves and the outer world that we always experience the riddle of how it is that we can't see through into the true being of the outer world. This outer world appears before us in its phenomena and events and even if we are only slightly interested in how we know things, we have to assume that the true nature of reality lies hidden behind these phenomena in the colours, sounds and warmth of the world. Something like a veil is there and only behind this veil is the true nature of reality to be found. On the other hand there is a similar riddle in relation to our inner life. I pointed out during the last few days how the inside of our body reveals the riddle of our organs once we truly enter the depths of our organism. It nevertheless remains a fact that as far as ordinary consciousness is concerned we cannot penetrate deeply enough into our inner being to be able to perceive the nature of our lungs, liver and so on in the way that was described yesterday. Now the fact that there are two riddles, the riddle of the impenetrability of the outer world and the inscrutability of our inner world can be understood in the context of the wholeness of our human nature. Once we address this wholeness we will see that only one side of it appears to us here between birth and death, the other side lying between death and a new birth.

Let us begin by looking at what appears to us of our own nature between birth and death. We must rely on a fact of our inner life that belongs to our normal daily consciousness: our memory. I spoke yesterday of how this faculty of memory is really based on reflections from the surfaces of our internal organs. We need this faculty of memory for our inner life. I have often referred to facts that show how any interference with this faculty of memory can undermine our normal life between birth and death. This was to illustrate how our capacity for remembering can be extinguished. There are well-known cases of this happening. You can look up numerous cases like this in books on psychology. It is a well-known fact that this can happen and the phenomenon is much more widespread than we think. You have only to imagine that for such people (without their knowledge in the normal sense of the word) these processes are like your own experience of falling asleep to waking up every night: consciousness is extinguished. However, an abnormal discontinuity of consciousness like this has an extraordinarily significant impact on one's whole awareness of personality. The person concerned can no longer deal with the experience undergone; later in life it appears horrible. We can see from this how important it is for everyday life between birth and death to have continuity of consciousness, with the exception of when we are asleep.

Continuity of consciousness is connected with our memory. We need our faculty of memory to carry on with our normal lives. There is another fact to consider when one has undertaken an occult schooling. This is that one is obliged to develop powers of soul that can extinguish this normal memory for the moments when spiritual vision is experienced. As long as we are in possession of our ordinary powers of memory, we cannot look into the spiritual world. Students undergoing occult development usually have the experience that to begin with, as they embark on their process of development, they have certain visions. They complain later that they no longer have those visions, that they have ceased. That is due to the fact that there is no faculty of memory for such visions if they are true visions, and not hallucinations. It is not possible to remember a vision, because it is something real. If you look at a piece of chalk and then look away, you have the image in your memory. If you want to have the chalk before you, the real chalk, you will have to turn back to the sense perception. You have to have the real object in front of you. Your memory will be of no use to you for this reality. If you touch a hot iron, you will burn yourself. You can remember the heat as much as you like but you will not burn yourself. Since the vision brings you into contact with something real, not just an image, you will have to return to it. The issue is that one has to return to the vision rather than trying to remember it, since the vision is a genuine occult experience and cannot be a memory. One can only return to it indirectly. We can say to ourselves: Before I had the vision I went through the following experience in ordinary consciousness. That is something we *can* remember and we have to repeat this stage in the process until we reach the point where the vision came; then we arrive at that point. It cannot occur directly again but in a way we have to go back over the process. Many do not take account of that; they believe one can remember a vision like anything else. In the course of occult development one even has to undermine one's memory. That is absolutely necessary and cannot be avoided. It follows that people striving for an occult development of this kind must above all ensure that they are sensible in ordinary life, i.e. that they are in possession of sound common sense, a healthy memory and no quasi-mystical tendencies. Anyone who indulges in nebulous mystical dabbling in ordinary life is not suited to undergoing an occult development. One certainly has to be able to remember the events of the day quite clearly and then one can venture to pursue visions of the kind that are inaccessible to memory. The cautions that apply to an occult development have to do with the nature of the process itself. In summary: memory belongs to ordinary consciousness and to a normal life between birth and death.

Now I can sketch out for you how it is for a person in possession of the faculty of memory. I shall illustrate it roughly like this [see drawing on page 101]. What I am now outlining is not present as such but can be perceived within the etheric body. This line shows what is in fact spread out over the whole body and you would then have to imagine that everything that is outside the organs lies between the head, i.e. sense perceptions or sense impressions and this line.

This line is intended to represent the boundary line for the human organs: here things are reflected back and beyond this line you will find heart, lungs, liver and so on. Here [arrows] things are reflected back. Symbolically that line represents the boundary of our faculty of memory. You can literally imagine: inside us we have a delicate form of skin; it is actually the fine boundary line between the etheric and astral bodies. In reality it is not spatial but it can be represented like this in a sketch. Everything that we perceive is bounced back by the forces within the organs behind this boundary; it is thus reflected along this boundary line and we are then unable to see through it in ordinary consciousness. We cannot see through the skin of memory into what lies within us. Memory covers up the inner workings of the human being. It has to do this because we would otherwise be unable to live normally in ordinary life between birth and death. Memory closes off what lies within us from ordinary consciousness. The moment this memory is interrupted, i.e. the moment there is a tear in its fabric, as is the case with occult development, we become able to see into what lies within our organs in the way I described yesterday.

Now we have the answer to the riddle of why we are unable to look through to what lies within us. This inner aspect of ourselves needs to be covered over or we would not be normal during life between birth and death, since we do need our faculty of memory. The reflecting activity of our memory obscures the inner aspect of our self. That is what you need by way of an answer to this riddle.

Looking towards the other side, the side that faces the outer world, what we see spread out before us is the veil of the senses, which we cannot see through either. Let us look at it this way: how would it be if we could look into the world and instead of seeing the veil of the senses we could see through the multiple tears in it into the being of the world? We would constantly be flowing through the boundaries of our senses into the nature of things themselves. We would merge with them. We could not distinguish ourselves from them. What would then be the consequence? If we could no longer distinguish ourselves from the world around us we would be unable to develop feelings of love, because they depend on us not flowing into the other, but remaining an individuality, separate but nevertheless capable of feeling our way towards the other. We are organized so as to be capable of love between birth and death. In the process of

occult development this capacity for love must then be replaced by
Imagination, Inspiration and Intuition. In a sense we have to break
through our capacity for love. If it were not for love, our ordinary
life would be totally ruined; we would become cold-hearted. For that
reason it is essential that anyone undergoing occult development in
this direction above all else develops the highest possible capacity
for love. Once this has been developed to the extent that it cannot
be lost as a result of occult development, but on the contrary that
one can sustain it despite occult development, one can then brave
the task of penetrating through the veil of the senses and looking
into objective reality. The second riddle then lies open to your soul.
To be human, we must be organized so that we are capable of both
memory and love. Since we have to be capable of love we cannot
look beyond the veil of the senses and since we have to be capable
of remembering we cannot see into our own insides.

That is the truth in relation to the utterly false Kantian philosophy.
Kant wanted to examine human subjectivity and staked out a few
completely abstract concepts which are meaningless. The reality is
that we have to see ourselves as beings who are capable of loving and
remembering in our life between birth and death. That is how we can
learn what is alive in our feelings and what lives in love. That is also
what we have to carry with us through the gates of death. It is our
very reason for living on earth: to perfect these two faculties within
us. Given that we have to keep our perceiving and our thinking apart
by means of our faculty of memory and so are obstructed by the
veil of the senses, we develop our conscious life mainly by means
of our heads (and in a sense as human beings we are entirely head
organizations). This conscious life does not get beyond thoughts.
Each thought becomes an image in our memories. That is, however,
as far as we can progress. Our thoughts are stored in that way and it
is only because they are stored in that way that we can retrieve them.
Our thoughts are held up and our normal life between life and death
relies on us not letting our thoughts descend into our organs. The
forces at work in our thinking do descend, as I described yesterday,
but the thought itself, living in us in the form of an image, we cannot
release down. It is at the moment of death that our thoughts become

what they should not be in ordinary consciousness, namely Imaginations. The faculty of Imagination which we strive for so intensely during occult development becomes available to us when we die. All our thoughts become images. We inhabit a whole world of images, and we can only understand someone who has died once we have acquired the language of images. Immediately after death thoughts transform into images. We then spend some time with these images between death and a new birth. Gradually they turn into Inspiration. In this way the soul continues to grow. Then we begin to perceive the music of the spheres. The music of the spheres becomes a reality for us. We live in the world of cosmic sounds. Finally we grow together with the objectively spiritual cosmos.

That is also the point at which, after this experience of Intuition, the world Midnight Hour strikes which I spoke of yesterday. Now the journey back begins, and our Intuition is prepared to take into itself what we had gradually left behind from our time here on the earth. You see, once we have passed through the gate of death, we live by forces which are different from those that we describe as will forces here on earth. We live our way into forms which are more of a cosmic nature. Our own will is absorbed; it gradually fades away. But once we have reached the world Midnight Hour, having passed through the stages of Imagination, Inspiration and Intuition and reached the turning point of life between death and a new life, our Intuition begins to absorb will forces again. Our thinking takes on a quality of will, and this will increasingly fill the soul which now can wrestle its way through to Inspiration and then to Imagination. Once it has reached the stage of Imagination and has inhabited it for a while, our thinking ripens to the point where it can reincarnate. The metabolic/limb system of the previous life then emerges transformed from the world of images, as I described earlier. You can see how we pass through stages that are striven for in occult development, towards the world Midnight Hour and then descend in the opposite direction through to the stage of Imagination, and come to the formation of thoughts when we are embodied.

Throughout this whole process we have been absorbing will forces. Now, as we reappear in physical form, we can see what has

been working into us from the cosmos, what we have drawn from
our previous incarnation.

Welten ⁝ Mitternacht

Intuition .... Wille

Inspiration .... Inspiration

Imagination   Imagination

Tod   neue
                   Geburt

Tod = death; Welten Mitternacht = World Midnight;
Wille = will; neue Geburt = new birth

Once we have reached the point of a new incarnation, just before
conception, we have an Imagination and one that is saturated with
will. Our head and all that belongs to it emerges from the Imagination, having essentially already been there in the form of an image.
Our will takes hold of the new limbs and metabolic system. Our
head consists principally of crystallized, rigidified thoughts; what
remains in the rest of our human being is organized will. We can
only really be awake in our heads. After all, you are familiar with your
thoughts which appear in ordinary consciousness. This concept can
be put to any one of our contemporaries; what goes on in our will,
however, is just as unknown to people as what goes on in their sleep.
When you raise an arm, how much of what goes on in doing so are
we aware of in ordinary consciousness? We perceive that the arm
is raised, the concept is clear, but the act of will involved remains
asleep, comparable with our sleep experience between falling asleep
and waking up. We can say then that in respect of our metabolic and
limb systems we are also asleep by day; it is only in our heads that we
fully awaken. These elements all work together.

Conventional science today speaks of a certain kind of logic, such
as concept, judgement and conclusion. The well-known conclusion

that features in all accounts of logic refers to the famous logical personality: all men are mortal—Caesar is a man—therefore Caesar is mortal. That is the conclusion. Each element of the conclusion is also a judgement: all men are mortal is a judgement—Caesar is a man—is a judgement; therefore Caesar is mortal—is a judgement. The whole thing is a conclusion. Man, Caesar are concepts.

If we were to ask an intelligent and well-educated person today (we must always refer to such clever people for they set the tone of debate) this person would say: All this takes place in our nervous systems. Our nervous system is the medium for concept, judgement, and conclusion, even of our feelings and our will. The facts, however, do not match the conventional view. Only ideation as such is actually the business of our head. When you make a judgement you have to feel your way through your ether body into your legs to find out where you stand. Your judgements are not carried out by your head but by your legs, specifically your etheric legs. Anyone making a judgement even when lying down, stretches out his etheric legs. Making a judgement is not a function of our head but of our legs. No one would believe this today, but it is nevertheless true. Coming to a conclusion is a function of our arms and hands; all that lifts a human being up beyond what an animal also has. An animal can stand on its legs, and an animal is itself a judgement, but it cannot come to a conclusion. We can. That is the reason for our arms being free, that is what they are for, not walking. We have our arms free so that we can come to conclusions. What takes place when we stand with our etheric legs in the process of judgement, what takes place when we move our astral arms in forming a conclusion are both only reflected in our heads as ideation and remain there as such. For judgement and conclusion to come about in us we need to involve the whole human being, not just our nerve-sense nature.

If you take that into account you will see that we come to judgements and conclusions by means of our limb system. Fundamentally these are acts of will and this will emerges from a more ill-defined part of us than the faculty of ideation. Our experience when we come to a conclusion is just like when we wake up in the morning. A conclusion has been drawn up from the very depths of our being;

that part of our life which has grown old in the passage from our previous life into this one and is now active in our heads, is what makes us capable of ideation. This aspect of us is old in relation to the cosmos when we are born. Conversely, the fact that our powers of will have been renewed relates to our growing young in relation to the cosmos. The head that we carry is always a reminder of our previous incarnation. It represents what is old. Our metabolic/limb aspect is what our will has captured on its way into this incarnation, and is passed on through the mother's body. Our other aspect, the head, is in fact formed within our mother out of the cosmos. One need only study conventional, empirical embryology to find this confirmed. Our head is an image of the cosmos and is formed by external forces. To deny this is the equivalent of saying that it is nonsense to maintain that the earth's magnetism sets the needle on a compass. If a physicist wants to explain the movements of the needle on a compass, he will start with the needle; similarly a physiologist, an embryologist or a biologist will focus on the mother's body if they want to explain the embryo. That is as pointless as trying to explain the movements of the needle on a compass on the basis of the needle alone; we have to take into account the whole cosmos. Only our head is initially fully developed and the rest of our body is simply appended. That in turn is what our will has taken by conquest, having attempted to seduce the forces of Imagination during its passage through life between death and the new birth from the moment of the world Midnight Hour onwards.

If we look at the human being sketched out here we will find everything that relates to thinking and perception above the delicate skin of memory and everything that relates to our will below. Our will works its way up out of the unconscious and can only be found in the way we set out yesterday. That is where our will works upwards. We are asleep in relation to our will. We thus have the human being appearing as a duality in life between birth and death. Whilst it is true that we are monads, we have this quality in respect of the whole cosmos and it is one which we have to keep developing in our process of evolving. It must be continually renewed. For all practical purposes we are dualistic between birth and death: on

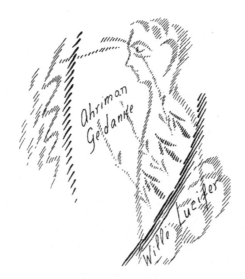

Gedanke = thought; Wille = will

the one hand thinking and perception, on the other will and natural disposition.

This leaves us in reality as the point of intersection between two worlds. If you take an honest look at yourself and at what is in your consciousness at any given moment in your life, you will find that it is a collection of your memories, all that you have experienced in the time since your second to sixth year. What pours out from below there, what pours out from our will is love, the capacity for love. In this sense we exist at the intersection of memory images and love.

Fundamentally we consist of this: up here is a world of cosmic thought and below it there is a world of cosmic will. As human beings we are continually under attack by Lucifer from the aspect of our will and by Ahriman from the aspect of our thinking. [See illustration above.] Ahriman is constantly trying to turn us into nothing but heads. Lucifer is constantly trying to knock our heads off so that we cannot think and so that everything flows out in warmth via the heart, overflowing with cosmic love which then pours itself out into the world as a cosmically rapturous being.

In our present-day much-vaunted culture we are largely under the influence of Ahriman. These ahrimanic influences have always been felt, particularly by sensitive people. When I was very young I once spoke to an Austrian poet who was very well-known at the time. He had a fine sense for trends in our culture and he expressed it in the form of a metaphor which he experienced as a reality. He said to me—I can still hear it as if he had said it today:

> People of our time are heading towards a terrible fate, a terrible fate that will befall us if we continue as we are. People will gradually lose their physical skills. They will no longer be able to walk properly; they will always be on wheels and moving about mechanically; they will also lose the dexterity of their hands, everything will become technical. Just as a muscle wastes away when it is not used, all our limbs will gradually shrivel up and we shall be just heads. These heads will become ever bigger and in the end we shall all be rolling about with the crippled remains of the rest of our organism.

This was the nightmarish vision of the Austrian poet—Hermann Rollett was his name—and he depicted it quite graphically because he was so troubled by the idea that our culture would one day turn us into rolling heads. Yet there is something very true about this. The truth is that there are indeed extraordinarily powerful forces at work in our time which would like our heads to become more and more developed. They are not having much success with our physical heads but are doing much better with our etheric heads. The fact is that the ahrimanic forces at work in our time are trying to turn us entirely into head people, so that they can completely transform us into just thinkers.

In a person developing healthily the opposite pole is her will pole which is constantly counteracting this tendency when we die so that the will can take hold of our thinking. Our thinking is not yet ready to be isolated. When we are born we have gathered new will forces, but our thinking detaches itself and finds our head. Our will forces take hold of the rest of our bodies. While we live on earth there is a constant interaction of will and thought within us. Our will takes hold of our thinking and we have to carry this composite of think-ing and willing back through death again. Ahriman would like to prevent us from doing this. He would like our wills to remain separate so that only our thinking becomes fully developed. In that case we would lose our individuality. If in the end it really came to that, which is what Ahriman wants, we would completely lose our individuality. We would arrive at the moment of death with a highly exaggerated, instinctively developed power of thought. But we would not be able to hold on to it and Ahriman would be able to take hold of it and integrate it into the rest of the world so that this thinking would continue to work on in the world left behind at our death. This really is the fate that threatens humanity if the materialism of our day continues unchecked. The ahrimanic powers will become so strong that they will be able to steal the human faculty of thinking and integrate it into the earth in such a way that it will go on working and that the earth which is supposed to pass away will be consolidated and remain earth. Ahriman is working to counter the words: 'Heaven and earth will pass away, but my word will not pass away.' His intention is that these words will be thrown away and that heaven and earth will remain. This can only be achieved if human thinking is stolen from us and we are deprived of our individuality.

If Ahriman were left to continue working in the way he has been since 1845 in particular, our brains would become increasingly rigid and we would live as if within a framework of compulsive thoughts, materialized thoughts, as I set out yesterday. This would become evident in education where people would be guided in a way that no longer left them scope for mobility in their thinking and left them with completely fixed ideas once they had reached a certain age. Now I ask you, have we not already reached a point where this has been realized in many respects! Consider how fixed our ideas already are today; is it still possible for people to learn anything much? Their thoughts have become so rigid, so fixed, that there is not a great deal they can be taught. Their thoughts are already in the service of Ahriman, who is making every effort to enhance this process, turning thoughts into compulsive thoughts. One very effective way in which these thoughts have a compelling influence, particularly in the sciences, is through the concept of atomism. According to this, what lies behind the veil of the senses is not the spirit but all kinds of atoms: swirling, whirling atoms. There is of course no other way of passing through the veil of the senses than by thinking, but Ahriman has confused people to such an extent that their thoughts have become materialized. People no longer believe that this world of atoms is a man-made thought construct, but think of it as a reality; this is how they project their thoughts into the world around them. This is the world made ahrimanic. Our science today is ahrimanic through and through.

From time to time in the course of life this is brought to our attention in a most terrible way. For example, I was given a manuscript some time ago, perhaps 35 years ago. It was a very learned manuscript. It was supposed to categorize human differential—this is a true story—which when integrated would result in a human being. Thus integrating components from feet to head would produce a human being. The doctor who brought this to my attention went on to say: 'I can introduce you to the author; I worked with him at the clinic.' When I did meet him he said: 'Yes, that is correct. I have experienced this myself. I am composed entirely of differential atoms and they are everywhere to be found. I myself am really an integral.' He imagined himself as being composed entirely of atoms; a form of consciousness that was intellectually ahrimanic. This is, one could say, simply a rigidified atomistic system. When this manuscript was brought to me I was reminded that there is an all-encompassing formula devised by Laplace: namely that it should be possible to calculate, starting from processes at an atomic level not just by integrating from foot to head but by integrating from the beginning of the world to its end, by inputting certain data when Caesar crossed the Rubicon and that sort of thing![19] Simply by arranging data within a global formula. This whole way of thinking is appallingly similar to the account this man gave of himself as an integral enclosed between feet and head. This alone gives us a glimpse (if we look at it rightly) into the ahrimanization of our culture.

It needs to be countered of course and that can only happen if we bring an imaginative quality to our concepts, so that they do not remain purely abstract. That will mean that when we cross the threshold of death we already bring a picture consciousness with us and can find a connection with what the world needs. The alternative would be that humanity runs the risk of losing itself and that what should develop into the will flowing into our thinking life and becoming individualized, will then become mineralized, no different from earthly matter. The earth would become a cosmic being but the soul life of humanity would end up in a great cemetery.

One has from time to time to see the development of culture from a wider perspective, particularly so in our own time. Anyone who is in a position to see trends in human development more exactly will know how rapidly we are in fact approaching this ossification of our culture. I should take this opportunity to mention that until the year 869 AD and the eighth General Ecumenical Council in Constantinople, our understanding of ourselves included body, soul and spirit. Now at this Council for the Occident it was stated that we should not believe that we are composed of a body, soul and spirit but only of body and soul, with the soul having some spiritual qualities. This then became generally accepted. During the Middle Ages it was heresy to believe that we are composed of body, soul and spirit. Today professors of philosophy will state as a matter of objective science that human beings are beings of body and soul. This 'objective' science is nothing more than a resolution of the Eighth Ecumenical Council. The ultimate objective is still to be realized. It would be true to say that as a consequence of this eighth Ecumenical Council, humanity has lost its awareness of the spirit which must now be regained by our own efforts. If, however, we continue in the direction I have outlined, we shall also lose our awareness of our human soul.

This awareness had already been lost to the materialists of the nineteenth century to such an extent that it was said: our brains secrete thoughts in the way that our liver secrets gall.[20] Only physical processes were taken into account. Moreover there are already tendencies unknown to most people, but working underground where all kinds of societies are operating with this in mind, towards bringing about something similar to the Eighth Ecumenical Council of Constantinople, namely to declare that we are not beings with a body and a soul, but a only a body, and our soul is something that develops out of our body. It follows that it is impossible to educate the human soul. Some material means must be found to inject into us so that after a certain age we can receive what it takes to unfold our talents. This tendency is certainly present in our time. It is the next step on the ahrimanic path of development: no longer to found schools for teaching to take place but to facilitate the injection of certain substances. This can be done. There is no question of it not being possible. It can be done but the result would be to turn us into automata. This would enormously accelerate what otherwise could only be achieved by means of thought control, an education aimed at controlling how we think.

Substances are already available that would enable us, if injected with them at let's say seven years old, to skip primary school; our thinking would, however, be automated. We would become extremely clever, but would have no awareness of it. This cleverness would simply be a fact of life. There are already people who do not care whether someone has an inner life or not, so long as the person goes about his business outwardly and gets this or that done! People of our time who have a preference for ahrimanic culture (and they do exist) see this as an ideal to be striven for. What could be more attractive to people with this attitude, which is becoming increasingly widespread, than to find a vaccine rather than to have to bother with teaching children year after year! These things have to be expressed in drastic terms. Failing that, people of our time will not awaken to the direction in which we are heading. A vaccine of this kind would have the effect of loosening our etheric body within the physical. The moment that happens the interplay of the universe and the etheric body would become extremely active and we would become automata. Here on earth our physical bodies need to be educated by an act of spiritual will.

The educational methods employed in Waldorf Schools were devised in full awareness of present-day intentions to automate us. In this respect they are indeed intended to be a cultural driving force leading humanity back towards spirituality. In essence it can be said that the most important thing in our time is to take particular care that cultural life among us becomes spiritual in nature. We should therefore have the courage to pay careful attention to every sign of improvement in the self-development of individual people. I have often emphasized in other contexts how people have the tendency today to strive to establish a routine rather than a conscious way of life; a routine is essentially a mechanization of life.

I was recently very pleased to read that there are still people who value a conscious way of life over and above everyday routine. There was an item in the news about how Edison tested his people for qualities that would prove valuable in practical life. He wasn't in the slightest interested in whether or not a sales person was good at bookkeeping. That he said, was something one could learn in three weeks if one was otherwise skilful and clever. All these specialisms were of no interest to him; they could all be developed in time. He was right. What he did present people with, if he was interested in knowing what they could achieve in practical life, were questions like: 'How big is Siberia?' So if he wanted to see if someone was a good bookkeeper, he would not ask if the person could draw up a balance sheet, but 'How big is Siberia?' or: 'If a room is five metres long, three wide and four metres to the ceiling, how many cubic metres of air does it enclose?' There would be other, similar questions. He put questions such as: 'What stands at the place where Caesar crossed to the Rubicon?'—questions of general knowledge, and depending on how well the candidate could deal with questions of general knowledge like that, Edison would hire them as bookkeepers or to some other position. He was not at all interested in whether or not someone was good at bookkeeping, since he knew that if the candidate could deal with a question like that, it would be proof that she had not wasted her time at school but had as a child grown up with mobility of thought, and that was what he required.

That is the direction in which practical life should go. Recently we have been heading in the opposite direction, constantly on the lookout for specialists, so that in the end one could despair of finding someone to deal with practical tasks. People could no longer be found who would contemplate anything outside the box in which they had chosen to be confined. It has to be said that here too we must work towards mobility of thinking. Once we are moving in that direction our thoughts will not become sclerotic and Ahriman will have a challenge on his hands. You will see for yourselves however, how few Edisons there are in life who work on such practical lines. What matters is working towards imaginative concepts; anyone following that course will be unable to say he could not understand spiritual science. It is precisely the nudge that we have to give ourselves to shift from the abstract to imaginative concepts that will enable us to understand something like this: the Earth developed out of the Moon, Sun and Saturn. At the same time feelings will begin to infuse our inner life with imaginative concepts and Imaginations.

It was recently reported here that a critic of anthroposophy had said that it was not a science because it drew on the whole human being for its research; any science as such should, however, be based solely on our intellect. You can see here that the critique starts with the definition of what a science is, i.e. that it should not be based on the faculties of the whole human being, and then goes on to say: If it is drawing on all our faculties, it is wrong. Using this approach one could of course define anything out of existence. The whole point is that we must extend our one-sided culture of the head into one that encompasses the whole human being. It is essentially just a flaw in our consciousness that leads to this head culture which then extends into practical life. The mistaken belief that we come to judgements and conclusions with our heads is what leads us to this head culture. We come to judgements with our legs and conclusions with our arms. Once it is known that the whole human being is involved in coming to a judgement and a conclusion then there will be no further resistance to the idea that genuine truth must be founded on the whole human being. That is what I wanted to bring to your attention today.

LECTURE 8

In preparation for our next two sessions we shall devote our attention to aspects of the human being that relate to our nature as thinking beings. It is just this aspect of our nature that science misunderstands or characterizes quite wrongly. People think that thoughts as we experience them arise in us, as if we were in a way the bearers of these thoughts. It comes as no surprise that people hold this view, since our true nature is only accessible to a more subtle observation. Our true nature is withheld from a crude approach to observing it.

If we see ourselves as thinking beings it is because while we are awake, (between waking up and falling asleep) we can see that our other experiences are accompanied by thoughts, by the content of our thoughts. These experiences in thought seem to us to arise within us somehow and then somehow to cease in the period spent between sleeping and waking, during sleep that is. It is because we take the view that our experience of thinking only takes place while we are awake and that it disappears into the unknown during sleep, about which we do not take the trouble to find out, we cannot come to an understanding of ourselves as thinking beings. If we adopt a more subtle approach, even one that does not go as far as the region I have described in my book *Knowledge of the Higher Worlds* we will see that our thinking life is nothing like as simple as we tend to imagine. We only have to begin with a comparison of our basic everyday way of thinking between waking and sleeping, we all know it, with the admittedly problematic state we are in when dreaming.

When we talk about dreaming, most people are generally satisfied with a rough characterization of the dreaming state. A comparison of our dreaming state with wide awake thinking shows that dreams contain what we might call random associations, images appearing in a sequence, one after the other, without the connection appearing that one would see in the world around us. Alternatively one might relate what is going on in a dream to the outer world, and notice how it stands out in contrast and seen as a whole will simply not fit in with the processes of the world outside.

It is true, these are observations that one can make which lead to fine results. What goes unnoticed, however, is that when we cease to concentrate for a moment and give our thoughts free rein something not unlike our dreaming state blends with our waking consciousness, which otherwise follows the outer course of events. In the time between waking up and going to sleep, whilst we make every effort to adapt to the outer events in which we are involved, a vague dreaming also takes place. It is as if there were two streams present in us: the upper one which we can control as we wish and the lower one which takes its course like dreams themselves, with images following each other at random. One does have to be a little attentive to one's inner life to observe what I am describing, but it is always there. You will invariably notice that there is an undercurrent present. Thoughts go swirling about just as full of images as they do in dreams, all kinds of things one after another. A variety of reminiscences appear which, just as in a dream, attract other thoughts with perhaps only similar sounding words to link them. People who are content to let their thoughts have free rein or who are unwilling to make the effort to link them with what is going on around them, may notice that there is an inner urge to give way to such daydreaming.

These daydreams only differ from normal dreams in that the images are paler and more like thoughts. With regard to how these images relate to each other, however, there is little difference between daydreaming and so-called real dreams. People range in their relationship to daydreams from those who have no idea that such daydreams are present as an undercurrent in their consciousness, and who let their thoughts be guided entirely by outer events, to those who completely abandon themselves to their daydreams and allow their thoughts to mingle and become entangled with them. Between the extremes of such dreamy characters and those who are quite dry and will accept nothing but what corresponds exactly to a given sequence of facts, there are all kinds of different tendencies. We should add that a substantial part of what nourishes art and poetry etc. comes from this undercurrent of daydreaming during the course of the day.

That is one aspect of what we are considering and it should definitely be taken into account. It would then become clear to us that there is a constant ebb and flow of dreams within us which we can only control by means of dealing with the outer world. It would also become clear that it is essentially our will that takes its lead from our surroundings and which brings system, coherence and logic into our otherwise anarchic inner thought processes. It is our will that brings logic into our thinking. That is, however, only one side of the issue.

The other side is the following: we need only to have made an initial acquaintance with the regions I described in my book *Knowledge of the Higher Worlds* to become aware of how when we awake in the morning we bring something with us from the condition we were in between falling asleep and waking up. We have only to add a little consciousness to what we perceive at that moment to realize very clearly that at the moment of awakening we are waking up out of a sea of thoughts, as it were. We are by no means waking up out of something indistinct or darkness, but actually out of a sea of thoughts, thoughts that leave the impression that they were very clear indeed whilst we were asleep, but which can no longer be grasped or carried over into waking consciousness.

Taking this further we will begin to notice that these thoughts, brought with us, as it were, out of sleep, are very similar to new ideas or solutions that we have to something that we have to deal with in the outer world, indeed that they are very similar to moral intuitions as I have described them in my *Philosophy of Spiritual Activity*.

While we may always have the feeling that the kind of weaving thoughts that accompany our consciousness as a kind of undercurrent confront us with ourselves as bubbling and simmering daydreams, we cannot say that of what we mentioned earlier. On the contrary, we have to say to ourselves: when we return to our bodies, taking hold of them for our daily tasks, we are not capable of retaining what we experienced in our thought life between falling asleep and waking up.

Once we have become fully aware of these two aspects of human life we will no longer regard thoughts as the products of our physical organism. The state we emerge from at the moment of waking up cannot be seen as just some product of our physical organism but rather as something that we have experienced between falling asleep and waking up when our astral body and I were separated from our physical body.

Where are we then? This is a question we have to ask ourselves. Our I and our astral body are outside our etheric and physical bodies. If we are prepared to look at life with an open mind, a simple consideration we must inevitably come to will reveal the following: when we are outside ourselves in this way we are in fact in the midst of all that appears to us when we direct our senses to the outer world, to the veil of the senses, to all that our senses can reveal to us. At the same time however, our ordinary daytime consciousness is extinguished. We can feel why our consciousness is extinguished when we wake out of this state in the morning. The feeling we have in our body on awakening is that it is too weak to keep a grip on what we experience between falling asleep and waking up. Our I and our astral body cannot retain their experiences as they dip back into our physical and etheric bodies.

The moment they take part in the experiences offered by our physical and etheric bodies they can no longer retain what they experienced between falling asleep and waking up. It is only when we have new ideas relating to the world around us, or moral Intuitions, that we experience something like what would appear to us directly if we were conscious of our surroundings during the time between falling asleep and waking up. Taking this into consideration we have a very clear contrast between our inner and outer worlds. In a way this sheds light on the expression we often use, namely that the outer world as it appears to us between sleeping and waking is a kind of illusion or Maya. In fact we only truly inhabit the world which reveals itself to us in this way when we are asleep. Then we submerge ourselves in the world which otherwise only reveals itself to us through our senses. We might then say that the world that reveals itself through our senses has hidden depths within which lie contained its primal causes, its being. In our normal consciousness we are too weak to perceive these causes and beings directly.

Unprejudiced observation will, however, take us quite far into those regions I have described in my book *Knowledge of the Higher Worlds*. What I might represent in a diagram as follows will be clear to an open-minded observer. To represent what goes on in our everyday life of thought I would include everything we inwardly experience in our thoughts between waking up and going to sleep in relation to outer perceptions or to our pains and pleasures. I would represent our experiences in ordinary consciousness like this [see drawing, white, p. 114]. Beneath it there would be what I first described [red, below it] which is like a daydream, living and weaving without being subject to the laws of logic. Opposite this, in the outer world we pass into between falling asleep and waking up, we find ourselves once more in a world of thoughts which we can reach in the form of reminiscences on awakening, a world of thoughts which are not within us but which receive us into themselves. In this way, using our ordinary thinking, we have distinguished two separate worlds of thought: an inner one and an outer one, a world of thoughts which is filled by the cosmos once we have fallen asleep. We could call this the cosmic world of thought. The previous one referred to is some other world of thought which we will examine more closely during the coming days.

So within our ordinary world of thought we are placed within a general world of thought which is, as it were, divided by a boundary, the one part being inside us, the other outside. The one that is inside us appears to us very clearly as a kind of dream. In the depths of our soul there lives a chaotic web of thoughts, which we could say is not imbued with logic. The outer world of thought, however, can't be perceived in ordinary consciousness. The only way we can see

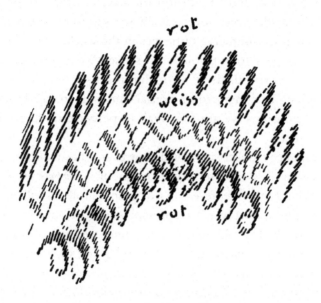

rot = red; weiss = white

and experience the nature of this outer world of thought directly is by means of genuine spiritual second sight which can penetrate more deeply into the regions I describe in my book *Knowledge of the Higher Worlds*. We then discover that the world of thought we dive into between falling asleep and waking up is one which is not only just as logical as our everyday world of thought but also contains a much higher logic. To avoid any misunderstanding I shall call this a super-logical world of thought. One could say that it lies just as far above our ordinary logic as the nebulous world of our daydreams lies below it.

As I indicated earlier, this can only be explored with spiritual second sight. There is another way to test the results of spiritual research on this point. It will be obvious to you that there are certain areas of our organism that we do not have access to with our ordinary consciousness. I have referred to them frequently in recent lectures. I pointed out that the faculty of memory that we have in our ordinary consciousness involves having a kind of skin covering our internal organs. We cannot directly perceive the nature of our internal organs, such as lungs, liver and so on. I also added that the kind of mysticism which fantasizes about what lies within us and is expressed in the words of Saint Teresa[21] or Mechthild of Magdeburg with all kinds of beautiful poetic images— their beauty is undeniable—is nevertheless a false and nebulous one, consisting of nothing more than organic secretions.[22] If we pursue real spiritual science, rather than this nebulous mysticism, we shall penetrate through what lies within the human being to genuine knowledge of the organs. We will then have the faculties to grasp the spiritual significance of our lungs, liver, kidneys and so on, having spiritually penetrated through the fine skin of memory and attained a spiritual grasp of our inner nature. This cannot be achieved with our ordinary everyday consciousness. We can only observe the organs outwardly by means of anatomy which will show us how they behave when they are considered only as belonging to the ordinary physical and mineral world. Only fully developed spiritual powers of vision will be able to observe them from within, seeing the forces with which they are imbued, what is at work in them.

So there is something within us that we cannot reach with our ordinary consciousness. Why not? Because it does not belong to us alone. What we are able to observe with our everyday consciousness belongs to us alone. What is coursing through our organs down there does not belong to us alone but to our cosmic human nature, and thus both to us and to the cosmos at the same time.

This can perhaps be explained most clearly as follows: looking at ourselves schematically we can take any given organ like our lungs or liver and see that there are forces at work within it. These forces are not simply our own internal forces but belong to the entire cosmos. Moreover, when the whole outer physical world that we can observe with our senses will one day have disappeared as the earth reaches its natural end, these forces within our internal organs will continue to work on. We could say that everything that our eyes can see, that our ears can hear, the whole outer world, will pass away in time with the earth. On the other hand what we bear within us beneath our skin contains something that will outlive the earth. These are the centres, the forces that will continue to work beyond the earth's existence. Our position as human beings in the world is not just to be a vessel for our organs but also to be a vessel within which the whole cosmos can take shape. Thus within what is inaccessible to our everyday consciousness we encompass something that belongs not just to us but to the entire cosmos. The question is, is it composed of the chaotic processes that take place in our daydreams, our waking dreams?

We have only to consider these chaotic processes at work in our waking dreams to conclude: the whole structure of what we can observe as an underground current in our consciousness is certainly not the basis of our entire organism, including each individual organ. It would be a sight to behold if the chaos rumbling through our subconscious life were to be the architect of our organs, let alone our entire organism! You would be astonished by the caricatures that would result if we were the products of what goes pulsing through our subconscious life. No, we are made up of the same external powers of thought which shape the outer world, inclining its outer surface towards our senses, i.e. those at work in the world which we experience between falling asleep and waking up and which we are unable to reach with our everyday consciousness. So if I wanted to represent what we are in the form of a complete picture I would have to do it a little like this: [see diagram on p.117] that is the world of thoughts surrounding us [red]. This enveloping world of thought shapes our human organism and this in turn, floating above it, as it were, creates the upper world of thoughts [white] which leans towards the external Maya which we perceive with our senses between our thoughts and the surrounding world [blue]. Now try to become fully aware of how small that part of us is which constitutes our consciousness, and how large that part of us is which is formed by the same outer world into which we plunge between falling asleep and waking up. This can also be seen from a different perspective by an open-minded observer.

In our ordinary consciousness we are only fully aware of
our thoughts. Our feelings swim
along like dreams, as it were,
beneath them. Feelings rise up
and ebb away. We are unable to
capture them with the same clarity as our thoughts and concepts.
What we experience between
falling asleep and waking up
closely resembles our experience of will at work during the
day. What, after all, do we know
about what is taking place when
our will is at work in the movement of our hand or an arm! This
is easy enough to understand conceptually; we are initially aware:
I wanted to move my arm. That is an idea. Then we recall how we
look once we have moved an arm: another idea. Everything we are
aware of in our ordinary consciousness is a web of ideas; beneath
this web there is a flow of feelings. But the will within us is just as
unconscious during our waking state as we ourselves are between
falling asleep and waking up.

rot = red; blau = blue; weiss = white

What is it exactly that sleeps within us? What the cosmos around
us has built into us and is now asleep is just as asleep as the plants
and minerals are from our waking perspective. In effect, we cannot
penetrate into them from outside; we cannot see through into the
cosmic nature that we have in common. We live and weave in this
cosmos between falling asleep and waking up. The degree to which
we are able to penetrate through the surface of the outer world of
the senses corresponds to our ability to consciously inhabit our own
organization. The extent to which we are able to cease having mere
memories or reminiscences of the events we have experienced in
daily life corresponds to our ability to consciously experience the
forces at work in building up our lungs, liver, stomach and so on. To
the same extent that we learn to see through the phenomena of the
outer world, we can learn to experience consciously our own piece

of the cosmos, the one we live in, that is enclosed within our skin, without us being aware of it in ordinary consciousness.

What do we bring with us out of this cosmos on awakening? An open-minded observer will see at once that what we bring with us is very definitely will. Our waking thoughts essentially only differ from what flows through our dreamy subconscious life in that they are imbued with will. It is our willpower that introduces logic and this logic is not actually a system of thought but reflects the way our will orders us and controls our thought images in such a way that they correspond to the outer ways of the world.

When we wake up from a dream we are particularly aware of the swirling jumble of chaotic and illogical pictures that live within us and we can then notice how our will takes hold of it and organizes it in a logical way. What we carry with us into the day, however, is not the cosmic logic referred to earlier as super-logic but the logic of our own will.

How is it possible then for our will to bring this logic to bear within us? The underlying cause is an exceptionally important secret of human nature. It is this: when we are submerged in the cosmic state of being which does not exist as far as our ordinary consciousness is concerned, we are submerged within the entirety of our organization and there we can sense within our will that is spread out within it, the cosmic logic of our organs.

It is extremely important to realize that when we wake up in the morning, rejoining our bodily nature, we are forced by this bodily nature to give shape to our will in a particular way. If our body had not itself taken on a certain shape, our will would swirl around in all directions like jellyfish at the moment of awakening. The only thing that prevents this is our present human form. Our will dives down and assumes this form in all its elements; that is what gives it its logical structure. It is our own body that makes it possible for our will to give logical coherence to the thoughts which would otherwise swirl around chaotically. During the night, when we are asleep, we are contained within the super-logic of the cosmos. We are, however, unable to retain it, so when our will dives back down into our physical body it takes on its form. Just as when you pour water into a vessel and the water takes the shape of the vessel, our will takes the shape of our physical body. Not only does it take the overall form of our body but it flows into its every detail right down to the tiniest capillaries. The vessel cannot move and so the water takes on the resting form of the vessel it is poured into, touching only its outer walls. In our case, however, our will immerses itself completely in every nook and cranny of our body and from there exercises its control on the otherwise chaotic sequence of images.

What we are aware of as a kind of subconscious undercurrent is in a sense released from the body. It really is released from our body. Whilst it does remain connected it is constantly trying to release itself from the form of our body. On the other hand, what we carry with us into the cosmos at the moment of falling asleep and which bears our human form, merges with the cosmos but still remains subject to the laws of this form.

Now despite the complexity of the way our head is organized, we are only able to form images with it. In terms of physiology it is only a matter of prejudice that leads us to believe that our heads enable us to form judgements and come to conclusions. It is in fact only thoughts that are enabled by our heads. If we only had heads and the rest of our bodies were not involved in the process of thinking we would all be daydreamers. All that our heads are capable of is remaining awake while we dream. So when we return to our bodies via our head in the morning, our head lets us become aware of our dreams. It is only when we penetrate more fully into our body, when our will takes on the form both of our head and the rest of our organization, that our will is once more able to restore logic to the otherwise chaotically swirling image-forming forces within us.

This brings us to something I raised in the earlier lectures. We have to be clear about the fact that our thoughts are facilitated by our heads and that strange and paradoxical as it may sound, in reality our judgements and conclusions are formed by our arms and legs. That is how judgements and conclusions are arrived at. When we have a thought it is only an image, mirrored back to us in our head. Our whole being on the other hand is involved in arriving at judgements and conclusions. This does not mean that if a person is deformed he is also unable or disqualified from forming a judgement or of coming to a conclusion. What matters is a person's predisposition, irrespective of the loss of one limb or another.

We will have to learn that what we are in soul and spirit must be seen in the context of our wholeness. This will involve seeing that logic is brought into our life of thought from the very regions that we are unable to reach with our ordinary consciousness, and which are occupied by our feeling and willing natures. Our judgements and our conclusions take place within the sleeping regions of our soul from which sound our feelings and our will impulses.

Of these the mathematical region is the most peculiar. The mathematical region is not accessible to us merely in our resting state, but also involves us as we walk about. Somehow or other we are always in movement when dealing with mathematical figures. When we look at someone walking about from outside, we see the person in spatial terms. When we experience mathematics inwardly we experience cosmic mathematics at work within us and at the same time building us up. The directions of space outside us also build us up and we experience them within us. In the process of experiencing them, we convert them into abstractions, take the images which are reflected in our brains and weave them together with what the world reveals to us externally in space.

It will be necessary for us to become aware today that what we place into the world by means of doing mathematics is of the same cosmic nature as the laws that apply to ourselves. The nonsense promulgated by Kantianism portrays space as a subjective form. It is not a subjective form, but something that we experience in all reality in the very region where we experience our will nature. That is where it radiates up from. As it radiates up it becomes a world which we can then imbue with what is presented to us from outside.

Today's world is a long way from being able to study the way in which we are inwardly interwoven with the cosmos, how we stand in relation to the cosmos. This is something that I presented with particular clarity in my *Philosophy of Spiritual Activity* which contains notable passages where I show how in ordinary consciousness we are connected with the entire cosmos, and that it is from the seedbed of the entire cosmos that the individual person blossoms whom we are then able to apprehend with our normal consciousness. It is this passage in my *Philosophy of Spiritual Activity* that has been least understood; most people did not know what it was about. It is perhaps not surprising that in an age in which abstraction has flourished to the point of admiring Einstein's ideas, an age in which this admittedly extraordinarily clever but nevertheless extreme abstraction is presented to the world as something special, there is no understanding for what is aiming to lead us into true reality.

One has continually to emphasize that it is not sufficient for something to be logical. Einstein's ideas are certainly logical but they do not correspond to reality. No form of relativism as such corresponds to reality. The kind of thinking that does correspond to reality involves not letting go of reality while in the process of thinking. People today for example are quite happy to read or to hear in a lecture by Einstein: 'How would it be if a clock flew out into the cosmos at the speed of light?'—people are quite happy to listen to this kind of thing.[23] For someone whose thinking and soul life are in touch with reality, this is the equivalent of saying: 'How would it be for a person if I cut off his head and then his left hand or his right arm, and so on?' This person would then no longer be a human being. Similarly what we are entitled to think of as a clock ceases to be a clock once we start talking about it flying through the cosmos at the speed of light! It is not possible to think of it that way. We have to stick to reality if we want to develop valid thoughts. Something can be logical and even immensely clever without corresponding in any way to reality. Thinking that is rooted in reality is what we need in our time. Abstract thinking will in the end take us to the point where we are no longer able to see reality amidst all the abstractions. People admire abstractions today when they are presented in this way. Proving these abstractions logically is simply not relevant. What matters is that we learn to embed ourselves in reality to such an extent that we are no longer able to say anything other than what is founded in reality.

The ideas about our human nature that I have shared with you today are a kind of guide to a thinking that is in touch with reality. You will often encounter mockery from those who have been trained in our abstract thinking. Western civilization has been schooled in purely abstract thinking for the last three to four hundred years, but we are now living in an age where we will have to turn this around and find our way back to reality. People have become materialists, not because they have lost their connection with logic but because they have lost their connection with reality. Materialism is logical, spiritualism is logical, monadism is logical, as is dualism so long as they are not founded on errors of thought. The fact, however, that something is logical does not mean it corresponds to reality. Reality can only be found when we ourselves bring our thinking steadily more into the region to which I was referring when I said: 'When we are engaged in pure thinking we have caught hold of a tassel of the cosmic process.' That can be found in my epistemological writings and is the basis for an understanding of the world that we still have to acquire.

The moment we are still thinking, despite not having any sense impressions, is also a moment when we are thinking and willing together. There is no distinction between willing and thinking. Thinking is then an act of will and willing is then thought. When our thinking has become completely free of sense impressions is when we have caught hold of a tassel of the cosmic process. That is what we have to strive to achieve above all else: a concept of this pure thinking. We shall speak more about this tomorrow.

LECTURE 9

W E set ourselves the task a few weeks ago of cognitively placing ourselves as human beings in the context of the cosmos. Yesterday I tried to indicate how we are integrated in the cosmic world of thought which has shaped our entire organization. So when we consider what cannot be grasped consciously from within our ordinary experience and our sense perceptions we have to think of our organization as belonging to the cosmos. In terms of our self-awareness we can consider it as belonging between cosmic thought on the one hand and the kind of thinking which can be observed as an undercurrent beneath ordinary consciousness on the other. This undercurrent would be part of what we consider as belonging to our own selves. That is how we tried yesterday to shed light on our experience of having a thought or being embedded in the world of thought.

The more we can raise our awareness to gain this perspective, the more we shall learn how to position ourselves in the context of the whole cosmic process and see ourselves as an element of cosmic development. If we can focus our attention on that part of us that is composed of our ordinary experience of thought and the subcurrent that I characterized yesterday, we shall also be able to grasp how in acquiring this, as it were, protruding element of the cosmos we become free, autonomous beings.

This study can be taken further and today we shall try to place ourselves within the context of the other kingdoms of Nature. In doing so I should point out how wrong it is to compare ourselves with the animal kingdom purely in terms of today's anatomy and physiology. Certainly, if you look at the human form as a whole and how it is made up of individual organs, you will notice that we have roughly the same number of bones, muscles and so on as the higher mammals and that these organs or systems of organs are transformed or metamorphosed. You can place human beings within the animal kingdom. Something quite different becomes apparent when you take into account the very particular place that we occupy within the cosmos. You can see that the animal's spine or spinal column is basically horizontal, parallel to the earth's surface; our own spinal column is vertical to the earth's surface. If you don't take the view that everything is based on purely material considerations but have worked your way through to the perspective that everything that exists has its own place within a coherent world order, you will acknowledge that this particular orientation of the human spinal column has a meaning of its own. One consequence is that our head has a quite different relationship to the organization of our body as a whole. Moreover if you are open to the view that the cosmos is filled with weaving and working thoughts, then to the extent that it can be thought of in spatial terms you will see that there is some reality to the picture of currents of thought passing through the cosmos and that it is not a matter of indifference whether the current that runs along the human spinal column is situated in a radial orientation to the earth or, as is the case with animals, runs parallel to the earth's surface.

The fact that we are placed in the cosmos in our own particular way must also be seen in the context of our organization as a whole, including the individual organs. Each of our organs or each organ system has a different relationship to the cosmos compared to that of an animal. This is not contradicted by the objection that our spinal column is horizontal when we are asleep. What counts is how the whole system of organs has grown, one organ in relation to the other. Once we have acknowledged that the animal's spinal column is horizontal to the earth's surface and that our own spinal column is vertical to it, we will be able to form a right judgement about the processes that are taking place within us. Now I would like to direct your attention to a different soul system from the one we looked at yesterday. Yesterday we looked at our thought system. Today we shall consider our will system.

Here too we can observe that our life breaks down into a rhythmic sequence of being awake and asleep. When we are awake, we are completely given over to our bodily nature; when we are asleep our I and our astral body are outside our bodily nature, both etheric and physical. When we wake up in the morning, we only retain a faint memory at best of the thoughts at work in the cosmos. We can therefore say that for the whole time between falling asleep and waking up we were immersed in the surging sea of cosmic thoughts. What we do bring with us on awakening, however, is our will, and this determines what we are throughout the whole day. Our will takes us out of the sea of thought in the cosmos which was the element we were immersed in during the night, or the time we were asleep. We emerge with our will, which brings logic into our inner life of soul. It may be that on awakening we have a feeling from the dreams pressing in on us of what our soul life would be like if it were not for our will bringing logic into it as we wake up.

This will has an impact on what is surging and swirling within our human organism. Let us take a closer and more focused look at the impact of our will. It takes hold of the chaotic swirling of dream images and also of the dreamy weaving that goes on as an undercurrent to our normal consciousness. We can say then that while we are asleep this fabric of thoughts is released from the working of our organs, whereas normally it is drowned out by the fabric of thoughts which is imbued with logic in the waking state. So it is this chaotic swirling of dream images and dreamy thoughts in which the will that we bring into our organism as we emerge from the cosmos, establishes order. Let's look more closely at what our will brings with it.

The moment it asserts itself our will ensures that our thoughts do not pop up in the way they do in the chaos of our dreaming state. We would not get on very well in life if our thoughts cropped up as they do in the chaos of dreams. What state should thoughts be in when they occur to us in normal life? They must somehow connect with our normal life. You have to be able somehow to remember. That is the first thing that our will undertakes, in a way its first step, as it takes hold of our thoughts. It organizes them so that our memory is an accurate reflection of events. Looking at our sketch, we have there [in red, see p. 127] the chaotic fabric of thoughts emerging from our organism. This is particularly characteristic of dreamy people who are often not content with life's normal memories, but who delight in the way thoughts associate in all kinds of references and relationships before separating again. Such dreamy characters are overpowered by this fabric of chaotic thoughts.

Even someone who has a normal grasp of their consciousness will always notice how if he lets himself go for a moment during the waking state, this swirling around of thoughts is present as an undercurrent in the depths of his head. Where does this will power come from that takes hold of the fabric of our thoughts on awakening? Our physical body [blue in the diagram] and our etheric body [yellow] were lying in bed. What I have sketched on the board for you is essentially what we leave behind every evening when we fall asleep and encounter again on awakening. We let our will take hold and this I will characterize with these lines [see drawing, arrows from above down]. The first thing our will has to do is to take hold of and organize this chaotic fabric of thoughts and transform it into our everyday memory. As it takes hold, our will begins to reshape the fabric of thoughts into normal memory. So what we meet in the morning is the etheric body and the physical body, still very powerful in the formation of memory. They reflect these thoughts back to us. It is, however, our will that has work to do at that moment of taking hold. We can observe this. Just try carefully to observe one morning as you wake up how all kinds of swirling currents arise from within your soul and come up to meet you, such as an event which you experienced when you were 5, 6, then 7, then again when you were 15 or even 65, then 21, 17, 8 how all this is randomly swirling about, helter-skelter. That is where our will has to take a grip. It organizes all this so that it ends up as an ordinary memory, so that an event that took place when you were nine has not switched ahead of what happened when you were eight, and so on. That is where our will takes hold and shapes our memory out of this chaotic fabric of dreams. Observing our memory at work we will not see much of our will forces. Most people will not be open to seeing our will at work in our memory. Yet it is there, though this act of will taking hold of the shaping of memory is much less conscious.

The second aspect of the will at work is something that we ourselves can be more aware of. That has to do with what the will that we have brought with us on awakening actually does with this swirling of thoughts: namely creating the power of our imagination [see drawing]. This is the second element. There you will observe that you yourself can actively engage with it. Once the power of memory has been formed you remain subject to the compulsion of your organism. Your physical and etheric bodies have a strong influence on you; less so in the case of the power of imagination, you can exercise your own will in that area. There is nevertheless a huge difference between someone who is imaginative and a dreamy person who is simply given over to this swirling of random thoughts. Someone who allows his imagination to work knows that his will rules the flow of intermingling images and he shapes them according to his own will.

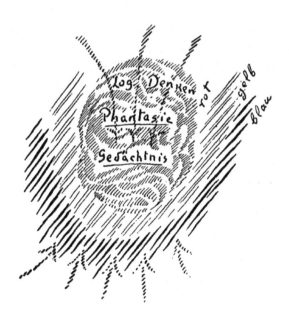

Log. Denken = logical thinking; Phantasie = imagination; Gedächtnis = memory;
rot = red; gelb = yellow; blau = blue

Now comes the third element. This is on the one hand completely dedicated to our will and on the other does not permit it to move as freely as it does in the case of imagination. This is logical thinking, which we depend on in life and for science. Our will is thoroughly engaged in this logical thinking; but it renounces its own freedom and submits to the laws of logic. It is a deed on the part of our will to submit to the laws of logic. That then is the third aspect: logical thinking.

Why is logical thinking so completely subject to our will? If we did not give shape to our logical thinking out of our will, our thoughts would be compulsive. We really do have to use our will to shape our logical thinking. In doing so, however, we have to take our lead from the world around us. The world around us is essentially our main teacher, also in matters of logic. We saturate the world of chaotic images with the laws of logic. In a sense we renounce our independence to a degree. On the one hand our will is free in the realm of thinking and on the other this freedom is renounced in favour of logic. Our will remains active in all these three areas of consciousness: memory, imagination and logical thinking. It is the same will that is not at work in our physical bodies or etheric organism during the time between falling asleep and waking up but which then takes hold of them at the moment of awakening and differentiates their rather inchoate flickering fire in the swirling of thoughts into memory, imagination and logic.

In regard to logical thinking it is true that we no longer exercise full sovereignty in our will. We don't. When we give free rein to our imagination in which we can clearly observe our will at work, we know how we feel in ourselves when we give way to logical thinking: we are no longer fully within ourselves. We know that we have to completely adapt to the cosmos, and not just to the cosmos beyond ourselves but to the whole cosmos that encompasses us too. Clearly logic does not apply only to the cosmos beyond us but also to the entire cosmos plus us as human beings. Logic is neither subjective nor objective but both at once.

We are now in a position to see the role played by what we bring with us out of the world of sleep and into our life of soul in the morning. We can also have an impression of what happens when the will that entered in with us withdraws back into the cosmic world of thoughts: it is then what rises up out of our physical and etheric bodies that holds sway within us.

This is, however, only one side of the will within us. One could refer to it as the cosmic aspect of our will, the aspect that we take out with us in the evening and bring back in the morning. Attentiveness to our inner life will teach us that the will that expresses itself mainly in memory, imagination and logical thinking is not the only one present in us. When we walk, when we take hold of something, when we make use of an instrument of any kind there is also an aspect of will at work in us. This will is not primarily active in our inner life as I have described above, but rather takes hold of our physical organization and etheric body. Thus I must characterize our will not just with these arrows coming from above, but also penetrating into the physical and etheric bodies from below. [see diagram].The conclusion is that our will is also present in what remains lying in bed during sleep. The will that has to be characterized in this way reaches out towards the other will which is not in our physical body during sleep. This latter will becomes essentially a physical activity. So this will that lives in our organs, in our physical and etheric organization, is called up by virtue of the other will reaching out to it. When we are awake and active, we can clearly distinguish between these two spheres of will.

Notice that will is at work on one side in opposition to will coming from the other side. We somehow incorporate the collaboration of two streams of will. The one swirls through our organism and the whole context tells us that we have to see it as whirling from below upwards. The other whirls its way down from above. That is when directions within the cosmos come into their own. That is when we notice that the situation has to be different in the case of animals, since the main orientation of their bodily organization happens to be perpendicular to the main orientation of our human bodily organization. The different directions of the will working in them are differently integrated in the cosmos. So if we take a closer look at the differentiations within the human being and once we have established how this human being is composed of individual streams, we realize the importance of how we are oriented within the cosmos.

Let's take our consideration of these two streams of will a little further. As with many things in spiritual science you will not be able to proceed, as it were, mathematically, by deducing one thing from another. Finding the truth in spiritual science is like this: one truth is next to another and one has to work out the connection later. Superficial commentators will quickly object that things are therefore not 'proved'. This would be like observing a horse and a cow standing beside each other in a meadow, for some good reason no doubt, and then requiring that one uses the horse as a basis for proving that the cow is standing beside it. There is of course nothing in the being of the horse that proves that the cow is standing next to it. Yet that is the basis on which very many people require proof within spiritual science.

I would now like to place another fact before you beside the one set out above which you will have gradually to try to relate to appropriately.

Everything that belongs to our soul nature is also expressed in our physicality. We are so organized that on waking up we kindle memory, imagination and logical thinking within us, and then let them come to rest during sleep. That is a kind of rhythm. This rhythm is opposite another: the rhythm that I have described as lying within our organs. The two streams opposite each other you will find reflected in the human being: you will find it if you look at the system of our breathing rhythm. I pointed out a few days ago how our breathing rhythm can be related to our sleeping and waking. Whilst it is true that breathing continues beyond sleeping you will see that there is nevertheless a connection through for example anything that interferes with calm breathing during sleep. The connection between breathing and the rhythm of waking up, going to sleep, waking up, going to sleep is not so obvious but it does nevertheless exist. If we look at our upward striving nature we shall have to consider our breathing system as one of its essential elements, also in terms of our speech organs. Breathing and speaking are essentially upwards, although the orientation of our throat turns forward for speaking. That is one form of breathing: uniform breathing.

We have another rhythm, namely the rhythm of our blood circulation which is expressed in our pulse, and we know that the ratio of pulse beats to our breathing is roughly four to one. You need only reflect a little in terms of anatomy and physiology to come to the conclusion that the pulsebeat, the rhythm of our circulation, is intimately connected with our metabolic and lymph system, essentially downwards. We have already linked the true rhythmic system with our breathing processes. The more we try to characterize our breathing system on the one hand and our circulatory system on the other, the more we will notice that everything that has to do with the organic basis for memory, imagination and logical thinking is connected with our breathing rhythm and that all the rest, which is connected to the will coursing through our organs, is linked to the pulsebeat as it is directed upwards. So just as the will that is in our organs coincides with the world that we bring with us from the cosmos on awakening, the breathing rhythm coincides with our pulse rhythm, with our circulation. We then find in the mutual interaction of our breathing rhythm with our pulsebeat the physical expression of what presses up from below in us and what beats down from above and they do so in such a way that what comes down from above is four times slower than what pushes up from below. If I draw this line as a timeline for the breathing rhythm I will have to assume four beats of the pulse.

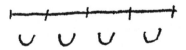

It is a fact that everything that we do in the way of art, as rhythmic art, is based on this relationship of pulsebeat to breathing rhythm. I have already drawn attention to this in connection with my remarks on the art of recitation.[24] One could go into more detail. One could imagine that if you emphasize the pulse rhythm more you will get: short syllable, long syllable. If you combine the breathing rhythm with the pulse rhythm you will get the hexameter and so on. All forms of metre are based on this rhythmic relationship which we have within us.

——————— ∪ ∪

Focusing more on the rhythm of our blood circulation we tend towards physical expression, focusing more on our breathing rhythm we tend more towards soul expression. The breathing rhythm is much more closely related to our soul than the blood rhythm. Our breathing rhythm is also open to what is outside us just as logical thinking is open to the outside. Irregularities in our lives are based on irregularities in these rhythms. As you can imagine, if there really is a ratio of four to one or one to four between these rhythms then it will mean something if, let us say, the breathing rhythm becomes too long or the pulse rhythm too short. Nevertheless, it can happen. It can even happen in a very insignificant way and will then immediately show itself.

Let me show you two radical cases of this. Imagine that someone gets excited. The person concerned becomes passionate. For some reason he begins to swear. He might even begin to rage. Alternatively the person might show symptoms like this: thoughts just will not come of their own accord, they come to a standstill; the person cannot think straight. Just as raging temper was the most radical example earlier of how passionate feelings can extend to swearing, hissing and fury, it can also happen that thoughts come to a standstill and eventually to a kind of powerlessness. The former example of passion and emotionality is related to the pulse rhythm becoming too fast. The seizing up, or paralysis of our thinking, relates to the breathing rhythm becoming too slow.

This shows how we are woven into the totality of cosmic rhythms, and the way a person is embedded in these rhythms determines how he may appear to us physically or in terms of soul expression. Our emotions do after all express themselves physically: the stream that passes through our organism from below up becomes too quick, it shakes up our organs and when we are in a rage, one can see how the organs are shaken up. Conversely when the stream that passes through us from above down becomes too slow, our thoughts will not come down from above. This is another example of how it is important to form a concept of how we are connected to the entire cosmos, embedded within it. It is childish to simply count up the bones, muscles and so on in our anatomy and declare: 'The human being is only a higher form of animal', without taking into account how we are integrated within the entire context of the cosmos.

Now I shall tell you something that seems very remote from what I have just been explaining. It will, however, make a coherent whole in the context of tomorrow's lecture. We are now moving on from being human to becoming human. You will know that we are presently living in the so-called fifth post-Atlantean epoch which began in 1415 or 1413 and is now continuing. It was preceded by the fourth which started about 747 before the mystery of Golgotha and before that again there was the third which goes back to the fourth millennium.

Looking at these epochs we can highlight the sequence with the illustration below. Imagine for a moment that the Atlantean epoch was preceded by the Lemurian, as I called it in my book *Occult Science*. I will only indicate the last phases of this Lemurian epoch here and I will go on to draw the sequence of seven cultural epochs that were part of the Atlantean age. Following that we have the ancient Indian, ancient Persian, Egypto-Chaldean, Graeco-Latin and now our own fifth post-Atlantean epoch. That would be the last epoch. These are all set out diagrammatically below:

You will know from my *Occult Science* and other descriptions I have given, that each one of these epochs lasts roughly as long as it takes the sun to progress from one vernal equinox right through the zodiac and back. This is only a rough indication, but it will do for what we are considering at present. In 747 before the event on Golgotha the vernal equinox took place in the sign of Aries. Before 747 it took place in the sign of Taurus, so that throughout the Egypto-Chaldean cultural epoch the spring rising of the sun took place in the sign of Taurus; hence the worship of the bull. Before that there was the ancient Persian epoch in which the sun rose in the sign of Gemini, the twins. In the ancient Indian epoch the sun rose in the sign of Cancer, the crab. Now we have reached back to the Atlantean era and to the seven cultural epochs that belonged to it. I would like to ask you to consider the following and place it before your soul as a question that we will simply hold for today.

Let us draw up the sequence of the signs of the zodiac. So we have: Aries, Taurus, Gemini, Cancer, Leo, Virgo, Libra, Scorpio, Sagittarius, Capricorn, Aquarius and Pisces. Now we will sketch out how they relate to the sequence of cultural epochs. We know that we are now in the sign of Pisces at the vernal equinox and are in the fifth post-Atlantean epoch. Going back [sketched in more darkly in the drawing on p. 135] we have: Aries—fourth post-Atlantean epoch, Taurus—third post-Atlantean epoch, Gemini—second post-Atlantean epoch and Cancer—first post-Atlantean epoch. Now we have reached back to the Atlantean era [lightly shaded]: Leo the 7th, Virgo the 6th Libra the fifth, Scorpio the fourth, Sagittarius the third, Capricorn the second, Aquarius the first; we have then reached back to the Lemurian era and return once more to the sign of Pisces.

You see, if you consider the important last cultural epoch of the Lemurian age and if you go over what I wrote about this important period in the development of humanity in my book *Occult Science*, you will be faced with a big question. If you take what I described in my *Occult Science* and what I wrote about subsequently in a separate publication entitled *Our Atlantean Forebears* [*Cosmic Memory*], you will see that we can only refer to humanity, in the sense that we are human today, from that point in our development and that is the period

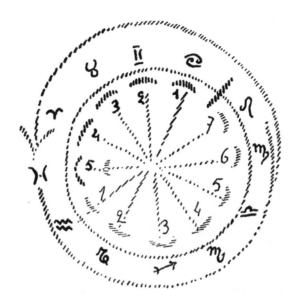

in which the vernal equinox was in the sign of Pisces, the same as now.[25] As a human race we have completed an entire circuit through the heavens and thus have in a sense returned to our starting point.

What I have just said relates to the process of becoming human. I have often tried to describe how human soul life has changed since the time of Atlantis. We know how different humanity's whole life of soul was in ancient India and how that in turn will have differed from human experience during Atlantean times. If you read my work about our Atlantean precursors you will see that during the era of Atlantis the human physical configuration corresponded to what was going on in people's souls. Whilst our soul experience has significantly changed in the post-Atlantean era in terms of its impact on our physical body, during the time of Atlantis our whole body was subject to metamorphosis. We are evolving more and more away from the region which I have characterized as belonging to the soul and towards the region down here which is primarily physical and is permeated by the other stream of will. Going further back into the time of Atlantis we reached the metamorphoses that relate to the forming of our bodies. During the passage of the vernal equinox through the sign of Pisces human beings were scarcely evident in the physical form as it is now [lightly shaded].[26] Here the form becomes increasingly physical [more strongly shaded] and only here does it begin to take on soul expression before returning here to the initial point of departure towards its physical form. One could then say that the passage through the signs of the zodiac from Pisces, through Aquarius, Capricorn, Sagittarius, Scorpio, Libra up to Virgo [lightly shaded] corresponds to the transformation of the human bodily form, and it is only in the upper zodiacal signs that we see the corresponding transformation of our soul being.

We have to look at these things in the light of spiritual science and then it will become clear that we have only now reached the point where we can form concepts and ideas about the nature of the human being. On the other hand we should at least be getting an inkling of what I have often said here, namely that we are living in a very important age. For during the whole period of our development on earth we have passed from the sun's spring rising point right through the cosmos and back to arrive in our time. There are tasks that we must now fulfil which derive from the fact that humanity has returned to its point of departure. Something must be initiated in our souls which corresponds to this return to our starting point. Today I just wanted to indicate the impact such considerations can have on our feelings when we look at the importance of the present age in the whole of human development. What I have said does admittedly only apply to the most advanced elements of civilized humanity but they will in the end be the determining factor in the development of humanity.

We shall have more to say about these things, particularly the latter, tomorrow.

LECTURE 10

At the end of yesterday's lecture I pointed out that the vernal equinox has made a complete circuit of the zodiac from Pisces to Pisces and that the starting point according to the findings of spiritual research was the beginning of humanity's development on earth. This must of course be understood in the right way. Looking at the evolution of humanity in its entirety we would have to say that it had its beginnings in the time of Old Saturn. The cycle we spoke of earlier is therefore only a part of the whole course of humanity's development on earth. We can also look at the process in this way: human beings took shape in significantly different ways in each of their phases of development from Saturn through Sun and Moon, none of which can be compared with the current human form. If we are now addressing the development of the human form on earth, it implies that the preparation for this physical existence took place at the end of the Lemurian age in the way I have described in my written works, and continued on through the Atlantean age, i.e. precisely for the time involved in such a complete cycle of the vernal equinox.

Today we shall expand a little on the circumstances affecting us during the time we returned to our point of departure. I would like to show you what I actually mean by this in the form of an illustration. It would not be correct to represent human development since the last part of the Lemurian era where the vernal equinox was in the sign of Pisces as a circle, simply returning on itself. That would be wrong. We have to think of this circle, which is of course only an image of the development process, as a spiral [see sketch on p. 138]. We have to think of it so that if the starting point of our development in the old Lemurian era was here, and then returned to its point of departure, with humanity having reached a higher state of development, in relation to the cosmos we have returned in the present age to our point of departure but at a higher level of development. We shall now consider how we have to live in these new surroundings.

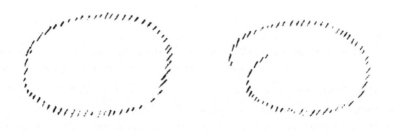

Some time ago I spoke to a smaller group in Stuttgart about a possible astronomical perspective on our world in its context.[27] I have shown how for a long time the Ptolemaic view of the world was considered the correct one. It was certainly intelligent and summarized in a series of geometrical lines what needs to be summarized if we want to express what we see of the stars in their positions, relations and movements in image form. Then due to a variety of circumstances which I have often referred to, the Ptolemaic system was replaced by the Copernican system which with certain substantial amendments is still regarded as correct today. In Stuttgart I showed that the Copernican system is likewise only a compilation of linear perspectives on what we see with our eyes or telescopes or anything else when we look out into the cosmos, and I went on to show that the Copernican system is by no means so very much more accurate a representation than the Ptolemaic system. It is only a different way of interpreting the phenomena. I then tried to summarize the phenomena myself, in relation to what we ourselves can experience when, for example, the earth moves in a certain way and carries us with it. Today I only want to present the result since the rest of the process is not important for us.

Now if we try to condense the phenomena down to a simple cosmic system that one could represent with a pencil or a globe, while avoiding the one-sided Ptolemaic or Copernican systems but taking into account all the phenomena that present themselves, it becomes so complicated that we would soon come to the conclusion that it simply can't be done. It is essentially impossible to summarize these things simply in the way we normally like to. As a result, we come to something quite remarkable which I would like to show you because however paradoxical it may seem to our modern consciousness, it needs discussion.

It is commonly held that present-day natural science is the cleverest thing that there's ever been and that essentially nothing could be cleverer. This belief, however, is leading us towards a cultural disaster. Somehow we will still have to find a way to present the reality. The more we take individual circumstances into account, the more likely we are to be overwhelmed by the complexity of the cosmos and to feel as we do when we have just woken up and experienced the chaotic images in our life of soul which I described to you yesterday and the day before as a kind of subcurrent in our consciousness. I illustrated the human organism in terms of an etheric body and a physical body and added: these chaotic images turn up which are in fact also always present during the daytime. They occur very actively in people who are inclined to be dreaming but we all find them deep inside us.

They are particularly noticeable in the morning when our ego and astral bodies dive back down into our physical and etheric bodies. What I am referring to is not the images themselves, which according to the state of development of the individuals involved can of course be poetic or imaginative or indeed be totally chaotic, which is more often the case—but rather the mood of soul that comes over us when as fairly logical people, used to thinking logically, we are immersed in this world of images. The mood of soul I mean is how one feels when one has put aside all prejudices and oversimplifications which tend to come up when one is trying to systematize the world, and simply approaches the task entirely without prejudice. Eventually the complexity and the way in which everything is interwoven will induce a kind of mood of soul.

Of course our culture has brought it about (and most people find it very reassuring) that every schoolchild knows: the sun is at the focal point of an ellipse, the planets revolve around it, the fixed stars do not move and so on. Every schoolchild knows this and it is very simple. However, if we look at the phenomena without preconceptions or any theoretical constructs we will find that they are not simple at all, but become increasingly complex and eventually we end up with the feeling I described earlier: we have to reach the point where we pass from the clearly determined to the indeterminate, from clearly defined lines to problematic ones. We begin to feel: what you are taking into your head is an image, a woven image, which you can of course simplify, just as you can make a sketch of one of Raphael's Madonnas, however, you would not then have the full Raphael Madonna before you, and similarly the Copernican system presents us with the cosmos in the form of an image which contains an infinite number of details and distinct elements. The moment you take this into consideration, you will realize: when eventually we have to admit to our limitations in the face of the complexity of the phenomena in the cosmos we will also have to admit that we are incapable of fully confronting reality as such. The mood in which we meet what is coming towards us is like the mood in which we meet the world of images when we wake up out of the cosmos every morning and enter into our bodies. So there is no question of us facing reality.

These are the sort of considerations we will have to take into account if we want to develop a mental picture in the true sense of the word of what is meant by the following: with our present consciousness we live in a world of illusion, of Maya. With the image we have constructed for ourselves of the cosmos and its phenomena, we are also living in Maya. The same is true of the impressions made on us by the world around us, woven together through our senses. We would certainly not develop the clumsy theory of knowledge that emerged at the end of the eighteenth century and on into the nineteenth century, constantly repeating the idea that the phenomena are out there, produced according to the laws of mechanics or dynamics and to be understood in terms of waves or, as is being said more recently, electrons which make impressions on our senses. What we perceive is thus only the effect of what is out there, and hence only the appearance of reality. To talk in this way about the appearance of reality really is a clumsy theory of knowledge, which can lead to all kinds of peculiar experiences.

These days we only need to make a couple of references here and there to the shortcomings of this theory of knowledge and someone will pop up and say: 'But Kant said...!' People have become so entangled in this web of Kantianism that they treat him like some kind of bible; at least many people do. They make certain adjustments, but on the whole he is regarded as a kind of bible. This can lead to strange encounters. I once gave some lecture courses on the topic in Berlin during the winter of 1900 to 1901, the very same winter in which Herr von Gleich proclaimed that a certain Winter had instructed me in Theosophy.[28]—He mistook the winter of 1900—1901 for a Herr Winter who is supposed to have given me instruction in Theosophy! I don't know if he had read it somewhere or if someone had told him that I gave these lectures in the winter which were subsequently published as having been given in the winter of 1900 to 1901 in Berlin and then the word winter was taken to refer to Herr Winter by name. Well, this argument is no more intelligent than the other stupid and untruthful arguments put forward by General von Gleich.[29] But there was also a dyed in the wool Kantian who actually attended these lectures. I can't say he was listening, since most of the time he was asleep and I don't know how many people are capable of listening while they sleep, but I did notice that this gentleman only woke up when he could make some reference to Kant. It then happened that I repeated an argument,—not one of mine—which maintained that if we really refer to the thing in itself in the way Kant did, i.e. that it is completely unknown, then it might consist of pins and that indeed pins might be behind all sense impressions. The moment I said this, the gentleman in question jumped as if he had been bitten by a tarantula and said: 'There is neither space nor time behind phenomena. Needles exist in space and so the thing in itself could not possibly consist of pins!' This is just one example of many incidents that occur when people believe that their bible, their Kantian bible has somehow been tampered with.

Now it really is not the case that somehow any old 'things in themselves' will throw effects into us which will then trigger sensory qualities in us, so that we are cocooned in our own sensory qualities; it's just not like that. The correct description is quite different. I would ask you to do the following: stand outside at 11am for example and look at your surroundings carefully, unlike the way some people sketch them. That approach is pointless because those sketches cannot render the sensory appearances correctly. Look at your surroundings at 11am and 12 noon including all the light effects playing on them. The entire sensory fabric will have completely changed at 12 noon and again at five and eight pm. The picture spread out before you is constantly changing. You are never dealing with anything other than interwoven effects. Take a tree—what part of the tree do you see? You see the light reflected back; you may see the leaves stirred by the wind, and so on. In short, you will never see anything constant. What you see will simply be an objective appearance. Where the clumsy theory of knowledge talks of a subjective appearance, you actually see an objective appearance and this naturally communicates itself to the eye. Just as a tree absorbs the rays of light in a certain way, reflects them and so on, your eye is in a particular relationship to the light rays and we can say: the world of phenomena, of appearances, surface reality, the Maya nature that is spread out in the world which we can sense around us is of course present in the subjective image we form; but because it is objectively changeable, our subjective image is also changeable.

This is just what I wanted to establish in the first section of my *Philosophy of Spiritual Activity* or in my little book *Truth and Science*. So even when we are looking at the world in front of us, we are not dealing with a permanent, lasting reality. We are dealing with what is coming and going at any given moment. We are concerned with appearances. If we wanted to construct this image theoretically we would be no better off than we were with a few lines sketched of the *Sistine Madonna*. That is how it is with everything that we relate to outside us. We are placed in a world of phenomena, of Maya, but despite the fact that we are in this world with all our sensory capacities we are not dependent on it. What is quite clear to us is that when we come out of the cosmos every morning and dive into our etheric and physical bodies with our astral body and I, what we are diving into is something objective and has its own truth. Of course, the chaotic images that swirl around us are only appearance on the surface, but what we are diving into contains something true in its essence. The moment we dive into our bodies, whether we say to ourselves: I want to move my limbs or I want my thoughts to become imaginative pictures or I want to organize my thoughts in some logical sequence—we know that what happens when we dive into our bodies is something that does not depend entirely on us. We receive it; it takes us into itself. The moment of waking up is the moment that gives us our feeling of identity.

This feeling of identity weaves and waves its course through our entire experience of thinking. Our thoughts themselves connect more with the world of phenomena, appearance, Maya. Let us now extend what I have described by means of our ordinary everyday experiences to encompass the whole human being.

Anyone who can contemplate the whole human being with the insights that can be gained from my book *Knowledge of the Higher Worlds* will soon see how our soul and spirit aspect passes through the condition we are in between death and a new birth, and then penetrates into the physical world. It embodies itself in order to experience the condition we are in between birth and death and then once again experiences the world between death and a new birth. I have already set out some important details of these processes in my recent lectures here. When we have developed our consciousness to the point where we can look back into the world that exists before our birth or conception, we will observe: the world that consists of what gives us our sense of identity is the one we have passed through on our journey between death and a new life. A true sense of identity that is not susceptible to feelings of doubt or scepticism can only come from an ability to look back into the world of our existence before our conception.

But now we come to a significant factor. You will find this in my lectures given in Vienna in the spring of 1914 but this time I want to present it in a different form.[30] It is revealed in something that comes towards us before we start our descent into physical embodiment and while we are still in the human condition between death and a new birth. What happens during this time is that we increasingly lose our appetite for existence, for being who we are. As we develop during the period between death and a new birth we go through a process of complete saturation with the experience of being who we are. This is one of the things that humanity attains between death and the new birth, namely that once we have passed through the first stages after death the relationship we have to the world we are entering involves us becoming deeply infused with a sense of being, a sense of being anchored in the being of the world. This becomes stronger and stronger to the point where we experience a kind of oversaturation with our sense of self and then, towards the end of the time between death and a new birth a complete oversaturation with our sense of self takes place. I could also put this in a different way. We begin to experience a real hunger for a feeling of non-existence. The beings of soul and spirit who come down to earth as human beings show a strong hunger for non-existence. This attitude of soul and spirit means that out of our hunger for non-existence we plunge into Maya, into the world that we see before us among the stars and in the phenomena of the earthly world. It is a yearning for a world of non-being, a world which affects us in the way the chaotic impressions do when we seek for what underlies it, a world that shows us a different face every time we look at it. As we live our way into this world, we find ourselves completely enveloped by surface appearances, the world of Maya. Our spiritual and soul nature wants to plunge into this world of Maya. That is what we have to face. Other aspects of our new existence are more or less side effects. It is the strongest impulse in our soul and spiritual nature as we approach our earthly existence: this yearning for Maya, this yearning for soft and permeable phenomena, as opposed to being saturated with the sense of our own being. The etheric and physical bodies that are then wrapped around us are born out of the cosmos. During the last few days I have explained how the embryo in our mother's body is formed out of the cosmos.

What we thus have to imagine is this: each of us actually comes from a completely different world, a world in which is developed this hunger for non-being, for a life within Maya as we approach physical existence. Our I and astral bodies [red and blue in the diagram below] are then received by our etheric and physical bodies [yellow and red]; these are formed out of the cosmos on conception as our earthly clothing. We have come from a world that has neither space nor time, which cannot be found in space, but are nevertheless clothed in space with what has been prepared in our mother's body. We dip back into this every time we wake up. As we fall asleep we emerge from it once more. We then develop a rhythmical relationship with our bodily nature, dipping into it and emerging from it.

rot = red; blau = blue; gelb = yellow]

Today's way of thinking makes it very difficult to deal with reality. It is hard to explain these processes appropriately to the science of our day because the necessary concepts are lacking: for example, how a completely different stream which a person has been following before coming to embodiment is linked to the outer garment in which the individual is wrapped, but with which the individuality had previously had no substantial connection. (I have explained how it really comes about on other occasions.)

The same is true in other contexts. When physiologists talk about light or colour today, they are primarily concerned with describing something or other that the eye does. In reality this is rather like someone wanting to describe one or other of the people sitting here and then mainly focusing on the carpenter's workshop here, because that is where the person came in. Essentially the light that enters the eye and has its impact on it has little more to do with it than you have with the carpenter's workshop once you have walked in and are enclosed within it. If someone is describing you and the workshop, both will naturally be described as a whole. But that doesn't happen. It remains a hard task to find the truth in the face of today's convoluted thought processes.

We can summarize the issue as follows: the spiritual and soul aspects of our being come to this earthly world primarily on account of this urge towards non-being. Then every waking moment experienced, that is in the time between waking up and going to sleep, is a new education towards being, a new imbuing of consciousness with being.

Human beings in the condition we were in between death and a new birth are so happy, so happy when they can come to their physical incarnation. I have often described how the brain floats in its cerebral fluid. If the entire weight of the brain (1,350 grams roughly) were to press down on the blood vessels beneath, they would be squashed and could not function, but the downward pressure amounts to no more than about 20 grams. Why? Because our brain is floating in cerebral fluid. You will be familiar with the Archimedean Principle. It was Archimedes who discovered it. He was in a bathtub one day and noticed how he became lighter and lighter in the bath and was so delighted by this discovery that he jumped out of the bath at once and ran through the streets naked, (a scientific researcher would have found it easier to do that in those days than in ours) shouting: 'I've got it, I've got it!' This was the principle that if you have a vessel with water in it, then place a solid object into it, the object will become lighter than it is outside the vessel and by the weight of the water it has displaced. If you imagine it as  made of water, it would have become lighter by its own weight in water. In this way the brain loses all but 20 grams of its weight, pressing down with only 20 grams, because it is floating in cerebral fluid. Our brain is thus not constrained by its own full weight. It is buoyed up. The force that brings this about is also known as buoyancy. As we incarnate we look forward to coming into something that draws us upwards, really draws us upwards. We learn what it is to be heavy from the remaining 20 grams, and heaviness teaches us to feel our own selfhood. We are once more imbued with the sense of self between birth and death. It is then extended and increased in the development we go through after death.

This has lapsed from the consciousness of modern humanity to such an extent that the greatest philosopher at the time this newer awareness was dawning, Cartesius or Descartes, coined the phrase *Cogito ergo sum*—I think, therefore I am. This is the most nonsensical phrase one could imagine, for it is precisely in the act of thinking that we cease to exist. We are outside existence at that moment. *Cogito ergo non sum*—is the true reality. We are so far removed from true reality today that the greatest philosopher of the modern age could formulate the truth as its opposite. We acquire our sense of self precisely when our thinking experiences itself within our organism, when it feels embedded in what is heavy. This is not merely a popular image, it is the reality expressed in the phenomena.

Moreover, this can teach us how from our position before conception we knowingly make our way down to earth, submerge ourselves in Maya and from within Maya learn what we are going to need again after death: the experience of selfhood. What I am describing to you now is something that is specifically human in our development. This rhythmic passing from a sense of being to non-being is something you could imagine as part of a meditation in the following way: when you are merely concerned with your thoughts: I am not—when you are living in your will, which physically lives in your metabolism and limbs, you could say: I am. What lies between our metabolic human nature and our purely brain-bound nature (which will say 'I am not' if it fully understands itself, for it is only images that live in the brain) is the rhythmic alternation between: I am and I am not. The outer physical expression of this is the breathing process. Our exhalation fills our breathing process with what comes from our metabolic process with carbon dioxide. I am is exhaling. I am not is inhaling

> I am not
>
> I am　　　–　　　I am not.
>
> Exhalation　–　　Inhalation
>
> I am

The inhalation is related to the: I am not—of thinking. Inhalation involves drawing breath into our ribcage, pressing the water in the arachnoidal cavity upwards and thus also the cerebral fluid. We bring the oscillation of our breathing process into our brain. That is the organ of thinking. The inhalation process transmitted to the brain: I am not. Breathing out again—the cerebral fluid presses down through the arachnoidal cavity onto the diaphragm. Exhalation, (air turned into carbon dioxide). I am—from the depths of the will. Exhalation—out of the will.

All this is a purely human process if regarded in this way. Anyone who wishes to attribute this to animals, since they also breathe, is like someone taking a razor blade to cut their meat with on the grounds that it is a knife. Of course animals breathe too, but animal breathing is quite different from human breathing, just as a razor blade is different from a table knife. Making definitions on the basis of external appearances only will never lead to any useful understanding of the world. Death is different in each case as human beings, animals and plants. If you start with the definition of death your explanation will be no more useful than defining a knife as something that is so thin on one side that it cuts through other objects. The general concept is all very well but does not help us to understand the actual reality. What I have just described to you are specifically human processes. These are processes that human beings have gone through during the time the vernal equinox passed from the sign of Pisces and back again to the sign of Pisces. This is precisely the period of the earth's development during which peoples at the forefront of the process went through the most essential aspects of what I have just described to you and indeed everything that enables us to see what happens when we descend into the physical world through birth, plunge into Maya and are then born out of Maya at the moment of death, enriched by the sense of self that will be needed for life going on after death. This is an extremely important fact: being born out of life through death and with a sense of self and on the other hand how coming to birth on earth is a plunging of our soul and spiritual being into the world of Maya. It is precisely the fact that we are plunging into Maya, a world of images, that enables us to be free.

We could never be free if we lived in a world of facts with the consciousness we have between birth and death. We are only free in that we live in a world of images. Images in a mirror do not determine us causally. A world of facts would. What you bring towards the picture hanging in front of you must come from you. The world of appearances here does not determine us in respect to what in my *Philosophy of Spiritual Activity* I describe as pure thinking which does not emerge from our organism. What comes out of our organism, as you will have seen, is saturated with a sense of self, although in the case of our brains it is present in such a small percentage that it amounts to roughly 20 parts to 1,350. We have to constantly take that into consideration when we think of how we develop this yearning for Maya as we are born into this earthly world and how living on the earth teaches us to develop a sense of our identity. That is what we have been going through during the time between the last Lemurian epoch and our own, amounting to a solar cycle of 25,920 years, a great world cycle.

Now we have reached the time in which this period of development has returned to its point of departure and as I indicated it should be represented diagrammatically in spiral form rather than as a circle. Developing humanity has returned to its point of departure, but on a higher level. What is meant by this higher level? It means that until now we humans have plunged into Maya at birth and have then acquired a sense of our own identity out of this physical existence. However, the earth itself has also undergone a transformation and is no longer the same organism that it was in the Lemurian or Atlantean epochs. Today, the earth is in a process of dissolution.

This is also known to geologists. Read the beautiful geological writings of Eduard Suess, *The Face of the Earth*: 'The Earth is in a process of crumbling, a process of dissolution.' The effect of this is that we now no longer have every opportunity to adequately develop our sense of individual being. Now that we have completed a cycle in the way I described yesterday and today, we face the danger of going through death without having developed a sufficient sense of our own individual being, because the earth no longer provides the necessary intensity of individual experience. This new period which I have now described to you as a period affecting the entire cosmos confronts humanity with the prospect of going through death with too strong a feeling of levity, if I may put it like that. We may become more and more materialistic, but the consequence will be that we will have an inadequate sense of our own weight, of our own individual being, on passing through the threshold of death.

This is already quite clear today to anyone who is familiar with how things are in the cosmos of our time: souls are now passing through the gate of death who are in a sense being borne aloft by their own feeling of non-being, so that they experience the opposite of someone falling into the water who is unable to swim, and sinks. These souls 'sink' upwards when they pass through the gate of death owing to their own lack of gravity. The way in which the term gravity is used in the spiritual world is illustrated at a significant moment in my Mystery Plays. 'They rise up and are lost.'[31] This can only be prevented if people are prepared to make the effort to rise above the concepts that come of their own accord and feature throughout our lives, and strive towards what requires a certain amount of exertion in physical life: i.e. concepts that do not derive from physical life alone but which have to be acquired through spiritual science.

What do people tend to say about spiritual science who wish to stay with the conventional way of thinking of our day? They will tell you: 'Well if you take for example what is described in Steiner's *Occult Science*, it's fantasy, it's random, it's impossible to imagine it!' Why do people say this? They can see chalk, tables, legs, and they can only imagine what appears before them in this way; they don't want to imagine anything other than the outer physical reality they are used to. They don't want to become inwardly active in their thinking. If you want to study *Occult Science*, you will have to exert yourself. If you stare at an ox, you will be facing a reality, it is true, but you will not need to make any effort; you will only need to stare at the ox and then form a so-called concept, which is not really a concept at all. The point is that these concepts indicated by spiritual science, such as for example my *Occult Science* or *Theosophy* or the other books, require this inner activity. With humanity having become so extremely materialistic today, a large number of people, spiritualists, are particularly reluctant to engage with thinking through, working through the content of *Occult Science*; they prefer to have something conjured up for them by Schrenck-Notzing, or others like him: humanoid lumps or things of that nature so that they can remain completely passive; no effort is required of them.[32]

The problem is that one then becomes increasingly lightweight, working against continued existence after death. On the other hand, fully engaging with the activity necessary to penetrate into spiritual science requires us to exert ourselves physically more than we normally would in so-called normal circumstances. One is obliged to give the concepts more weight. That has the effect of enabling us to carry our sense of self with us through death and being capable of facing life after death.

This is what people like so much today: adding nothing to what life brings towards them. If they have to add something, become inwardly active, they immediately start to feel uncomfortable. In society in general, people have always tried to learn as much as possible on the basis of the templates prescribed by the State; when we have happily reached the age of 25 or 26 and are student teachers, articled clerks or graduate trainees, we are pushed into some scheme or other and are entitled to a pension after so and so many years: then we are secure. Although we are only in our 20s, we are assured for the rest of our lives. We have our bodies pensioned—that is assured from the outset—then comes the Church according to our faith, which also demands no more from us than that we passively devote ourselves to what is on offer. The Church then provides the pension for our souls when we are dead.

This is assured without us having to do anything, other than keeping the faith, just as our bodies were covered by a pension earlier. This is something that must be broken with if we are not to see culture go into total decline. What is required is inner activity, active inner collaboration with what people are able to make of themselves, even with regard to their immortal beings. We must work for our immortality. That is what most people would prefer to have conjured magically away. They believe that knowledge can only teach us about what already exists and at best can only tell us that we are immortal beings. There are people who say: 'Well this is where I live with whatever life brings; as to what happens after death, well, we'll see when the time comes.'

They will see nothing, absolutely nothing! This argument is about as intelligent as the one advanced by Anzengruber's character: 'Sure as there is a God in heaven, I am an atheist.'[33] The logic behind both positions is the same. The fact is that as far as our spirit and soul nature are concerned we help our spirit to grow and mature by including it in our search for knowledge and so prevent it from going through the opposite experience of someone who is sinking while swimming, i.e. rising up with no sense of their own being. We must work at our own being to ensure that it can pass through death in the right way. Acquiring spiritual knowledge is not acquiring abstract knowledge but involves penetrating our spirit and soul nature with the forces that overcome death.

In truth that is the essence of the Christian doctrine, after all. Thus we are not merely to believe in Christ, as more recent confessions would have it, but rather to take to heart the words of Saint Paul: 'Yet not I but the Christ in me.' We must want to develop the power of Christ in ourselves and to form it within ourselves! Belief is not in itself sufficient to save us. Only inner collaboration with the Christ, inner work at acquiring the power of Christ, which is after all always present when we wish to develop it within ourselves, but which has to be worked for. We will have to fill ourselves with initiative and activity, and we will have to recognize that purely passive belief will simply make us too light, so that immortality on earth would gradually die out. That is what Ahriman is working towards. We shall find out the extent to which this is Ahriman's intention in the next lecture, since we are now placed between the conflicting powers of Lucifer and Ahriman. Just as we have to some extent preserved our unconsciousness while the vernal equinox completed a full cycle, we shall have to embark on the next cycle in the full knowledge of what is weaving through the being of worlds: the battle between the ahrimanic and luciferic spirits. Spiritual science leads us into reality, not into a purely abstract knowledge. More of this the next time we meet.

LECTURE 11

Today I will summarize a few truths which will then help us give a direction to what we will cover in the next few days. When we look at our soul life we can see that there is one pole devoted to our thinking and that the other contains our will element and between the two lies the element of feeling and what we might call our disposition. In our soul experience during the waking condition we will never find just the one element, thinking or will, at any given time because they are always in connection with each other, playing into each other. Let us assume that we have a very calm approach to life so that one could say that our will is outwardly not very much in evidence. We will still have to be quite clear that whilst we are thinking in such moments of calmness, our will is at work in our thinking; as we connect one thought with another, will is at work in our thinking. Thus even when we are apparently in a purely contemplative state, just thinking, our will is at work within us. Similarly, unless we happen to be raving mad or sleepwalking, our will cannot be active without our will impulses being infused with thoughts. Our will activity is always penetrated by thinking. Thus our will is likewise never acting alone within our soul life. Nevertheless what is never acting alone within us can also have a different origin from the other elements of our soul life. The thinking pole within us comes from a totally different source from our life of will.

Even looking at everyday life we can see that our thinking always relates to what is already present and has its own preconditions. Thinking is usually retrospective. Even when we are anticipating something, when we are thinking of some undertaking that we intend to carry out later with our will, this anticipatory thinking will still be based on experience which we will use as a guide. This kind of thinking is also reflective. Our will cannot be directed to what is already there. It would otherwise always be too late. Our will can only orient itself towards what is to come, towards the future. In sum, if you give a little thought to the inner aspect of our thinking and to the inner aspect of our will, you will find that even in everyday life, thinking relates more to the past and our will to the future. Our feeling disposition lies between the two of them. Our feelings accompany our thinking. Thoughts can delight us or repel us. Feelings in turn guide our will impulses into life. Our feeling, the content of our soul's disposition, stands in the middle between our thinking and our will.

Just as these things are hinted at in ordinary life they are also to be found in the greater scheme of things. There we find that the foundations of our powers of thought which enable us to think, are laid in the life before our birth, or rather conception. The seeds of all the thought capacity that we are able to unfold in life are to be found already in the little child before us. The child uses these thoughts as guiding forces in developing its body. For the first seven years leading up to the change of teeth, a child uses these powers of thought as guiding forces with which to build up its body. Thereafter they emerge gradually as powers of thought in their own right. Prior to that they have been embedded in us from the moment we embark on our physical, earthly lives.

Impartial observation will show us that the powers of will emerging in the child have little to do with its thinking capacities. Just look at the wriggling, constantly moving infant in its first few weeks of life and you will see that this wriggling, chaotically moving quality of the child is the result of its soul and spirit being wrapped in the physical body from its physical surroundings. It is in this physical nature that we gradually develop from the moment of conception and following our birth that our powers of will are to be found, and slowly and steadily this will is captured by the powers of thought that we have brought with us into physical existence. Just observe how the child initially moves its limbs quite randomly out of the natural liveliness of its physical body and then how gradually thinking takes hold of these movements so that they become purposeful. This thinking is pressing and pushing its way into the child's will life which is completely embedded in the protective embrace within which we live from the moment we are conceived. Its will life is completely contained within it.

We could illustrate this in a diagram showing how we bring our thought life with us as we come down from the spiritual world [yellow in the diagram below]. We put our will life in place in the physical body which is given to us by our parents [red].

gelb = yellow; rot = red

That is where our will forces are to be found, expressing themselves chaotically. Here are our thought forces [arrows] which initially serve as guiding forces, penetrating our will in its physical setting. They fill it with spirit in the right way.

We become aware of these will forces when we go through death and into the spiritual world. This time we experience them as highly ordered. We have carried them through the gates of death and into our life in the spirit. During the course of our lives we will have lost the forces of thought which we bring with us into earthly life.

It is different in the case of people who die early, but for the present we shall focus on the normal person. A normal individual who has lived beyond their 50s will already have lost the real forces of thought which they had brought with them from life before birth, and will have kept the direction-giving powers of will which are then carried over through death into the life we embark on as we pass through the gate of death.

It can be assumed that people will now be thinking: 'So we will have lost our powers of thinking after we reach 50 years old!' In a sense this is absolutely true of most people today who have shown no interest in spiritual matters. I would urge you to make a point of noticing how many original, authentic thought impulses have come from people today who are over 50! Generally it is the automatic thought processes rolling on from previous years which have imprinted themselves on our body which then automatically keeps them going. It is after all an image of our life of thought and we tend to carry on with the old thought processes according to the law of inertia. There is hardly any other way today of pro-tecting oneself from the treadmill of these old thoughts running on than by taking up thoughts of a spiritual nature during our lifetime which are similar to those forces of thinking in which we were immersed before our birth. The consequence is that the time is drawing ever closer when older people will be mere automata unless they take the trouble to engage with the forces of thinking that have a supersensible origin. Of course we can continue to think automatically and even look as if we are being actively thoughtful. It is, however, only an automatic movement of the organs in which the thoughts have embedded themselves, or woven themselves, unless we are gripped by the youthful element that comes when we engage with thoughts deriving from spiritual science. This is by no means a theoretical activity, but one that has quite a deep effect on our lives.

It becomes particularly significant when we consider our relation-ship to the world around us. By the world around us I mean every-thing that reaches our senses between waking up and falling asleep. One could look at it like this: one could cast an eye (a spiritual eye, I mean) over what it is that we see. We call it the veil of the senses. I'll illustrate it in a diagram like this:

rot = red; Gedanken = thoughts; blau = blue

Behind everything that we see, hear, experience as warmth, the colours of Nature etc. (I shall now draw an eye to represent what is perceived), behind this veil of the senses there is something definite. Physicists or people with our current perspective on things will say: 'There are atoms whirling about behind what we see, and then there is no veil of the senses but somehow these atoms call forth colours and sounds in our eye or our brain.' Now imagine that you start thinking quite dispassionately about this veil of the senses. Once you have started to think about it and if you don't fall prey to the illusion that you could determine this gigantic army of atoms disposed in military array by chemists, let us say for example there is NCO C, then two privates C,O,O, and then another private H, you see, then we have them all arranged in military order: ether, atoms and so on. Now if we do not succumb to this illusion, but stick with reality, we will know: the veil of the senses is spread out before us; there are the different qualities of the senses and what I can grasp of what lies within these sensory qualities with my consciousness is essentially thoughts. In reality there is nothing behind this veil of the senses other than thoughts [blue]. What I mean is that behind the phenomena of the physical world you will find nothing but thoughts. We shall talk about the fact that these are carried by beings later. It is, however, only with our thinking that we can get behind what we find in the physical world. The power of this thinking is something we have brought with us from our life before conception. Why is it then, that we penetrate through this veil of the senses with this power of thought?

Let us try to become really familiar with the thought process I have just embarked on and try to set out the question on the basis of what we have just indicated and in the context of our studies to date. How is it that we are able to reach behind the veil of the senses with our thoughts, if these thoughts come to us from our life before birth? It is very straightforward: because what lies behind it is not in the present, but in the past. It belongs to the past. What lies behind the veil of the senses is in fact of the past and our view of it is only correct if we recognize it as from the past. The past works on into our present and what we see in the present is sprouting up towards us out of the past. Imagine a meadow covered in flowers. You see the grass as a green covering and you see the flowery decoration of the meadow. That is all in the present but it is growing up out of the past. If you think that through in detail, what you will have is not an atomistic present but the past as an underlying reality which is related to that part of you which has its origins in the past.

It is interesting: when we begin to reflect, the world that is revealed to us is not the present but is the past that reveals itself. What is the present? The present has no logical structure at all. A ray of sunshine falls on the flower and gleams there. The next moment, when the ray of sunshine has changed direction, it gleams in another direction. The picture changes from moment to moment. The present is such that we cannot grasp it with mathematics, nor with thought constructs. What we can grasp with the structures of our thinking is the past, working on into the present.

This is something that can reveal itself to us as a great and significant truth: when you are thinking, what you think is essentially only the past; if you are weaving logical thought structures, you are basically only thinking about what is past. If you can grasp this thought, you will no longer look for marvels in the past. For whilst the past is weaving its way into the present it must remain as it was in the past even in the present. Just think: if you had eaten cherries yesterday, it was an action in the past. You cannot change the fact that it has happened, because it is a past action. But if the cherries were in the habit of leaving a sign somewhere, before they disappeared into your mouth, this sign would remain. You could do nothing to change this sign. Now if every cherry had registered its past in your mouth after you had eaten cherries yesterday, and someone came along and wanted to cross out five of them, he would be able to cross them out, but the fact of the matter would not change.

Similarly there is no way in which you could produce any kind of miracle out of natural phenomena, since they are all reaching into the present from the past. Everything that we can grasp with the laws of Nature is already in the past; it no longer has anything of the present about it. The present can only be grasped by means of images. It is fluctuating by nature. If a body lights up here, a shadow will arise. You have somehow to allow the shadow to determine its own contours. You can construct the shadow. For the shadow to arise in reality you have to devote yourself to a study of the image. So we can conclude: even in ordinary life, setting boundaries, I could also say logical thinking, relates to the past. Imagination on the other hand, relates to the present. We always have Imaginations in relation to the present.

Just think how it would be if you wanted to live in the present logically! It's true isn't it, living logically means developing one concept out of another, following strict laws from one concept to the next. Now place yourself back in real life. You see one event: is the one that follows it logically connected with it? Can you deduce the next event logically from the previous one? If you look at life as a whole, are not the images within it similar to a dream? The present is similar to a dream and it is only the fact that the past gets involved in the present that gives the present its lawful, logical structure. If you want to divine anything of the future in the present, even if you want to think of something that you intend to do in the future, then initially nothing concrete happens inside you at all. What you will experience this evening is not there as an image within you but as something even less substantial than an image. At best it will be an Inspiration. Inspirations relate to the future.

Logical thinking:	Past	
Imagination:	Present	} Intuition
Inspiration:	Future	

We can clarify what is meant in the form of a simple diagram. I'll represent the human being in this eye [see diagram p. 163] and as we look at the veil of the senses we see it in its constantly changing images. Now we introduce laws into this world of changing images. A specific science emerges. Now consider how this science is developed. We research and we do so by thinking. If the aim is to develop a science of what is manifesting in the veil of the senses, a science that is based on logical thought, you will find it impossible to derive these logical thought processes from the outer world itself. If the thoughts underlying the laws of Nature—and the laws of Nature are after all also thoughts—emerged from the outer world itself, it would not be necessary to learn anything about the outer world. Anyone looking at that light over there would have as precise an understanding of the laws of electricity etc. as the person who had studied them! Similarly, unless you have learned the relationship of the radius to the circumference you are unable to say anything about it. The thoughts that we transfer to the outer world emerge from within us.

That is how it is: the thoughts that we carry into the world around us are brought with us from our own inner life. We ourselves are the human being who is built as a head person. This person looks at the veil of the senses. Within the veil of the senses itself lives what we are able to reach with our thinking [see diagram page 163] and between that and what we are unable to perceive lying within us there is a kind of underground connection. That is how it comes about that what we do not perceive in the outer world, because it links up with what lies within us, is brought out of our own inner life in the form of thoughts which we then bring out and project into the outer world. Counting would be a good example of this. The outer world does not do any counting for us; but laws of number lie within us. This is due to there being an underground or sub-corporeal connection between what is to be found in the outer world and the earthly laws that apply to ourselves. That is how we produce numbers from within ourselves. They also match what is outside us. The pathway linking them does not, however, go through our eyes or any of our senses but through our organism. Our whole human constitution is thus involved in our learning process. It is not true to say that we grasp any natural law by means of our senses; we grasp it with the whole of our human nature.

rot = red; weiss = white

These are the things we have to take into account if we wish to acquaint our inner, feeling disposition rightly with how we stand in relation to the outer world. We are constantly immersed in Imaginations and all we need to do is to draw an unprejudiced comparison between everyday life and a dream. While the dream is in progress it certainly behaves quite chaotically, but is nevertheless much closer to real life than logical thinking. Let us take an extreme example.

I'm assuming a conversation between two sensible people of our time. You are listening in and can contribute to the conversation. Now consider the context of a half-hour conversation in terms of its coherence from the perspective of a dream sequence or from the perspective of its logical sequence. If you were expecting a logical sequence to emerge you would probably be rather disappointed. The world of our time clearly reaches us in the form of images with the result that we are basically constantly dreaming. If we want logic it has to be introduced. We wrest logic from our pre-birthly state; we first of all connect it with the things around us and then in doing so encounter the past in these things. The present we access through our Imaginations.

If we take a look at this imaginative life that constantly surrounds us, we can say: it is given to us. We have to make no effort of our own to access it. Now just think how much effort you have had to put into acquiring logical thinking! There will have been no need to exert yourself to enjoy life or to contemplate it; it reveals itself to you of its own accord. So we are well served in ordinary life in terms of how our surroundings reveal themselves to us in pictures. All we need now is to acquire the capacity to form pictures out of our own inner activity as we otherwise would do with our thinking. Then we would not only see our surroundings in picture form but would extend this pictorial consciousness into our life before we were conceived. Once we can perceive that in the form of images, our thinking will become populated by these images and our life before we were born will become a reality. By developing the faculties I describe in my *Knowledge of the Higher Worlds* we can become accustomed to thinking in pictures without these pictures presenting themselves to us involuntarily in the way they do in everyday life. If we can turn the world of images in which we live in ordinary life into our own inner life, we shall be looking into the spiritual world and we will see how our life truly unfolds.

Today it is regarded (largely without exception) as spiritual if someone despises material life and says: 'I am striving towards the spirit and matter is far beneath me.' That is a weakness, for one will only attain a spiritual life if one does not have to leave matter behind but can see it in the spiritual aspect of its activity. One will need to see all matter as spiritual in its origin and likewise recognize everything spiritual in its material manifestation. This will be particularly significant when we come to look at thinking and willing. There remains only language, which after all contains a hidden genius, that has something of the quality within it which can lead to knowledge in this field.

Let us look at the foundations of our will activity in ordinary life: you will know that it is initiated by desire; even the most ideal aspiration of the will begins in desire. Now let us take the most basic manifestation of desire, which is—hunger. We can deduce that everything that stems from desire, is essentially linked to hunger. From what I shall be indicating today, you will gather that the opposite pole is thinking, which will therefore work in the opposite way to desire. What we can say then is that if we recognize desire as the foundation of will, it will be satisfaction that underlies thinking; satisfaction as opposed to hunger.

The facts correspond to this at the deepest level. If you take the human head organization and the other organization that hangs from it, the fact is that we perceive. What exactly does this mean? We perceive through our senses. As we do our perceiving, something is constantly being worn away in us. Something comes from outside into what is inside us. The ray of light that penetrates into our eye actually wears something down inside us. It is as if a hole is being drilled into our material substance [see diagram on p. 166]. Where there used to be matter, a ray of light has now drilled a hole, now there is hunger. This hunger must be appeased and it is appeased out of the organism by the available nutrients; i.e. this hole is refilled by the nutrients that lie within us [red]. Now we have thought, we have thought what we have perceived: as we think, we are constantly filling up the holes that sense impressions have made in our substance with a satisfaction that arises out of our organism.

It is fascinating to observe what happens in our head organization when we place matter from the rest of our organism into the holes that arise through our ears, our eyes, our sense of warmth etc. As we think, we completely refill the holes that have been drilled into us [red.]

rot = red

It is similar when we exert our will. The difference is that it is not holes being drilled into us from outside, but what is coming from within. When we exert our will, hollow spaces arise in us everywhere; these must likewise be filled up with matter. So there are negative effects, hollowing us out, coming both from outside and within us which have constantly to be filled up by our own material substance.

It is these extremely subtle effects, these hollowing out activities that actually destroy our whole earthly existence. As we receive the ray of light or hear the sound, we are destroying our whole existence on earth. Of course we react to it and replace what has been destroyed with earthly substance. Our lives are thus spent between the destruction of our earthly existence and its replacement. Luciferic, ahrimanic. The luciferic element is constantly trying to make something partially non-material out of us, to lift us completely out of our earthly existence; if he could, Lucifer would like to completely spiritualize us, i.e. dematerialize us. But Ahriman is his opponent; he ensures that everything that Lucifer hollows out is filled back in again. Ahriman is the continual refiller. If you were going to make a sculpture of Lucifer, and make Ahriman capable of being moulded into shape, and the substances used could blend with each other, you could very well press Ahriman into the hollows created by Lucifer or cover them over with Lucifer. Since there are also hollow spaces within, one would have to fill these in too. Ahriman and Lucifer are the opposing forces at work within us. We ourselves must hold the balance. Lucifer with his constant dematerializing processes results in Ahriman who is constantly rematerializing. When we perceive something at work, it is Lucifer. When we reflect on what we have perceived: Ahriman. If we have the idea that we should wish for this or that: Lucifer. If we really wish to realize something on earth: Ahriman. That is how we are placed between the two. We swing between the two of them and need to be aware that we are positioned in the most intimate way between ahrimanic and luciferic elements. We can really only understand ourselves once we take this polarity within us into account.

This is an approach that is neither purely abstract nor spiritual—for abstract spirituality is nebulous mysticism—nor purely materialistic. Everything that has a material effect is simultaneously spiritual. We are always with the spirit. We can see through matter and its effects by seeing how the spirit is everywhere at work within it.

Imagination always comes towards us in the present of its own accord. If we artificially develop Imagination, we are looking into the past. If we develop the power of Inspiration we are gazing into the future rather in the way that one can predict solar eclipses or lunar eclipses, as opposed to delving down into every detail. We can see the overarching laws at work in the future on a higher level.

Intuition encompasses all three faculties; we are in fact constantly subject to the power of Intuition but sleep through it. When we are asleep, our I and astral body are completely within the embrace of the world outside us; there we exercise the intuitive activity which we would otherwise have to carry out consciously with the faculty of Intuition. At present our organization is too weak to allow us to be conscious when we are intuiting; however, we do in fact intuit during the night. Thus during sleep we intuit, and in the waking state we exercise logical thinking, up to a point of course; between these two states we have Inspiration and Imagination. As we emerge from sleep into waking consciousness, our I and astral body enter into our physical and etheric bodies; what we bring with us is Inspiration. So during sleep we are in an intuitive state, while awake we make use of logical thinking; as we wake up we bring with us Inspiration and as we fall asleep Imagination. You can see then that the higher cognitive faculties are not remote from everyday life, but are present every day. They do, however, have to be raised into consciousness if we wish to develop higher knowledge.

Awakening
Inspiration

Awake　　　　　　　　　　　　　　　　　　　　　*Sleeping*
Logical thinking　　　　　　　　　　　　　　　　　*Intuition*

Falling asleep
Imagination

We have to remind ourselves again and again that in the last three or four centuries natural science has accumulated a huge number of purely material facts and has ordered them into laws. These facts have in turn to be penetrated by the spirit. However paradoxical it may sound, it is good that materialism came about since we would otherwise have fallen prey to nebulous ways of thinking, and would eventually have lost all connection with our earthly existence. When materialism came about in the fifteenth century, humanity was on the brink of succumbing to luciferic influences and so had become increasingly hollowed out. Then followed the ahrimanic influence and in the last four to five centuries they have reached a kind of peak. Today they have become very strong and the danger is that they overshoot the mark unless we confront them with what deprives them of their energy: unless we confront them with what is spiritual.

It then becomes important to develop the right feeling for the relationship of the spirit to matter. There is a poem from ancient German culture which was entitled '*Muspilli*' and was first discovered in a book that was dedicated to Louis the German in the ninth century, though it had much earlier origins.[34] This poem contains something essentially Christian: it depicts the battle between Elias and the Antichrist and is reminiscent of the battles depicted in the ancient sagas, between the inhabitants of Asgard and those of Jotunheim, the kingdom of the giants. All that has happened is that the kingdom of the Aesir has been transformed into Elias and the kingdom of the giants into that of the Antichrist.

The way of thinking that we meet in this poem obscures the true facts less than later ways of thinking. Later worldviews always represent things in terms of a duality between good and evil, God and the devil and so on. These do not, however, correspond to the earlier perspective.

The people portrayed in the battle between the home of the gods and the home of the giants did not have the same view of the gods as a Christian of today would have of the kingdom of God. Instead these older ideas placed Asgard (the kingdom of the gods), above and Jotunheim (the kingdom of the giants) below. Between these was the realm of human beings—Midgard. That is simply a Germanic/ European portrayal of what is found in the ancient Persian Ormuzd and Ahriman. In our terms that would correspond to Lucifer and Ahriman. We would have to speak of Ormuzd as Lucifer and not simply as the good god. The great error that we make is in portraying this dualism as if Ormuzd were merely the good god and his opponent Ahriman the bad one. Their relationship is much more like that of Lucifer to Ahriman. In Midgard, at the time this poem was composed, the picture was not yet fully clear: Christ lets his blood ray downwards. In this case, however, it is Elias who lets his blood ray down from above. The place of the human being lies between them. At the time Louis the German probably wrote this into his book the idea was more correct than the later one. Later on people had the strange idea of ignoring the Holy Trinity. This meant considering the higher gods who live in Asgard and the lower gods, the giants who are in the ahrimanic realm, as the entirety of the cosmos, with the higher gods, the luciferic ones, considered the good ones and the others the bad ones. This idea came to be accepted later; the earlier view of the opposition of Lucifer and Ahriman was correct and thus placed Elias with his emotional prophecy and what he was able to announce at the time in the luciferic kingdom, for the reason that it was intended to place Christ in Midgard, in the middle kingdom.

Asgard
Lucifer—Ormuzd

Jotunheim
Ahriman

We shall have to return to these ideas in full consciousness or, if we continue to speak only of the duality of God and the devil, we shall not be able to return to the Trinity: the luciferic gods, the ahrimanic powers and between them what belongs to the realm of Christ. Unless we are able to progress to that view we shall not be able to come to a true understanding of the world. Just think, therein lies the pro-found secret of how European civilization developed historically: the ancient Ormuzd was turned into the good god, whilst he was actually a luciferic power, a light bearer. This did admittedly give people the satisfaction of tarnishing the name of Lucifer as much as possible; since the name Lucifer did not seem to fit the figure of Ormuzd, it was transferred to Ahriman, turned into a hotchpotch which still worked on in Goethe's portrayal of Mephistopheles, where Lucifer and Ahriman are once again muddled one with another, as I spelled out in my little book on Goethe's *Geistesart* [*Goethe's spiritual signature*]. The European peoples and their civilization as we see them today have got into a state of great confusion which is inevitably reflected in all their thinking. This can only be redressed by leading people out of this duality back into the Trinity, for all dualism is bound to result in a polarity that allows no space for humanity. What is needed is the prospect of finding a polarity within which we can hold the balance: Christ holding the balance between Lucifer and Ahriman, between Ormuzd and Ahriman and so on.

This was the topic I wanted to broach and which we shall be able to develop with its various ramifications in the days to come.

LECTURE 12

DORNACH, 16 JULY 1921

YESTERDAY I closed with the remark that in more recent times
a confusion arose in relation to what the polarity of Ormuzd and
Ahriman in the Persian view of the world actually is. I pointed out
how we can go back to ancient European-Germanic views as they
are represented for example in the poem which has come to be
known as the '*Muspilli*'. It deals with the firmament and the earth
in an entirely Christian way, expressing the opposing principles of
Lucifer above and Ahriman below. I say entirely Christian, because
it had not been infected by what has since been lost of the Muspilli
attitude of soul in respect of the above and below, for it was not
at that time assumed that the Christian principle was assigned to
the upper spirituality, but instead placed the Elias principle there
and it is Elias then who fights the Antichrist, his blood dripping
downwards as he does so. The Antichrist figure is a Christianized
expression of the ahrimanic principle. There was then still a clear
consciousness evident in those ancient European-Germanic ideas
that one had to distinguish between an upper principle and a lower
principle, higher forces and lower forces, with the Christ principle
holding the balance and harmonizing them. Once this Elias principle has been assigned to the upper realm and the Antichrist principle
to the lower, it will be easy to see how the upper principle is oriented
towards a moral impulse to the world order and the ahrimanic principle towards the intellectual impulse in the world's development.

This sense of an above and below was seen as a polarity which
is present in the world. It is also in a way projected onto the human
being. We know that we determine what is above and below with
reference to the main orientation of our spine, which is vertical. That

is how we come to an above and below, a concept that is entirely relative. What we are considering today, quite apart from the above and below, is a polar opposition. The way in which this manifests in the human being is extremely complex. We can, however, also study this polar opposition as it appears more externally in the world around us. It is very useful to look at the world in a way that allows it to reveal the secrets at work within it by means of particular phenomena in which certain forces come to expression quite radically.

There is a certain polarity expressed perhaps less clearly in us but which can become very apparent once we take a comprehensive view of how we are formed. Like us, the bird family has emerged from the wholeness of the world order. What is more, the bird family reveals certain secrets at work in the world much more clearly than they appear at first glance in us, where their manifestation is altogether more complex.

What is characteristic of the bird family? The main feature is that birds first appear before us, to the extent that they can do so in physical form, in the shape of an egg from which they then emerge before the public at large so to speak. Birds first make their appearance in the form of an egg. Then the egg has to be cracked open. The birds then begin their development outside the egg and you will have seen how it is only once they have left the egg that their feathers begin to grow etc. Now this polarity of being enclosed within the egg and then continuing its existence outside with a coat of feathers is at first sight not so clearly expressed in us as human beings. We do not emerge into the world in the form of an egg and we are spared from continuing our development in the world wearing a coat of feathers. But what is revealed to us by the bird family in terms of the egg shape and their subsequent appearance?

Looking at the egg quite externally, it is naturally the calcareous shell that stands out. This calcareous shell has a certain form. Nevertheless it cannot be considered essential to a bird's existence, since it is allowed to fall away. It is not an essential part of a bird. Putting it trivially, one could call it a protective sheath around the young creature. Whatever we might call it, there is nothing localized within the calcareous shell that works on into the form of a bird. What we have then is this secretion of matter in the outer shell. It is, as it were, ejected by the bird's organization like something that has been shed, which is no longer required for its later development; it is therefore thrown out. There must then be forces at work within the bird that secrete and later dispose of what constitutes the shell.

rot = red

Looking at the phenomenon in this way, natural laws at work on the earth will not help us understand what is going on. We will have to look at what is said in *Occult Science* for an explanation. There is an indication there that at a certain stage in the development of our earth, the Moon was secreted by the earth, its matter was secreted by the earth. What we have been looking at is an imitation of this process. Just as the formative forces of the whole earth's cosmos once secreted the Moon forces, the substance of the bird secretes the calcareous shell as something, let's say, super-mineral. What was it then that initially lay within the calcareous shell? [See diagram above, red.]

What lay within it was at first protected by the shell from the forces at work in the earth's surroundings. If the chick had been exposed to these forces too early, let us say to the Sun's rays, it would of course have died. It could not have withstood the forces at work within the earth's surroundings. The fact is that the creature that is being protected by the calcareous shell is living in a world that is not really of the earth.

What kind of a world is it then living in? It is the world that we ourselves have evolved through via Saturn, Sun and the Moon and which has ceased to exist. It is no longer present as a developing process on the earth. It is an element of the past that is still there in the present. If we then say that everything that is outside the eggshell belongs to the earth, then what is inside the eggshell is essentially what does not belong to the earth. It does not want to have anything to do with the earth itself. In a sense it does not want to participate in the earth's development. It must first mature, then break through the shell to be ready for development on the earth.

This is where we can introduce a further aspect. Not all creatures that start out in the form of an egg are actually born. A number of birds' eggs are destroyed, not to mention fish eggs and others. Moreover—and I don't know if it is always suitable to put these things out there so dryly, since there is so much that people prefer not to be made aware of, but in view of what lies ahead of us there are things that we simply have to know, and can no longer close our minds to—moreover, a large number of birds' eggs are lost because we eat them. They do not come to fruition. Now the question arises: What is going on with all these eggs that do not mature into fully-grown chickens, other birds or fish?

The common materialistic response might be: 'Well that is Nature at work, irrationally producing an overabundance at random and so much of what Nature produces simply goes to waste.' That is, however, not correct. The essential substances that are somehow contained within the eggshell do not mature for earthly existence, but the forces that work in them are ripe for pre-earthly existence, the existence that we as beings of the earth went through during our Saturn, Sun and Moon epochs. That is the luciferic state of being. They become substances from which luciferic existence continues to draw nourishment. Everything that is destroyed in the egg state gives nourishment to certain spiritual beings. Now we shall turn our attention to what concerns the earth.

Looking at the bird family, we first of all have the luciferic element contained in the egg, the aspect that does not wish to have anything to do with the earth, that does not wish to be on the earth and so surrounds itself with a wall against the laws of the earth, which can only come into play when the warmth and light that are otherwise at work on the earth have broken the shell.

What triggers this process? The opposite forces. If you place a bird's egg in front of you, you could say: inside it is in essence Lucifer. If you plucked all the feathers off a bird, you could say: here I have the purest image of the directing forces of Ahriman. These are ahrimanic forces at work, even in the delicate, downy feathers found on the emerging chick; ahrimanic forces have already been able to exert their influence through the shell. They were in combat with what was totally against carrying feathers. Thus when you look at a bird's coat of feathers you have in front of you the purest image of Ahriman at work.

Taking this idea further, you could say: 'If I look at an egg, I see Lucifer in disguise.' Lucifer's disguise is merely the outer form of the material secreted by him, as it were. Whether it is an eggshell or a snakeskin that is shed, they are shed by the luciferic principle, the luciferic forces at work. These cast-offs can also reveal something of the gesture of luciferic forces at work. In their purest form they manifest in spirals. On the other hand the coat of feathers or any other natural phenomenon that inserts itself into the physical body from the outside reveals the ahrimanic principle. The direction of that gesture is tangential. Take a peacock's tail-feather, look at it carefully and consider this: it is the purest image of the trajectory of ahrimanic forces.

We must of course be clear that Lucifer and Ahriman are interweaving and intermingling everywhere and that we therefore only have images to go by. These are, however, most beautifully displayed in the bird family. We need only look at examples in the way I have described.

The forces at work inside the eggshell are also at work in the bird itself. So the bird has the forces from the eggshell within it [red] and coming in from all around the ahrimanic forces [blue]. In the example of the bird we also have the opportunity of clearly localizing both the etheric and the physical aspects. If you consider what a bird keeps of the luciferic forces that were inside the egg, the growth potential, you will find the basis of the etheric body. These are shown in red on my sketch. What a bird inherits from the egg constitutes its life forces, its etheric. Conversely, the mantle of feathers it adopts is under the sway of physical forces [arrows]. What lies between them in the form of flesh, muscles and so on is influenced throughout the course of its life by astral forces [yellow]. Birds as examples thus enable us to localize the astral forces in the flesh and muscles, the physical in their feathers and the etheric in the growth forces inherited from the contents of the egg.

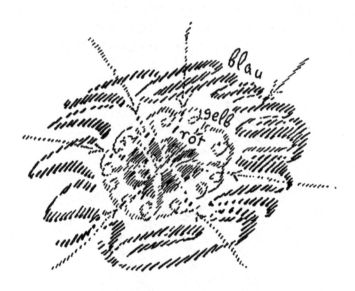

blau = blue; gelb = yellow; rot = red

It is much more complicated in the case of human beings. We do not manifest outwardly in the form of an egg. The luciferic qualities that the egg projects outwardly, we develop in the womb. That is also the reason why Ahriman does not yet have an influence on us in the womb. Birds can show us how they carry the luciferic influence out in the world without it going astray, and also how they take on the ahrimanic influence there. Individual details of this are apparent in us with particular clarity. We can then place the family of mammals between birds and human beings.

One distinction in particular stands out between human beings and birds. Look at a bird's legs. Compared with human legs they are generally pretty stunted organs. Why might that be? Look at a sparrow's legs: what pathetic little sticks they are next to our own proud legs! You might argue that the whole rather bony form of a bird is due to the fact that it is designed for flying, for taking to the air, hence the lightweight legs. It is as if they are mere indications of its connection with the earth.

weiss = white; rot = red

We on the other hand do not lift our legs off the earth, neither can we fly. Our legs stand like proud pillars on the earth. As such they are a gift of the earth. Birds do not receive this gift, since they are not tied to the earth in the same way. They are somehow separated off from the earth. Bearing this gift from the earth, a human being is also more tied to the earth and to ahrimanic forces than a bird. A bird does not receive its ahrimanic forces so directly from the earth as we do. Ahriman shoots and sprouts into us through our legs and from there into every other aspect of our organism. In birds you will only find Ahriman shooting in through their feathers.

Turning back to ourselves and the way we relate more to the earth through our legs, you might ask: Why do we not have feathers? The reason is that we are not built for the earth in the way birds are. If we were to fly around in the air, we would also have feathers, since the ahrimanic forces would work up into us from a quite different direction. As it is we have only a hint of ahrimanic forces working on us, evidenced by our hair. That is the extent of the ahrimanic tendencies that we have. They are at their strongest in the human head. Our head has a great deal about it that is ahrimanic, as we have seen elsewhere in our studies.

When we look at mammals, we come to the view that they are even more closely tied up with the earth than we are. They are also bound to the earth in a way that we are not, namely through their forefeet, for example. Apes only rarely walk upright and even dogs can do that when they are begging, but it does not lie in their nature. It is not even natural for gorillas to walk upright since they are essentially climbers. Their forearms are for grasping and moving along with. Human beings on the other hand are halfway lifted from the earth; birds are completely lifted above the earth and mammals are bound to the earth with those forelegs and hind legs. They are in a sense entirely creatures of the earth. We have liberated ourselves from the earth by our upright posture and the orientation of our spine, where mammals are completely bound to the earth. The rest of a mammal's form also exemplifies this. Where a bird's feathers come from is where the mammal's coat of fur comes from, built into the organism from the outside, as it were.

Taking all this into consideration, one will be able to arrive at the form of a mammal, bird or a human being or indeed other living creatures from an understanding of their relationship to the earth. One can use this understanding to construe the form a creature will take. One could say that birds embody the luciferic principle, which abhors the earth, and so separate themselves from the earth as long as possible inside their eggs. They can thus ensure that the earth has the least possible influence on them. Their legs remain stunted and the forces nearest to the earth, but above the earth, constituting its mantle of warmth, are those that influence birds more. They thus have the form that they do: stunted legs and so on. We on the other hand are bound to the earth by our lower limbs and can liberate ourselves from it in our upper limbs. Mammals are firmly embedded in the earth standing on it with the four pillars of their legs and taking their form from out of the earth. It is primarily the forces working out of the earth that give mammals their shape.

Such things were known to an older, more instinctive understanding of the world. This meant that the human head could be seen as a bird, as an eagle, because our head is shaped most independently of the earth and is really only a metamorphosis of our previous earth life. By contrast our metabolic and lymph system which is completely oriented towards the earth, could be seen by this earlier form of understanding as an ox or a bull or a cow, because this animal is likewise organized so as to be completely oriented towards the earth. The middle part of the human being which acts as a kind of bridge between the eagle and the cow was seen as a part which releases itself a little from the earth precisely by means of its metabolism; you might see how this manifests in the fact that a lion has a very short intestine. Its metabolism is extraordinarily basic, whilst by contrast its chest and heart systems are particularly well developed. Hence also its passion, its fury and so on. The earlier way of understanding such phenomena saw the lion in the middle part of the human being.

Now we shall have to return to such perspectives in a more conscious way. We must be clear for example that we human beings differ from all animals in that we have an I. For the vast majority of people this I is still largely a dormant organ. To believe that our I is very strongly awake is to be mistaken. As I have explained earlier, we are asleep in our will and when our I exerts its will we relate to its activity much as we do to the night. Although the night is dark, we count on its being there in our lives. If you truly look back over your life, you will see that it consists not only of what is clear as day, but also of all the nights. These nights are somehow always cancelled out of our perception of the passage of time. The same is true of our I. In terms of our ordinary consciousness it is remarkable for its absence. It is in fact present, but not in our consciousness. Something is missing there and that is how we are aware of our I. It really is as if one had a white-painted wall and one part of it had not been painted white; what we then see is black. That is also how it appears to our ordinary consciousness: as something that has been extinguished. The same holds good for our waking hours: our I is initially always asleep, but whilst asleep it shines through our thoughts, ideas and feelings and is thus perceived in ordinary consciousness, or rather it is considered that we are aware of it. We can say therefore that our I is not perceived directly to begin with.

There is a prejudiced psychology that believes that this I is located within the human being in the same place as our muscles, flesh, bones and so on. If one took a broader view of the phenomena of life, one would soon become aware that it is not the case. It is difficult, however, to put the case for this to a wider audience. I tried it in 1911 in Bologna where I gave a lecture to the conference of philosophers.[35] No one has yet understood this lecture. I tried to show there what the nature of the I really is. In reality our I is to be found in every perception that we have, in everything that makes an impression on us. My I is not to be found in my flesh and bones but in what I can perceive with my eyes. If you see a red flower somewhere you will not be able to separate the red from the flower, neither in your I nor in the whole experience that you have when you devote your attention to the flower. All this is the basis of your I. Your I is connected with the content of your soul. The content of your soul in turn is spread out in all that is around you. This I is less even than the air within you which you are just breathing in, less than the air that was previously in you. The I is connected with every perception and in essence with all that is outside you. It is active within you because it sends into you the forces of what it is perceiving. Moreover the I is also connected with something else: you need only walk, i.e. to express your will forces. Your I accompanies this movement, participates in the movement and whether you are creeping, running, hopping like a bird, twisting and turning, dancing or jumping, the I will accompany every movement. Whatever activity you wilfully engage in will be accompanied by your I. There again, however, the I is not within you. Imagine it is carrying you along with it. If you are dancing a round dance, is that inside you? There would be no room inside you for that! How could there be? But your I is engaged with it; your I is dancing along. So your I is present in your perceptions and in your movement. It is actually never within you in the true sense of the word, as for example your stomach is inside you, but is always outside you. It is just as much outside your head as it is outside your legs, except that it engages very strongly with your walking, with the movements that your legs are making. Your I is really very strongly engaged with the movements your legs are making. This is less so with your head.

In what other ways are our legs or indeed any of our limbs and our metabolic system different from our head? Our etheric and astral bodies are relatively independent of our head, which belongs mainly to our physical body. This head of ours, which is such an ancient fellow that he comes from our previous incarnation, is really the most totally uncompromising inhabitant of the earth. Our legs and our metabolic system on the other hand keep their physical aspect closely connected to the etheric and astral bodies. In short: our legs keep closely connected with the etheric and astral bodies and only our I is relatively free of our legs, only accompanying them when they are in movement. The same is true of our metabolic system: our metabolic organs are essentially bound to our etheric and astral bodies.

We could now go on to ask: in what ways does our head differ from our limbs and metabolism? Our etheric body, astral body and I are all free of our head; our metabolic and limb systems within our physical body leave only the I free, whereas the etheric and astral remain closely tied to the physical. They are not free of it.

The following will make this clearer. Imagine that your etheric body or your astral body which have the task of caring for your physical body, come up with the idea of treating your metabolic and lymph systems in the same way that they do your head; that they wanted to be free of it. Let us say for example, that the astral body belonging to your metabolic and lymph system wanted to behave in the same way

Aeth. L = etheric life; Astr. L = astral life; Ich = I

that its colleague is allowed to do in relation to your head. It is only another part of your astral body, which is why I use the word colleague. What would happen then? It would be counter to the way the human body is constructed—our abdomen would be wanting to behave like our head. It would become apparent that what is characteristically healthy for our head makes our abdomen ill. It is characteristic of all abdominal illnesses that our abdomen takes on the configuration of our head.

This can be illustrated by a particular case I described in a lecture in Stuttgart or Zurich of a carcinoma which began to form in a part of the body where there should not normally be any sense organs directed inwards, and suddenly the astral body started to want to develop sense organs.[36] A carcinoma is essentially an ear or an eye wishing to form in an inappropriate part of the body. It grows inwards. An ear or an eye wants to develop there. Thus when this astral or etheric body belonging to the abdomen wants to behave like its equivalent in the head an illness of the abdomen results.

The opposite is also true. If our head wants to live like our abdomen—one can see it initially in migrainous conditions—and wants to draw the etheric body or astral body into its business, the result is illness in the head. If it wants to draw in the etheric body, migrainous conditions follow; if it wants to draw in the astral body then even worse conditions follow.

These examples go to show how complicated our human nature is. It cannot be studied in the way today's trivial science does. It has to be studied in all of its complexities. One has to be able to see that our head cannot be like our abdomen, since if it were it would only become ill. Thus if for example the cerebrum begins to develop its metabolic processes too strongly, begins to secrete too much, then illnesses will be the result. These strong processes of secretion derive from the fact that our head is placing excessive demands on our etheric body. Similarly the moment our abdomen is left to its own devices, i.e. become more head like and tends towards developing sense organs, illness will follow. In short: the human head has a free etheric body, a free astral body and a free I. Our metabolic/ limb system has our etheric and astral bodies bound to it and leaves only the

I free. The human being of the middle, the rhythmic human being has its etheric bound in but leaves the astral and I free.

Head:	free etheric body, free astral body, free ego.
Rhythmic human:	bound etheric body free astral body, free ego.
Metabolism-limbs human:	bound etheric body, bound astral body, free ego.

Here you have an overview of the human constitution from a perspective which is particularly important, because it gives you an impression of how the I stands in a free relationship to the whole human being, how it works into us from waking up to falling asleep and always remains relatively free. You will also see how your I is connected with your outer sense perceptions and with the movements you make, but does not actually completely unfold within your bodies. Where does the human I live? Are we able somehow to see where the human I lives?

To some extent we can already see it in what develops in birds' feathers. We do not have feathers, but our I lives in the forces that are in our surroundings and in the case of birds these give direction to how they come by their feathers. That is where our I lives externally. Moreover, there are ways in which we can see these directional forces even more clearly. In a bird's plumage we see them somehow captured by the bird's body, but these forces also give direction to freely moving creatures: insects. When you see insects buzzing about and grasp their movement imaginatively you will have there before you an image of where your I lives. Imagine insects buzzing about in your surroundings: beetles, flies, beautiful butterflies, ugly horse-flies and bumblebees, all kinds of insects; imagine all these things swirling about you in every direction; that is where you will find the outer manifestation of where your I in fact lives. It is more than a mere picture when we say: ugly thoughts live there like bumblebees and horse-flies, but also beautiful thoughts like butterflies; many a human thought will bite like a nasty fly and so on. The difference is that the one is spiritual, the other physical. The human I really does live in our surroundings.

This has very important implications and true knowledge and understanding of the world depends on us being able to correctly evaluate what it is that we see. We should not waffle on about the spirit in generalities but be able to see in image form around us what we inwardly experience in a more abstract and spiritual form. Everything that exists in the spirit can also be seen as an image in the world around us. There is always a place where what exists in a purely spiritual form may be seen in the form of a picture. We simply have to be able to interpret what is contained in the picture correctly. Thus when ahrimanic elements come into our I, when our I finds an image of itself in butterflies, or birds' feathers outside us, i.e. the directing forces within them, then our I will acquire the capacity to develop all kinds of forms from within. We can inwardly construct a circle, an egg shape, a triangle; we can create a whole world from within ourselves. If we then research further into this we will find: these are the very forces that have been ejected by the luciferic principle.

I recently said that when mathematicians study space they should consider the hen's egg in relation to the dimensions of space: something very interesting would then emerge. The polarity we are considering is this: our I lives both in the forms that we can construct within the world in this way and also in what is constructed out of the world itself. On the one hand we live in what shields itself from the world within an eggshell, within the luciferic element and on the other we experience what inserts itself into the bird's body in the shape of feathers and what flies around us in butterflies and insects in general as our I, as we do in our sense perceptions and our participation in the movement of our limbs.

Indeed, anyone who understands the wonderful diversity of the world of birds around us will also understand many things about the nature of the human soul in its relationship to the world. What a bird turns out towards the world in its plumage, what comes shimmering towards us from the birds also streams into the sense perceptions of our I as glimmering, iridescent, sparkling impressions from outside inwards.

This is how we have to try to grasp the world with the aid of images. Today's abstract science is only able to grasp a tiny proportion of the real world.

LECTURE 13

THE view that Ormuzd and Ahriman are polar opposites has led to the misunderstandings arising, as I described yesterday and the day before, which have obscured many of the laws and secrets of world existence in the consciousness of humanity. It has been the root of modern materialism, which could otherwise not have arisen, and which now imbues modern consciousness with the following idea: there are polarities all around us which are investigated by the science of today and which will gradually enable us to achieve an understanding of the universe. A simple consideration can show us that it will never be possible to grasp the universe in this way. Think back if you will to some of the things I explained to you a couple of weeks ago and take them into consideration in the right light.

Consider how those who think of themselves as natural scientists today will only view the human being as a creature who will be a corpse after death. All the other laws of Nature and natural phenomena which apply to and pervade us once our physical body is a corpse can be explained in terms of conventional natural science. This is, however, resisted and opposed by what lives in us between birth and death. If it were possible today to take a dispassionate, unprejudiced view of the phenomena on the basis of genuine evaluation one would draw the conclusion that between birth and death, indeed from the very first beginning of development in the embryo, we are battling against all that is governed by the laws of Nature as they are currently understood.

Take the phenomena of Nature around us and everything that we are told about them by physics, chemistry, physiology, biology and so on; take stock of them all and of what we are told about them and then consider the human being living life between birth and death, and you will come to the conclusion: the whole of this life is a battle against the kingdom of Nature as governed by these laws of Nature. It is only because our human organization is at odds with these laws of Nature, and battles against them, that we can be truly human between birth and death.

From this it will already be apparent that if human development is to be integrated into the cosmos it is necessary for the cosmos to incorporate a different set of laws, a different form of development. The laws of Nature that we recognize today posit a world which does not include the human being, indeed not even plants or animals. Today we shall only focus on human beings in relation to the rest of the natural world. We are not to be found in the natural world as it is currently grasped by science. Indeed, we rebel against this natural world with every last breath in our bodies.

Nevertheless we are able to speak of the cosmos, since we ourselves have emerged from the womb of this cosmos, in the way we appear to each other in physical form. What is required is that we think of this cosmos as having a quality of being that differs from what we inwardly experience when we think of it in terms of the natural science of today. We can form an idea of what this means in practice if we allow the following fact, determined by spiritual science, to pass before our souls.

Let's consider the moment at which a person dies, either young or after having reached the normal age. The corpse is left behind. We could compare this process, and it would be more than a comparison, with a snake shedding its skin or a bird emerging from its egg. The corpse is shed and the remains are dealt with, just like the snakeskin, which according to the laws that we recognize in today's natural science, from then on no longer follows the laws governing the growth of the snake. What we leave behind as a corpse is dealt with by the laws of the earth. However, we did have the human form in our time between birth and death: human stature. This now dissolves, ceases to exist. In a certain sense the corpse still retains this form but only as a kind of imitation of the form it had in life. The form that the corpse retains is no longer the same as the one we had between birth and death. That form is capable of enabling us to experience ourselves within it and contains forces which come into play when we move. None of that is possible when only the corpse remains. What truly gave the corpse its form has now left; it disappeared at the moment of death. We do not take it with us. What we do take with us for a while is our etheric body, but we shall ignore that for the present. The key point is that our physical form, our physical stature does not go with us. In a sense we lose this physical form. One could spell out the details as follows: if we could follow a person's movements and their agility after the body has been left behind, once we had passed through the gate of death we would find them different from those expressed in the physical body.

Thus what is actually present in our physical form can no longer be seen from outside once we have passed through the gate of death. The corpse is left with only the form. This form is gradually lost since it no longer belongs to the corpse. If I may make a rough comparison it is as if you had a pot which you tipped up over the dough for a cake: the cake would then retain the form but it has nothing of the form of the pot itself and one could not say that the cake you are left with has achieved this form through its own matter; no, it received it from the pot that was tipped up over it. Just as this cake retains the form of the pot when you remove the pot, the corpse retains the form of the human being when that form is removed. The form itself, however, which is the one with which we move about, ceases to exist when we cross the threshold of death. The fact that we have this form, that it takes shape according to the laws of the cosmos, as for example a crystal does, is a property of the laws of the cosmos themselves. We might wonder: What happens to this form? Spiritual research shows that it provides nourishment for the spiritual hierarchy which we call the archai, the primal beginnings. Thus something of the human form passes on into the realm of the archai.

The fact is that the physical form that we take on at our birth and which we shed when we pass through death, comes to us from the realm of the archai, the primal beginnings or primal forces; we receive our physical form as a result of being in the embrace of a spiritual being from the realm of the archai. We are encompassed by a spirit that came from the realm of the archai and which now takes back what was lent to us for the course of our life. This is another example of how we belong to the whole cosmos.

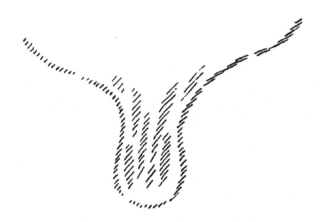

It is as if the archai were to stretch out their feelers somehow. If we take this [see diagram above] as one of them, it is stretching out creative force, which gives shape to the human form, within which the human being is to be found. You will only imagine your existence within the cosmos correctly if you imagine that you are enclosed in an outcrop of an archai. If you now imagine that it is only in the Lemurian age that we appear—as I have set out in the last few days—as the kind of being that belongs on the earth, gradually emerge and gradually take on this form, then you will have what I was able to describe in my *Occult Science*. You will have a description of what the archai actually do. It is a depiction of how the archai reach down from their realm into the earthly realm and there metamorphose the human form. This continuing metamorphosis of the human form from the Lemurian age until the time when it will disappear from the earth is directed in every way from out of the realm of the archai. As the archai work at the human being in this way, they bring forth the zeitgeist, the spirit of the age in the truest sense of the word. This spirit of the age is intimately bound up with the human form in the sense that our skin is in a way given a particular shape. The spirit of the age is essentially located in the outermost sphere of our sensitivity. Once we understand how these archai work, we will also understand how it is not only human forms that are in a process of transformation during their time on earth, but also those of the archai.

Now you will know that in the ranks of the hierarchies the spirits of form, the exusiai, are behind the archai. If you look up from our earthly existence to what constitutes our archetypal form, to what belongs to the whole of the earth's development from its beginning to its ending we will find more comprehensive cosmic laws at work than those already containing the human form. The earth's development can be described as initially an echo of Old Saturn, which we call the era of Polaris; an echo of Old Sun, the Hyperborean epoch; an echo of Old Moon, the Lemurian epoch. Only then do we reach the earth evolution proper, of which the first epoch is the Atlantean. We are now living in the post-Atlantean era. Only now have we unfolded our human form. The earth must have more comprehensive laws than those expressed in the portion of its development which enables us to manifest in human form and its metamorphoses today. We must look back to the earth's earliest beginnings when we were not yet fully formed, but were still present only as spiritual and etheric beings, and we also have to look at what will happen on earth after a series of millennia, when we will have disappeared from the earth as physical beings. The physical earth will continue for a while, and will even be inhabited by human beings who will, however, no longer appear physically but as etheric beings.

If we take the whole forming process of the earth, including ourselves, but going on beyond us, if we cast our spiritual eye over the laws at work within it, of which the natural science of our day constitutes only the tiniest portion, then we will find what belongs to the realm of the exusiai. The earth took shape from the realm of the exusiai and humanity in turn from the realm of the primal powers, bringing with us all that must be present on the earth for us to be able to exist. Looking ahead, the form of the earth will, once it has dissolved, return to the realm of the exusiai.

If we now focus on the second member of the human being, our etheric body, we will find that we cannot regard it as entirely our own. Just as our physical form in fact belongs to the realm of the archai with us being housed in a protuberance of their realm, with our etheric bodies we belong within a protuberance of the realm of the archangels. That means that when we pass through the gate of death we retain this etheric body for a short while. We know that this will then dissolve, although this does not mean that it dissolves into nothingness, but rather that it returns to the realm of the archangels.

The human astral body has a similar relationship to the realm of the angels as the etheric body to the archangels and the physical to the archai. Our astral body is likewise not entirely our own. It is a protuberance of the angelic realm. That in turn means that after death something of our astral body passes over into the realm of the angels. Like the other parts of our being, our astral body is clothed in the substance of a higher being, in this case the angels. The fact that we are subject to the laws governing the earth, that we can walk about on the earth as human beings, can exert our will, do things on the earth, all subject to the laws governing the earth, all this means that we play our part within the realm of the exusiai, the spirits of form, the elohim.

Now we come to a significant point. Consider your physical form in its sleeping state: when your body is lying in bed, it retains its form. You will find it again in the morning. This form is by no means dissolved yet, nor could one say that it is a corpse, that it merely retains the shape given to it by the pot, as it were. Its form is there in reality. This means that the archai remain connected through this form with what we have as physical beings on earth. The same is true of the archangels in relation to our etheric body—they remain connected. This is not true, however, of our astral bodies. Between going to sleep and waking up again in the morning, our astral bodies are in no way connected with our physical human form; our astral body is in completely different surroundings between our falling asleep and waking up from those we are familiar with between waking up and falling asleep. The fact is that whilst the archai principle is bound to our physical form from birth to death, and similarly the archangel principle to the human etheric, the angel principle is obliged to accompany the human individual from one condition to the other and back. The angel principle or angel being has to accompany us into sleep and back into wakefulness.

You see then that a new element appears in this process when we are talking about the angels. The fact is that it depends on us—on our attitude, on our ability to direct the whole world of our feelings towards the spiritual world—whether or not our angel accompanies us out of our physical and etheric bodies when we are asleep. Children are accompanied, but once adults have reached a certain level of maturity it really does depend on their attitude and on whether they have been able to inwardly develop a relationship with their angel. If this relationship is not there, if an individual only believes in the material world and thinks only of material things, then the angel will not come along.

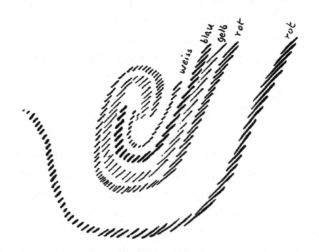

weiss = white; blau = blue; gelb = yellow; rot = red

If you take the whole human being into account [see illustration above] with the earth as the work of the exusiai [outer red] the human physical body as the work of the archai [inner red], the human etheric body as the work of the archangels [yellow] and now the human astral body as the result of the work of the angels [blue], if you take all this into account, you can see that for as long as we are awake our angel is in the embrace of the archangels, the archai, the exusiai and indeed all the higher spiritual beings. When we then leave our physical and etheric bodies but with a materialistic attitude, our angel would be denying its relationship to the hierarchies of the archangels, the archai and the exusiai by accompanying us. You can see then the situation where our attitude determines the outcome of an extremely important event in human life, namely whether or not we are accompanied by our angel whilst sleeping. No, our angels will not accompany us at night if their existence is denied by day! This is the key to very profound secrets of human life and will at the same time demonstrate how our attitude to life will have its influence in the whole body of cosmic laws as for instance does our blood circulation in the context of what is understood, or rather not understood, by natural science.

Our I and its expectation of becoming an independent being is thus included in the entirety of the cosmos. It was only in the course of our existence on earth that we attained this I consciousness. Moreover, we did so very slowly. If we look back to ancient times where humanity still had so-called instinctive clairvoyance, we did not yet have complete awareness of I consciousness. When these ancient inhabitants of the earth had their particular visions, their instinctive visions, they were not truly their own visions, for their I was not awakened. It submitted instead to what its angel thought, to what the archangel felt and to what the archai willed. It lived so to speak in the bosom of these higher beings. We look back to this primal wisdom with wonder today but it is not human wisdom in essence. Rather it is a wisdom that came down to earth by virtue of the fact that we were in the embrace of archai, archangels and angels who then released their primal wisdom into human souls, a wisdom that much higher beings had acquired before the earth had become the earth. It is now our task with the help of our angel, to whom we must have a collaborative attitude, to acquire our own wisdom. We are moving towards this time. We are now also in a period of time where having become increasingly awake in our I we are bereft of what the archangels and angels once thought within us.

The fact, however, that we have been deserted by these angels has meant that our connection with our earthly existence has become all the stronger. This connection has meant on the one hand that we have the potential for freedom and on the other hand that we must inwardly reach up towards what we can enable the higher hierarchies to bring about within our consciousness. We must strive towards once more having thoughts that will allow the angels to live with us. These are thoughts that we can only have by means of the Imagination of spiritual science. Moreover, if by having such thoughts we become able to reorient our whole life of feeling towards the world, we will be able to reach the realm of the archangels. We currently face the danger that when we return to our physical bodies at the moment of waking up we will have no idea that we have an etheric body or that the substance of the archangels is at work in this etheric body. We will have to relearn this. Likewise relearn the fact that the primal forces, the archai, are at work in our physical form. We will have to develop an understanding of the moment of falling asleep and the moment of waking up.

Moving forward to acquire our own I, to experiencing our own I, we came out of the realms of the higher hierarchies, we became independent beings. However, this also meant that we entered another realm, the realm of Ahriman. Our I is now entering, and in full consciousness, into the realm of Ahriman.

> The earthly form goes into the realm of the exusiai.
> Something of our human form goes into the realm of the archai.
> Something of our human etheric body goes into the realm of the archangels.
> Something of our astral body passes over into the realm of the angels.
> Our I goes into the realm of Ahriman.

The danger of falling into Ahriman's realm was at its greatest around the year 333 before the Mystery of Golgotha. It was at that time that the transition was made to mere intellect, mere logic. Then the Mystery of Golgotha took place and immediately began to come to life in humanity as a whole. It is from the year 333 after the Mystery of Golgotha that the period began during which we must consciously strive towards the realm of the higher hierarchies.

It has to be said that we have not yet raised ourselves back out of the realm of Ahriman, since intellectualism only really took hold from the fifteenth century. The fact, however, that we have been living in our intellect, i.e. not in complete reality, means that we are living in a world of images, in Maya. That is also our good fortune. We are not living in the real realm of Ahriman, but in the Maya of Ahriman, in mere outward appearance in the way I have described in the last few days. This means that we can find our way out and turn back again. But it can only be done in freedom. We are living in Maya, in a world of images; our whole intellectualistic culture consists only of images. Since AD 333 it has lain within the power of humanity to strive back up again. The Catholic Church made every effort to prevent this; it must in the end be overcome to enable this striving to happen. We must strive upwards towards the spiritual Worlds.

333 BC
333 AD
666

If you add these two numbers together, you will get 666. That is the number of the beast, during which period humanity was most exposed to the real risk of sinking into the animal world. We remain exposed to this risk even after 333 AD if Ahriman's Maya has come about, if we do not strive upwards. The issue is that since we have sailed into the realm of Ahriman, right into his Maya we have become free beings. No providence, no cosmic wisdom could have prevented us from sailing into the realm of Ahriman, or we would have been left unfree.

Now bear in mind that it is one thing for us to acquire a spiritual attitude to the world and thus maintain our astral body's connection to our angel during sleep, and another to fail to acquire a spiritual attitude to life, so that our angel does not accompany us through sleep, for in that case what we bring back out of sleep will be the inspiration of Ahriman. That is how things stand today: the whole materialistic way of thinking, this tendency of humanity to be preoccupied with materialistic thoughts, is emerging more and more quickly from our sleeping condition in the present age. Our only defence against the fact that as we emerge from sleep we are condemned to materialism, i.e. being earthbound, to passing over into matter and the death of our souls, is to fill our attitude to the world with what wells up within us when we engage with the concepts of spiritual science. The sleeping condition in itself is now bringing up materialism within us. Ahriman is also trying to estrange us from our angel in other ways, and the resultant pressures are piling up. They were particularly bad in 1914 when Ahriman's forces dulled the consciousness of humanity. Our sound common sense was taken from us so that we were in a position where our angels no longer accompanied us and ahrimanic influences grew increasingly. This was the reason why I said to so many people that a right view of the origins of the war in 1914: we should not believe for example that a right view of the origins of the war in 1914 will ever be able to emerge on the basis of external documentation. Prior to that it had been possible to do research on the basis of documents in archives. What happened this time was actually more of a spiritual nature, originating in the spiritual world, and a large proportion of those who took part in events at that time did so without being fully conscious, but were led by ahrimanic influences into paralysis of their consciousness, so that the realm of the angels could no longer engage with them. It has now become necessary, if we want to understand the times we are living in, to take into account the way in which the spiritual world is influencing the course of events. This has really become a necessity.

Moreover there are many other ways in which from the depths of Ahriman's realm efforts are being made to loosen humanity from its connection to the realms of the angels, archangels, archai etc. and to draw people towards Ahriman, to draw humanity towards an ahrimanic culture. Just think of how often we hear today—I have said this for many years now—when someone has told a lie, a bare-faced lie: 'Well, he believed what he was saying and said it to the best of his knowledge and belief.' Now that makes no more difference to the objective facts than if you put your finger in the fire to the best of your knowledge and belief, no amount of divine providence will prevent you from being burned, even if you do so to the best of your knowledge and belief. Appeals to the best of your knowledge and belief are just as useless in world affairs—and it would be a sad thing if they were not. People simply do not have the freedom to be untruthful to the best of their knowledge and belief. On the contrary we have a duty to ensure that what we say is in fact true. We must be connected to the world in such a way that the thoughts that occur to us are born out of the world and not held by individuals on their own, detached from the world. Anything that is said to the best of one's knowledge and belief, and yet is not true, is invariably the result of being detached from the world. After all if someone writes: 'There is a sculpture in the building over there which has luciferic traits at the top and ahrimanic traits at the bottom'—and when others maintain, as continually happens, that he said so to the best of his knowledge and belief, it means that as a result of this attitude Ahriman has been declared the ruler of the world. For anyone who makes this assertion has a duty to check for themselves whether what they have said is true or false! It is an ahrimanic influence reaching even into our jurisprudence today if we fail to pursue rigorously something that has been asserted, but is a lie, adding that it was said in good faith. This good faith is the very worst kind of ahrimanic temptation and seduction. There is essentially nothing more seductive or tempting than these words 'in good faith'. This good faith is nothing more than a feeble excuse in the strictest sense of the word for a laziness in people who do not feel obliged to check whether something is true or false, factual or not, before stating it.

Anyone who seriously wants to counter the risk of Ahriman gaining the upper hand, quite concretely, will have to start by taking on this: 'something was said in good faith'; this appeal to good faith cuts us off from our objective context within the world. Anything that lives in us so strongly that we feel authorized to assert it must be coherent with its context in a wider world; it should not just be based on our position; everything else in the outer world has been deserted by the angels, is left to Ahriman. Any untruth put forward 'in good faith' is the most powerful means of driving us towards Ahriman, a remorseless net drawing us into his clutches. Any appeal to 'good faith' today in dealing with untruths is the best way to surrender world civilization to Ahriman.

When you can see what is at work in the world, this is the kind of thing you have to understand. It does not involve general fantasizing about angels, archangels, archai and so on in nebulous mysticism, sticking to mere theories, but does involve taking hold of the world where it really is. For it is in fact the case that humanity is losing the support of the angelic world by lazily relying on 'in good faith' with regard to matters that have not been checked, but are nevertheless asserted.

These things show how an inner determination to imbue ourselves with spiritual truths and knowledge plays out into every detail of real life. Spiritual truths and research into them must send their power down into the details of life.

This is just what makes so many people hostile to spiritual science: it is not a mere theory like other worldviews, but is alive and requires people to make the effort to overcome in themselves the laziness and inner decay evident in the tendency to appeal to 'in good faith' when representing an untruth. People do not like this and come up with all kinds of excuses for so and so having said something 'in good faith'. That is what makes our science, above all historical science, thoroughly corrupt. You can easily see that people who come up with mere assertions of the kind I described earlier lose all credibility, even if they go on to make some other assertion, when they represent conventional science for example; one has to check whether they have copied it from someone else, who perhaps belonged to the better generation, where people felt an inner obligation to test the veracity of what they wrote. When you see how people officially imitate Frohnmeyer and his kind, you will realize how much trust they place in the official scientific method and its representatives![37] It is of the greatest importance that we face up to these things. One can only hope, earnestly hope, that spiritual science will have supporters in our time who are deeply persuaded that serious devotion is needed to knowledge that will bring about profound change in the world. The issues we are dealing with today are not minor ones.

One can only wish that anthroposophy will find supporters glowing with enthusiasm to put it into practice. I mentioned in the building earlier that people who replicate lies by the dozen have today announced a forthcoming new, sensational, i.e. scandalous pamphlet. These people are hard at it. Why? Because they are capable of developing strong enthusiasm for the bad feelings in their souls. They can lie enthusiastically. We will have to get used to representing the truth just as enthusiastically or civilization will not progress any further, my dear friends!

Anyone looking out into the world today must be quite clear that we have to be serious about finding our way back to the hierarchies and out of the clutches of Ahriman. This involves pursuing issues in detail. Again and again it happens that when some unscrupulous opponent promulgates something or other to the public even our own supporters come along and say: 'We must first check whether or not it was some personal weakness that led to it.' There is unfortunately always a yearning in the Anthroposophical Society to complain about something that comes from a truthful source rather than about opponents, who out of dark impulses in their souls would trample any truth in the dirt. As long as it remains common practice in the Anthroposophical Society continually to express sympathy for untruth, we shall make no progress.

It has to be repeated from time to time, that we must recognize a lie for what it is; a lie provides a hiding place for Ahriman and it is usually a lie which when it has been uttered, will appeal to 'good faith' and 'to the best of our knowledge and belief'. I have given you plenty of examples of how people have claimed to be acting in good faith and appeal to the best of their knowledge and belief. But look at the facts and you will see the ahrimanic influence of good faith unswervingly working its way even into our courts of law. One could say that humanity has succumbed to Ahriman even in its jurisprudence. These are things that must be taken seriously if the Anthroposophical Society wishes to remain true to itself; it must be filled with a glowing sense of truth, for today that is identical with a glowing sense for the progress of humanity. Anything and every-thing else is merely filled with a leaning towards the forces of decline and will continue in that direction. What I am telling you today is not merely said for its own sake, but because the signs of our time are pressing for individual people to know this.

NOTES

Textual source: The lectures were recorded by the professional stenographer Helene Finckh (1883-1960). The printed version is based on her transcription.

1. *In the lecture cycle which I gave in Vienna in the spring of 1914*: The Inner Nature of Man and our Life between Death and Rebirth, 8 lectures, Vienna from 6 to 14 April 1914, CW 153.
2. *In the clutches of the power:* changed in line with the second transcript. Previous version 'in the clutches of the night'.
3. *Arthur Drews*, religious philosopher, in his book *The Christ Myth*, Jena 1909/1911.
4. *Professor Friedrich Traub:* 'The Teaching of Rudolf Steiner', article in the Sunday edition of *Schwäbischer Merkur* 30 April 1921.
5. *when I spoke to you here last time:* 14 December 1920, *Universal Spirituality and Human Physicality*, CW 202.
6. *70 elements:* See *Handbook of the natural sciences*, 2 vols., Jena 1912.
7. *precisely in the rhythms of the physical world* ...altered from transcript.
8. *'Not I, but the Christ in me.'* : Paul, Galatians 2:20.
9. *'Heaven and earth':* Matthew 24:35; Mark 13:31; Luke 21:33.
10. *Gustav Theodor Fechner, Professor Schleiden and the moon*, Leipzig 1856.
11. *what we have been considering in the last few weeks':* See lecture on 5 June 1921, *Materialism and the Task of Anthroposophy*, CW 204.
12. *'project into the outer world'* altered from typescript.
13. *published by a Swedish academic:* Theodor Svedberg, Swedish chemist. Presumably referring to his book *Matter*, 1912, in German 1914.
14. *Nikolai Lobachevsky: New Foundations of Geometry*, Kasan 1828. *Bernhard Riemann: On the hypotheses which lie at the foundation of geometry*, Göttingen 1854.

15. *Here I am repeating some of what I described in my public lectures,* CW 322, *The Boundaries of Natural Science,* 8 lectures, 27 September to 3 October 1920.

16. *In the cycle of lectures I gave in Vienna.* See note 1.

17. *(like the king who once ruled Spain):* King Alfonso X of Castile, 1226–1284. Compare Gottfried Wilhelm von Leibnitz, *Theodicee,* Part 2 para. 193, Hamburg and Leipzig 1744, p. 397.

18. See note 9.

19. *All-encompassing formula devised by Laplace:* Compare Rudolf Steiner's description in *The Riddles of Philosophy,* CW 18.

20. *our brains secrete thoughts..:* See Jacob Moleschott, *The cycle of life,* vol. 2, Giessen 1887 (5th edition) Ch. 18, p. 227.

21. *Saint Teresa:* Teresa de Avila, *Libro de la vida,* 1552–1565.

22. *Mechthild von Magdeburg: The flowing light of the Godhead,* Mela Escherich edition 1904 (in Rudolf Steiner's library).

23. *in a lecture by Einstein:* See Albert Einstein's 'Theory of Relativity' from a lecture given in a session of the Zürcher Naturforschenden Gesellschaft in Zürich 16 January 1911, published in *Vierteljahresschrift der Natur-forschenden Gesellschaft in Zürich,* 56th edition, vol. 2. pp. 1–14.

24. *I have already drawn attention to this: Poetry and Speech,* CW 281, *Creative Speech,* CW 280.

25. *'Our Atlantean Forebears':* in CW 11, *Cosmic Memory.*

26. *Scarcely evident in the physical form as it is now (lightly shaded).* Previously (darkly shaded).

27. *Some time ago I spoke to a smaller group in Stuttgart: Interdisciplinary Astronomy,* CW 323.

28. *I once gave some lecture courses on the subject in Berlin during the winter of 1900–1901: Mysticism at the Dawn of the Modern Age / Mystics After Modernism,* CW 7.

29. *Gerold von Gleich:* Major General, figured in lectures and pamphlets against Rudolf Steiner in 1921 and 1922.

30. *Lectures given in Vienna in the spring of 1914:* See note 1.

31. *in my Mystery Plays.:* In *The Soul's Awakening,* Scene 5 in Four Mystery Plays, CW 14.

32. *Albert Freiherr von Schrenck-Notzing:* Neurologist, researched hypnosis and mediums.

33. *Ludwig Anzengruber:* Viennese author. Quotation from *Ein Faustschlag*, a play, Act 3, Sc. 6.

34. *which was entitled Muspilli:* 'Muspilli', a fragment of an anonymous early Bavarian poem. Origin at the beginning of the ninth century. First edition by Andreas Schmeller, Munich 1832.

35. *in Bologna where I gave a lecture:* 'The psychological foundations and epistemological standpoint of Theosophy', 8 April 1911, reproduced in the volume Philosophy and Anthroposophy: Collected Essays, 1904–1923, CW 35.

36. *in a lecture in Stuttgart or Zurich:* On 14 January 1921, CW 73a; published in the journal *Gegenwart*, 14th edition, Number 4/5 July/August 1952 under the title 'Exploring the relationships of spiritual science to individual subject areas'.

37. *Frohnmeyer and his kind:* Pastor L. Johannes Frohnmeyer had written the following in his essay : 'The Theosophical movement, its history, description and evaluation' written in Stuttgart 1920: 'There is currently a 9m high statue of the ideal human being in Dornach, which is being chiselled with luciferic features at the top and with animal features at the base'. Frohnmeyer wrote to Rudolf Steiner in a letter dated 23 January 1921 that this description came from an article by Pastor Nidecker-Roos ('Christian Messenger from Basel'), 1920, dated 9 June and which he had not checked. Nidecker had made a mistake as a result of not understanding the word 'ahrimanic' and having taken it to mean 'animalic'. The publisher of the journal had changed the word to 'animal' in order to avoid using a foreign word.

Rudolf Steiner's Collected Works

The German Edition of Rudolf Steiner's Collected Works (the *Gesamtausgabe* [GA], published by Rudolf Steiner Verlag, Dornach, Switzerland) will be completed in the year 2025. The works are organized either by type of work (written, spoken, artistic creations), chronology, audience (public or other), or subject (education, art, etc.). For ease of comparison, the Collected Works in English (CW), listed below, follows the German organization and numbering.

The volumes that have so far been published in the English Collected Works edition appear *in italics with their published titles*; all other volumes, including those that have appeared in editions other than the CW, are set in Roman type with *literal translations* of the German titles. Published English titles are not necessarily the same as the German.

This list is current as of the date of this volume's publication.

A. Written Works

I. Writings 1884–1925

CW 1	Introductions and Selected Commentary on Goethe's Natural-scientific Writings
CW 1a–e	Goethe's Natural-scientific Writings
CW 1f	Editorial Afterwords to Goethe's Natural-scientific Writings in the Weimar Edition (1891–1896)
CW 2	*Goethe's Theory of Knowledge: An Outline of the Epistemology of His Worldview*
CW 3	Truth and Science
CW 4	The Philosophy of Freedom
CW 4a	Documents to 'The Philosophy of Freedom'
CW 5	Friedrich Nietzsche, A Fighter against His Own Time

CW 6	Goethe's Worldview
CW 7	Mysticism at the Dawn of Modern Spiritual Life and Its Relationship with Modern Worldviews
CW 8	*Christianity as Mystical Fact and the Mysteries of Antiquity*
CW 9	Theosophy: An Introduction into Supersensible World Knowledge and Human Purpose
CW 10	How Does One Attain Knowledge of Higher Worlds?
CW 11	From the Akasha-Chronicle
CW 12	Levels of Higher Knowledge
CW 13	Occult Science in Outline
CW 14	*Four Modern Mystery Dramas*
CW 15	The Spiritual Guidance of the Individual and Humanity
CW 16/17	*A Way of Self-Knowledge & The Threshold of the Spiritual World*
CW 18	The Riddles of Philosophy in Their History, Presented as an Outline
CW 18a	Views of the World and of Life in the Nineteenth Century
CW 19	Thoughts during the Time of War (1915) and Further Texts on the Events of the World War (1917–1921)
CW 20	The Riddles of the Human Being: Articulated and Unarticulated in the Thinking, Views and Opinions of a Series of German and Austrian Personalities
CW 21	The Riddles of the Soul
CW 22	Goethe's Spiritual Nature and Its Revelation in 'Faust' and through the 'Fairy Tale of the Snake and the Lily'
CW 23	The Central Points of the Social Question in the Necessities of Life in the Present and the Future
CW 24	Essays Concerning the Threefold Division of the Social Organism and the Period 1915–1921
CW 25	Three Steps of Anthroposophy. Philosophy – Cosmology – Religion
CW 26	Anthroposophical Leading Thoughts
CW 27	Fundamentals for Expansion of the Art of Healing according to Spiritual-Scientific Insights
CW 28	*Autobiography: Chapters in the Course of My Life: 1861–1907*

II. Collected Essays

CW 29	Collected Essays on Dramaturgy, 1889–1900
CW 30	Methodical Foundations of Anthroposophy: Collected Essays on Philosophy, Natural Science, Aesthetics and Psychology, 1884–1901
CW 31	Collected Essays on Culture and Current Events, 1887–1901
CW 32	Collected Essays on Literature, 1884–1902
CW 33	Biographies and Biographical Sketches, 1894–1905

CW 34   Lucifer-Gnosis: Foundational Essays on Anthroposophy and Reports from the Periodicals 'Luzifer' and 'Lucifer-Gnosis,' 1903–1908

CW 35   Philosophy and Anthroposophy: Collected Essays, 1904–1923

CW 36   The Goetheanum-Idea in the Middle of the Cultural Crisis of the Present: Collected Essays from the Periodical 'Das Goetheanum,' 1921–1925

CW 37   Writings on the History of the Anthroposophical Movement and Society 1902–1925

III. Publications from the Literary Estate

CW 38/1   Complete Letters, Vol. 1: Weimar Period 1879–1890

CW 38/2   Complete Letters, Vol. 2: Weimar Period 1890–1897

CW 38/3   Complete Letters, Vol. 3: Early Berlin Period 1897–1905 [forthcoming]

CW 38/4   Complete Letters, Vol. 4: Activity within the Theosophical Society 1905–1912 [forthcoming]

CW 38/5   Complete Letters, Vol. 5: From the Founding of the Anthroposophical Society to the Opening of the Goetheanum 1913–1920 [forthcoming]

CW 38/6   Compelte Letters, Vol. 6: The Last Years 1920–1925 [forthcoming]

CW 40   Truth-Wrought Words

CW 40a   Sayings, Poems and Mantras; Supplementary Volume

CW 41a   Translations and Free Renderings from the Old and New Testaments

CW 41b   Translations and Free Renderings of Various Works

CW 42   Stage Adaptations I: Dramas by Édouard Schuré

CW 43   Stage Adaptations II: The Oberúfer Christmas Plays

CW 44   Sketches, Fragments and Paralipomena on the Four Mystery Dramas

CW 45   Anthroposophy: A Fragment from the Year 1910

CW 46   Posthumous Essays and Fragments 1879–1924

CW 47/48   Notebooks and Notepads (digital edition)

CW 49   Notes for and about Helmuth and Eliza von Moltke and Relatives, 1904–1924 [forthcoming]

CW 50   [Blank number]

B. Lectures

I. Public Lectures

CW 51   *On Philosophy, History, and Literature: Lectures at the Worker Education School and the Independent College, Berlin, 1901–1905*

CW 52   Spiritual Teachings Concerning the Soul and Observation of the World

II. Lectures to the Members of the Anthroposophical Society

The Theosophy in the Gospel of John

CW 254   The Occult Movement in the 19th Century and Its Relationship to World Culture. Significant Points from the Exoteric Cultural Life around the Middle of the 19th Century

CW 255b   Anthroposophy and Its Opponents

CW 256   [Blank number]

CW 257   Anthroposophical Community-Building

CW 258   *The Anthroposophic Movement: The History and Conditions of the Anthroposophical Movement in Relation to the Anthroposophical Society: An Encouragement for Self-Examination*

CW 259   The Year of Destiny 1923 in the History of the Anthroposophical Society. From the Burning of the Goetheanum to the Christmas Conference

CW 260   The Christmas Conference for the Founding of the General Anthroposophical Society 1923/24

CW 260a   The Constitution of the General Anthroposophical Society and the School for Spiritual Science. The Rebuilding of the Goetheanum

CW 261   *Our Dead: Memorial, Funeral, and Cremation Addresses 1906–1924*

CW 262   Rudolf Steiner and Marie Steiner-von Sivers: Correspondence and Documents, 1901–1925

CW 263/1   Rudolf Steiner and Edith Maryon: Correspondence: Letters, Verses, Sketches, 1912–1924

CW 264   *From the History and Contents of the First Section of the Esoteric School: Letters, Documents, and Lectures: 1904–1914*

CW 265   *Freemasonry and Ritual Work: The Misraim Service*

CW 265a   Teaching and Instruction Lessons for Members of the Knowledge-Cultic Section of the Esoteric School 1904–1914 [forthcoming]

CW 266/1   *From the Esoteric School: Esoteric Lessons 1904–1909*

CW 266/2   *From the Esoteric School: Esoteric Lessons 1910–1912*

CW 266/3   *From the Esoteric School: Esoteric Lessons 1913–1923*

CW 267   *Soul Exercises: Word and Symbol Meditations*

CW 268   *Mantric Sayings: Meditations 1903–1925*

CW 269   Ritual Texts for the Celebration of the Free Christian Religious Instruction. The Collected Verses for Teachers and Students of the Waldorf School

CW 270   Esoteric Instructions for the First Class of the School for Spiritual Science at the Goetheanum 1924, 4 Volumes

III. Lectures and Courses on Specific Realms of Life Lectures on Art

CW 271   *Art and Theory of Art: Foundations of a New Aesthetics*

CW 272   *Anthroposophy in the Light of Goethe's Faust: Volume One of Spiritual-Scientific Commentaries on Goethe's Faust*

Lectures on Education

Lectures on Medicine

Lectures on Natural Science

Lectures on Social Life and the Threefold Arrangement of the Social Organism

CW 338   *Communicating Anthroposophy: The Course for Speakers to Promote the Idea of Threefolding*

CW 339   Anthroposophy, Threefold Social Organism, and the Art of Public Speaking

CW 340/41 *Rethinking Economics: Lectures and Seminars on World Economics*

Lectures and Courses on Christian Religious Work

CW 342   *First Steps in Christian Religious Renewal: Preparing the Ground for The Christian Community*

CW 343   Lectures and Courses on Christian Religious Work, Vol. 2: Spiritual Knowledge – Religious Feeling – Cultic Doing

CW 344   Lectures and Courses on Christian Religious Work, Vol. 3: Lectures at the Founding of The Christian Community

CW 345   Lectures and Courses on Christian Religious Work, Vol. 4: Concerning the Nature of the Working Word

CW 346   Lectures and Courses on Christian Religious Work, Vol. 5: The Apocalypse and the Work of the Priest

Lectures for Workers at the Goetheanum

CW 347   The Knowledge of the Nature of the Human Being According to Body, Soul and Spirit. On Earlier Conditions of the Earth

CW 348   On Health and Illness. Foundations of a Spiritual-Scientific Doctrine of the Senses

CW 349   On the Life of the Human Being and of the Earth. On the Nature of Christianity

CW 350   Rhythms in the Cosmos and in the Human Being. How Does One Come To See the Spiritual World?

CW 351   The Human Being and the World. The Influence of the Spirit in Nature. On the Nature of Bees

CW 352   Nature and the Human Being Observed Spiritual-Scientifically

CW 353   The History of Humanity and the World-Views of the Folk Cultures

CW 354   The Creation of the World and the Human Being. Life on Earth and the Influence of the Stars

C. Artistic Works

CW A 1–10; 57 The Architectural Work I: The Goetheanum and Its Predecessors

CW A 11   The Sculptural Work

CW A 12   The Goetheanum Windows. The Speech of Light. Sketches and Studies

CW A 13–16;
52–56   Painting Work
CW A 14   Sketches for the Painting of the Small Dome of the First Goethe-anum
CW A 27–43 The Architectural Work II: Commercial and Residential Buildings in Dornach and Other Places [forthcoming]
CW A 45   The Graphic Work
CW A 48   The Drawing Work
CW A 51   The Art of Jewellry as a Goethean Language of Form
CW A 54.0   A Path of Training in Painting. Pastel Sketches and Watercolours
CW A 54.1   Nature Moods. Nine Training Sketches for Painters

Eurythmy Figures

CW A 26   Skectches of the Eurythmy Figures
CW A 26a   The Eurythmy Figures of Rudolf Steiner, Artistically Executed by Annemarie Bäschlin
CW A 26b   Eurythmy Figures from the Time When They Were Created

Eurythmy Forms

CW A 23/1   Volume I: Eurythmy Forms for Poems by Rudolf Steiner
CW A 23/2   Volume II: Eurythmy Forms for the Calendar of the Soul by Rudolf Steiner
CW A 23/3   Volume III: Euythmy Forms for Poems by J. W. von Goethe
CW A 23/4   Volume IV: Eurythmy Forms for Poems by Christian Morgenstern
CW A 23/5   Volume V: Eurythmy Forms for Poems by Albert Steffen
CW A 23/6   Volume VI: Eurythmy Forms for German Poems by Fercher von Steinwand, Hamerling, Hebbel, C. F. Meyer, Nietzsche, among others
CW A 23/7   Volume VII: Eurythmy Forms for English Poems
CW A 23/8   Volume VIII: Eurythmy Forms for French and Russian Poems
CW A 24   Volume IX: Eurythmy Forms for Tone Eurythmy

Blackboard Drawings from Lectures

CW A 58/1   Volume I: 20 Plates from Public Lectures 1920–1924 in CWs 73a, 74, 76, and 84
CW A 58/2   Volume II: 38 Plates from Lectures in 1919 in CWs 191 and 194
CW A 58/3   Volume III: 34 Plates from Lectures in 1920 in CWs 196 and 198
CW A 58/4   Volume IV: 33 Plates from Lectures in 1920 in CWs 199 and 200
CW A 58/5   Volume V: 31 Plates from Lectures in 1920 in CW 201
CW A 58/6   Volume VI: 46 Plates from Lectures 1920–1921 in CWs 202–204

CW A 58/7   Volume VII: 38 Plates from Lectures in 1921 in CWs 205 and 206

CW A 58/8   Volume VIII: 42 Plates from Lectures in 1921 in CWs 207–209

CW A 58/9   Volume IX: 40 Plates from Lectures in 1922 in CWs 210–212

CW A 58/10   Volume X: 35 Plates from Lectures in 1922 in CWs 213–215

CW A 58/11   Volume XI: 41 Plates from Lectures 1922–1923 in CWs 216, 218–220

CW A 58/12   Volume XII: 37 Plates from Lectures in 1923 in CWs 221–225

CW A 58/13   Volume XIII: 38 Plates from Lectures in 1923 in CWs 227–230

CW A 58/14   Volume XIV: 36 Plates from Lectures in 1923 in CWs 232 and 233

CW A 58/15   Volume XV: 37 Plates from Lectures in 1924 in CWs 233a, 234, and 243

CW A 58/16   Volume XVI: 56 Plates from the 'Karma Lectures' in CWs 235–238 and 240

CW A 58/17   Volume XVII: 21 Plates from Lectures on the History of the Anthroposophical Society in CWs 257, 258, 260, and 260a

CW A 58/18   Volume XVIII: 33 Plates from Lectures on Art in CWs 271, 276, 283, 288–290, and 291

CW A 58/19   Volume XIX: 41 Plates from Lectures on Eurythmy in CWs 278, 279, and 315

CW A 58/20   Volume XX: 27 Plates from Lectures on Speech Formation in CWs 281 and 282

CW A 58/21   Volume XXI: 42 Plates from Lectures on Education in CWs 296, 303, 304, 306, and 311

CW A 58/22   Volume XXII: 46 Plates from Lectures on Medicine in CWs 312–315

CW A 58/23   Volume XXIII: 48 Plates from Lectures in 1924 in CWs 316–318

CW A 58/24   Volume XXIV: 39 Plates from Lectures on Natural Science and the Social Question in CWs 322, 326, 327, 339, and 340

CW A 58/25   Volume XXV: 33 Plates from the 'Workers Lectures' (Volumes 1 and 2) in CWs 347 and 348

CW A 58/26   Volume XXVI: 51 Plates from the 'Workers Lectures' (Volumes 3 and 4) in CWs 349 and 350

CW A 58/27   Volume XXVII: 35 Plates from the 'Workers Lectures' (Volumes 5 and 6) in CWs 351 and 352

CW A 58/28   Volume XXVIII: 42 Plates from the 'Workers Lectures' (Volumes 7 and 8) in CWs 353 and 354

CW A 58/29   Volume XXIX: 43 Plates from Lectures and Courses on Christian Religious Activity in CWs 342–344 and 346

CW A 58/30   Volume XXX: 27 Plates from CWs 255b, 324a, 337b, and 340, Corrigenda, Plates without CW Assignment, Copies

SIGNIFICANT EVENTS IN THE LIFE OF
RUDOLF STEINER

1829:	June 23: birth of Johann Steiner (1829–1910)—Rudolf Steiner's father—in Geras, Lower Austria.
1834:	May 8: birth of Franciska Blie (1834–1918)—Rudolf Steiner's mother—in Horn, Lower Austria. 'My father and mother were both children of the glorious Lower Austrian forest district north of the Danube.'
1860:	May 16: marriage of Johann Steiner and Franciska Blie.
1861:	February 25: birth of *Rudolf Joseph Lorenz Steiner* in Kraljevec, Croatia, near the border with Hungary, where Johann Steiner works as a telegrapher for the South Austria Railroad. Rudolf Steiner is baptized two days later, February 27, the date usually given as his birthday.
1862:	Summer: the family moves to Mödling, Lower Austria.
1863:	The family moves to Pottschach, Lower Austria, near the Styrian border, where Johann Steiner becomes stationmaster. 'The view stretched to the mountains . . . majestic peaks in the distance and the sweet charm of nature in the immediate surroundings.'
1864:	November 15: birth of Rudolf Steiner's sister, Leopoldine (d. November 1, 1927). She will become a seamstress and live with her parents for the rest of her life.
1866:	July 28: birth of Rudolf Steiner's deaf-mute brother, Gustav (d. May 1, 1941).
1867:	Rudolf Steiner enters the village school. Following a disagreement between his father and the schoolmaster, whose wife falsely accused the boy of causing a commotion, Rudolf Steiner is taken out of school and taught at home.
1868:	A critical experience. Unknown to the family, an aunt dies in a distant town. Sitting in the station waiting room, Rudolf Steiner sees her 'form', which speaks to him, asking for help. 'Beginning with this

experience, a new soul life began in the boy, one in which not only the outer trees and mountains spoke to him, but also the worlds that lay behind them. From this moment on, the boy began to live with the spirits of nature . . .'

1869: The family moves to the peaceful, rural village of Neudorfl, near Wiener Neustadt in present-day Austria. Rudolf Steiner attends the village school. Because of the 'unorthodoxy' of his writing and spelling, he has to do 'extra lessons'.

1870: Through a book lent to him by his tutor, he discovers geometry: 'To grasp something purely in the spirit brought me inner happiness. I know that I first learned happiness through geometry.' The same tutor allows him to draw, while other students still struggle with their reading and writing. 'An artistic element' thus enters his education.

1871: Though his parents are not religious, Rudolf Steiner becomes a 'church child', a favourite of the priest, who was 'an exceptional character'. 'Up to the age of ten or eleven, among those I came to know, he was far and away the most significant.' Among other things, he introduces Steiner to Copernican, heliocentric cosmology. As an altar boy, Rudolf Steiner serves at Masses, funerals, and Corpus Christi processions. At year's end, after an incident in which he escapes a thrashing, his father forbids him to go to church.

1872: Rudolf Steiner transfers to grammar school in Wiener-Neustadt, a five-mile walk from home, which must be done in all weathers.

1873–75: Through his teachers and on his own, Rudolf Steiner has many wonderful experiences with science and mathematics. Outside school, he teaches himself analytic geometry, trigonometry, differential equations, and calculus.

1876: Rudolf Steiner begins tutoring other students. He learns bookbinding from his father. He also teaches himself stenography.

1877: Rudolf Steiner discovers Kant's *Critique of Pure Reason,* which he reads and rereads. He also discovers and reads von Rotteck's *World History.*

1878: He studies extensively in contemporary psychology and philosophy.

1879: Rudolf Steiner graduates from high school with honours. His father is transferred to Inzersdorf, near Vienna. He uses his first visit to Vienna 'to purchase a great number of philosophy books'—Kant, Fichte, Schelling, and Hegel, as well as numerous histories of philosophy. His aim: to find a path from the 'I' to nature.

October
1879–1883: Rudolf Steiner attends the Technical College in Vienna—to study mathematics, chemistry, physics, mineralogy, botany, zoology,

biology, geology, and mechanics—with a scholarship. He also attends lectures in history and literature, while avidly reading philosophy on his own. His two favourite professors are Karl Julius Schröer (German language and literature) and Edmund Reitlinger (physics). He also audits lectures by Robert Zimmermann on aesthetics and Franz Brentano on philosophy. During this year he begins his friendship with Moritz Zitter (1861–1921), who will help support him financially when he is in Berlin.

1880: Rudolf Steiner attends lectures on Schiller and Goethe by Karl Julius Schröer, who becomes his mentor. Also 'through a remarkable combination of circumstances', he meets Felix Koguzki, a 'herb gatherer' and healer, who could 'see deeply into the secrets of nature'. Rudolf Steiner will meet and study with this 'emissary of the Master' throughout his time in Vienna.

1881: January: '... I didn't sleep a wink. I was busy with philosophical problems until about 12:30 a.m. Then, finally, I threw myself down on my couch. All my striving during the previous year had been to research whether the following statement by Schelling was true or not: *Within everyone dwells a secret, marvellous capacity to draw back from the stream of time—out of the self clothed in all that comes to us from outside—into our innermost being and there, in the immutable form of the Eternal, to look into ourselves.* I believe, and I am still quite certain of it, that I discovered this capacity in myself; I had long had an inkling of it. Now the whole of idealist philosophy stood before me in modified form. What's a sleepless night compared to that!'

Rudolf Steiner begins communicating with leading thinkers of the day, who send him books in return, which he reads eagerly.

July: 'I am not one of those who dives into the day like an animal in human form. I pursue a quite specific goal, an idealistic aim—knowledge of the truth! This cannot be done offhandedly. It requires the greatest striving in the world, free of all egotism, and equally of all resignation.'

August: Steiner puts down on paper for the first time thoughts for a 'Philosophy of Freedom'. 'The striving for the absolute: this human yearning is freedom.' He also seeks to outline a 'peasant philosophy', describing what the worldview of a 'peasant'—one who lives close to the earth and the old ways—really is.

1881–1882: Felix Koguzki, the herb gatherer, reveals himself to be the envoy of another, higher initiatory personality, who instructs Rudolf Steiner to penetrate Fichte's philosophy and to master modern scientific thinking as a preparation for right entry into the spirit. This 'Master' also teaches him the double (evolutionary and involutionary) nature of time.

1882:   Through the offices of Karl Julius Schröer, Rudolf Steiner is asked by Joseph Kürschner to edit Goethe's scientific works for the *Deutsche National-Literatur* edition. He writes 'A Possible Critique of Atomistic Concepts' and sends it to Friedrich Theodor Vischer.

1883:   Rudolf Steiner completes his college studies and begins work on the Goethe project.

1884:   First volume of Goethe's *Scientific Writings* (CW 1) appears (March). He lectures on Goethe and Lessing, and Goethe's approach to science. In July, he enters the household of Ladislaus and Pauline Specht as tutor to the four Specht boys. He will live there until 1890. At this time, he meets Josef Breuer (1842–1925), the co-author with Sigmund Freud of *Studies in Hysteria,* who is the Specht family doctor.

1885:   While continuing to edit Goethe's writings, Rudolf Steiner reads deeply in contemporary philosophy (Eduard von Hartmann, Johannes Volkelt, and Richard Wahle, among others).

1886:   May: Rudolf Steiner sends Kürschner the manuscript of *Outlines of Goethe's Theory of Knowledge* (CW 2), which appears in October, and which he sends out widely. He also meets the poet Marie Eugenie Delle Grazie and writes 'Nature and Our Ideals' for her. He attends her salon, where he meets many priests, theologians, and philosophers, who will become his friends. Meanwhile, the director of the Goethe Archive in Weimar requests his collaboration with the *Sophien* edition of Goethe's works, particularly the writings on colour.

1887:   At the beginning of the year, Rudolf Steiner is very sick. As the year progresses and his health improves, he becomes increasingly 'a man of letters', lecturing, writing essays, and taking part in Austrian cultural life. In August–September, the second volume of Goethe's *Scientific Writings* appears.

1888:   January–July: Rudolf Steiner assumes editorship of the 'German Weekly' *(Deutsche Wochenschrift)*. He begins lecturing more intensively, giving, for example, a lecture titled 'Goethe as Father of a New Aesthetics'. He meets and becomes soul friends with Friedrich Eckstein (1861–1939), a vegetarian, philosopher of symbolism, alchemist, and musician, who will introduce him to various spiritual currents (including Theosophy) and with whom he will meditate and interpret esoteric and alchemical texts.

1889:   Rudolf Steiner first reads Nietzsche *(Beyond Good and Evil)*. He encounters Theosophy again and learns of Madame Blavatsky in the theosophical circle around Marie Lang (1858–1934). Here he also meets well-known figures of Austrian life, as well as esoteric figures like the occultist Franz Hartmann and Karl Leinigen-Billigen (translator of C.G. Harrison's *The Transcendental Universe).* During this period, Steiner first reads A.P. Sinnett's *Esoteric Buddhism* and Mabel Collins's *Light on the Path.* He also begins travelling, visiting Budapest, Weimar, and Berlin (where he meets philosopher Eduard von Hartmann).

1890:   Rudolf Steiner finishes Volume 3 of Goethe's scientific writings. He begins his doctoral dissertation, which will become *Truth and Science* (CW 3). He also meets the poet and feminist Rosa Mayreder (1858–1938), with whom he can exchange his most intimate thoughts. In September, Rudolf Steiner moves to Weimar to work in the Goethe-Schiller Archive.

1891:   Volume 3 of the Kürschner edition of Goethe appears. Meanwhile, Rudolf Steiner edits Goethe's studies in mineralogy and scientific writings for the *Sophien* edition. He meets Ludwig Laistner of the Cotta Publishing Company, who asks for a book on the basic question of metaphysics. From this will result, ultimately, *The Philosophy of Freedom* (CW 4), which will be published not by Cotta but by Emil Felber. In October, Rudolf Steiner takes the oral exam for a doctorate in philosophy, mathematics, and mechanics at Rostock University, receiving his doctorate on the twenty-sixth. In November, he gives his first lecture on Goethe's 'Fairy Tale' in Vienna.

1892:   Rudolf Steiner continues work at the Goethe-Schiller Archive and on his *Philosophy of Freedom. Truth and Science,* his doctoral dissertation, is published. Steiner undertakes to write Introductions to books on Schopenhauer and Jean Paul for Cotta. At year's end, he finds lodging with Anna Eunike, née Schulz (1853–1911), a widow with four daughters and a son. He also develops a friendship with Otto Erich Hartleben (1864–1905) with whom he shares literary interests.

1893:   Rudolf Steiner begins his habit of producing many reviews and articles. In March, he gives a lecture titled 'Hypnotism, with Reference to Spiritism'. In September, volume 4 of the Kürschner edition is completed. In November, *The Philosophy of Freedom* appears. This year, too, he meets John Henry Mackay (1864–1933), the anarchist, and Max Stirner, a scholar and biographer.

1894:   Rudolf Steiner meets Elisabeth Fürster Nietzsche, the philosopher's sister, and begins to read Nietzsche in earnest, beginning with the as yet unpublished *Antichrist.* He also meets Ernst Haeckel (1834–1919). In the fall, he begins to write *Nietzsche, A Fighter against His Time* (CW 5).

1895:   May, *Nietzsche, A Fighter against His Time* appears.

1896:   January 22: Rudolf Steiner sees Friedrich Nietzsche for the first and only time. Moves between the Nietzsche and the Goethe-Schiller

Archives, where he completes his work before year's end. He falls
out with Elisabeth Förster Nietzsche, thus ending his association
with the Nietzsche Archive.

1897: Rudolf Steiner finishes the manuscript of *Goethe's Worldview*
(CW 6). He moves to Berlin with Anna Eunike and begins editorship of the *Magazin für Literatur.* From now on, Steiner will write
countless reviews, literary and philosophical articles, and so on.
He begins lecturing at the 'Free Literary Society'. In September,
he attends the Zionist Congress in Basel. He sides with Dreyfus in
the Dreyfus affair.

1898: Rudolf Steiner is very active as an editor in the political, artistic,
and theatrical life of Berlin. He becomes friendly with John Henry
Mackay and poet Ludwig Jacobowski (1868–1900). He joins Jaco-
bowski's circle of writers, artists, and scientists—'The Coming
Ones' (*Die Kommenden*)—and contributes lectures to the group
until 1903. He also lectures at the 'League for College Pedagogy'.
He writes an article for Goethe's sesquicentennial, 'Goethe's
Secret Revelation', on the 'Fairy Tale of the Green Snake and the
Beautiful Lily'.

1898–99: 'This was a trying time for my soul as I looked at Christianity.
. . . I was able to progress only by contemplating, by means of
spiritual perception, the evolution of Christianity. . . . Conscious
knowledge of real Christianity began to dawn in me around the
turn of the century. This seed continued to develop. My soul trial
occurred shortly before the beginning of the twentieth century.
It was decisive for my soul's development that I stood spiritually
before the Mystery of Golgotha in a deep and solemn celebration
of knowledge.'

1899: Rudolf Steiner begins teaching and giving lectures and lecture
cycles at the Workers' College, founded by Wilhelm Liebknecht
(1826–1900). He will continue to do so until 1904. Writes: *Literature and Spiritual Life in the Nineteenth Century; Individualism in Philosophy; Haeckel and His Opponents; Poetry in the Present;* and begins what
will become (fifteen years later) *The Riddles of Philosophy* (CW 18).
He also meets many artists and writers, including Käthe Kollwitz,
Stefan Zweig, and Rainer Maria Rilke. On October 31, he marries
Anna Eunike.

1900: 'I thought that the turn of the century must bring humanity a new
light. It seemed to me that the separation of human thinking and
willing from the spirit had peaked. A turn or reversal of direction
in human evolution seemed to me a necessity.' Rudolf Steiner finishes *World and Life Views in the Nineteenth Century* (the second part
of what will become *The Riddles of Philosophy*) and dedicates it to

Ernst Haeckel. It is published in March. He continues lecturing at *Die Kommenden,* whose leadership he assumes after the death of Jacobowski. Also, he gives the Gutenberg Jubilee lecture before 7,000 typesetters and printers. In September, Rudolf Steiner is invited by Count and Countess Brockdorff to lecture in the Theosophical Library. His first lecture is on Nietzsche. His second lecture is titled 'Goethe's Secret Revelation.' October 6, he begins a lecture cycle on the mystics that will become *Mystics after Modernism* (CW 7). November–December: 'Marie von Sivers appears in the audience. . . .' Also in November, Steiner gives his first lecture at the Giordano Bruno Bund (where he will continue to lecture until May, 1905). He speaks on Bruno and modern Rome, focusing on the importance of the philosophy of Thomas Aquinas as monism.

1901:   In continual financial straits, Rudolf Steiner's early friends Moritz Zitter and Rosa Mayreder help support him. In October, he begins the lecture cycle *Christianity as Mystical Fact* (CW 8) at the Theosophical Library. In November, he gives his first 'theosophical lecture' on Goethe's 'Fairy Tale' in Hamburg at the invitation of Wilhelm Hubbe-Schleiden. He also attends a gathering to celebrate the founding of the Theosophical Society at Count and Countess Brockdorff's. He gives a lecture cycle, 'From Buddha to Christ,' for the circle of the *Kommenden.* November 17, Marie von Sivers asks Rudolf Steiner if Theosophy needs a Western–Christian spiritual movement (to complement Theosophy's Eastern emphasis). 'The question was posed. Now, following spiritual laws, I could begin to give an answer. . . .' In December, Rudolf Steiner writes his first article for a theosophical publication. At year's end, the Brockdorffs and possibly Wilhelm Hubbe-Schleiden ask Rudolf Steiner to join the Theosophical Society and undertake the leadership of the German section. Rudolf Steiner agrees, on the condition that Marie von Sivers (then in Italy) work with him.

1902:   Beginning in January, Rudolf Steiner attends the opening of the Workers' School in Spandau with Rosa Luxemberg (1870–1919). January 17, Rudolf Steiner joins the Theosophical Society. In April, he is asked to become general secretary of the German Section of the Theosophical Society, and works on preparations for its founding. In July, he visits London for a theosophical congress. He meets Bertram Keightly, G.R.S. Mead, A.P. Sinnett, and Annie Besant, among others. In September, *Christianity as Mystical Fact* appears. In October, Rudolf Steiner gives his first public lecture on Theosophy ('Monism and Theosophy') to about three hundred people at the Giordano Bruno Bund. On October 19–21, the

German Section of the Theosophical Society has its first meeting; Rudolf Steiner is the general secretary, and Annie Besant attends. Steiner lectures on practical karma studies. On October 23, Annie Besant inducts Rudolf Steiner into the Esoteric School of the Theosophical Society. On October 25, Steiner begins a weekly series of lectures: 'The Field of Theosophy'. During this year, Rudolf Steiner also first meets Ita Wegman (1876–1943), who will become his close collaborator in his final years.

1903:   Rudolf Steiner holds about 300 lectures and seminars. In May, the first issue of the periodical *Luzifer* appears. In June, Rudolf Steiner visits London for the first meeting of the Federation of the European Sections of the Theosophical Society, where he meets Colonel Olcott. He begins to write *Theosophy* (CW 9).

1904:   Rudolf Steiner continues lecturing at the Workers' College and elsewhere (about 90 lectures), while lecturing intensively all over Germany among theosophists (about 140 lectures). In February, he meets Carl Unger (1878–1929), who will become a member of the board of the Anthroposophical Society (1913). In March, he meets Michael Bauer (1871–1929), a Christian mystic, who will also be on the board. In May, *Theosophy* appears, with the dedication: 'To the spirit of Giordano Bruno'. Rudolf Steiner and Marie von Sivers visit London for meetings with Annie Besant. June: Rudolf Steiner and Marie von Sivers attend the meeting of the Federation of European Sections of the Theosophical Society in Amsterdam. In July, Steiner begins the articles in *Luzifer-Gnosis* that will become *How to Know Higher Worlds* (CW 10) and *Cosmic Memory* (CW 11). In September, Annie Besant visits Germany. In December, Steiner lectures on Freemasonry. He mentions the High Grade Masonry derived from John Yarker and represented by Theodore Reuss and Karl Kellner as a blank slate 'into which a good image could be placed'.

1905:   This year, Steiner ends his non-theosophical lecturing activity. Supported by Marie von Sivers, his theosophical lecturing—both in public and in the Theosophical Society—increases significantly: 'The German Theosophical Movement is of exceptional importance.' Steiner recommends reading, among others, Fichte, Jacob Boehme, and Angelus Silesius. He begins to introduce Christian themes into Theosophy. He also begins to work with doctors (Felix Peipers and Ludwig Noll). In July, he is in London for the Federation of European Sections, where he attends a lecture by Annie Besant: 'I have seldom seen Mrs Besant speak in so inward and heartfelt a manner... Through Mrs Besant I have found the way to H.P. Blavatsky.' September to October, he gives a course of 31 lectures for a small group of esoteric students. In October, the annual meeting of the German Section of the Theosophical Society, which still remains very small, takes place. Rudolf Steiner reports membership has risen from 121 to 377 members. In November, seeking to establish esoteric 'continuity', Rudolf Steiner and Marie von Sivers participate in a 'Memphis-Misraim' Masonic ceremony. They pay 45 marks for membership. 'Yesterday, you saw how little remains of former esoteric institutions.' 'We are dealing only with a "framework" … for the present, nothing lies behind it. The occult powers have completely withdrawn.'

1906:   Expansion of theosophical work. Rudolf Steiner gives about 245 lectures, only 44 of which take place in Berlin. Cycles are given in Paris, Leipzig, Stuttgart, and Munich. Esoteric work also intensifies. Rudolf Steiner begins writing *An Outline of Esoteric Science* (CW 13). In January, Rudolf Steiner receives permission (a patent) from the Great Orient of the Scottish A & A Thirty-Three Degree Rite of the Order of the Ancient Freemasons of the Memphis-Misraim Rite to direct a chapter under the name 'Mystica Aeterna.' This will become the 'Cognitive-Ritual Section' (also called 'Misraim Service') of the Esoteric School. (See: *Freemasonry and Ritual Work: The Misraim Service,* CW 265.) During this time, Steiner also meets Albert Schweitzer. In May, he is in Paris, where he visits Édouard Schuré. Many Russians attend his lectures (including Konstantin Balmont, Dimitri Mereszkovski, Zinaida Hippius, and Maximilian Woloshin). He attends the General Meeting of the European Federation of the Theosophical Society, at which Col Olcott is present for the last time. He spends the year's end in Venice and Rome, where he writes and works on his translation of H.P. Blavatsky's *Key to Theosophy.*

1907:   Further expansion of the German Theosophical Movement according to the Rosicrucian directive to 'introduce spirit into the world'—in education, in social questions, in art, and in science. In February, Col Olcott dies in Adyar. Before he dies, Olcott indicates that 'the Masters' wish Annie Besant to succeed him: much politicking ensues. Rudolf Steiner supports Besant's candidacy. April–May: preparations for the Congress of the Federation of European Sections of the Theosophical Society—the great, watershed Whitsun 'Munich Congress,' attended by Annie Besant and others. Steiner decides to separate Eastern and Western (Christian–Rosicrucian) esoteric schools. He takes his esoteric school out of the Theosophical Society (Besant and Rudolf Steiner are 'in harmony' on this). Steiner makes his first lecture tours to Austria and

Hungary. That summer, he is in Italy. In September, he visits Édouard Schuré, who will write the Introduction to the French edition of *Christianity as Mystical Fact* in Barr, Alsace. Rudolf Steiner writes the autobiographical statement known as the 'Barr Document.' In *Luzifer-Gnosis*, 'The Education of the Child' appears.

1908:   The movement grows (membership: 1,150). Lecturing expands. Steiner makes his first extended lecture tour to Holland and Scandinavia, as well as visits to Naples and Sicily. Themes: St John's Gospel, the Apocalypse, Egypt, science, philosophy, and logic. *Luzifer-Gnosis* ceases publication. In Berlin, Marie von Sivers (with Johanna Mücke (1864–1949) forms the *Philosophisch-Theosophisch* (after 1915 *Philosophisch-Anthroposophisch*) *Verlag* to publish Steiner's work. Steiner gives lecture cycles titled *The Gospel of St John* (CW 103) and *The Apocalypse* (104).

1909:   *An Outline of Esoteric Science* appears. Lecturing and travel continues. Rudolf Steiner's spiritual research expands to include the polarity of Lucifer and Ahriman; the work of great individualities in history; the Maitreya Buddha and the Bodhisattvas; spiritual economy (CW 109); the work of the spiritual hierarchies in heaven and on earth (CW 110). He also deepens and intensifies his research into the Gospels, giving lectures on the Gospel of St Luke (CW 114) with the first mention of two Jesus children. Meets and becomes friends with Christian Morgenstern (1871–1914). In April, he lays the foundation stone for the Malsch model—the building that will lead to the first Goetheanum. In May, the International Congress of the Federation of European Sections of the Theosophical Society takes place in Budapest. Rudolf Steiner receives the Subba Row medal for *How to Know Higher Worlds*. During this time, Charles W. Leadbeater discovers Jiddu Krishnamurti (1895–1986) and proclaims him the future 'world teacher,' the bearer of the Maitreya Buddha and the 'reappearing Christ.' In October, Steiner delivers seminal lectures on 'anthroposophy,' which he will try, unsuccessfully, to rework over the next years into the unfinished work, *Anthroposophy (A Fragment)* (CW 45).

1910:   New themes: *The Reappearance of Christ in the Etheric* (CW 118); *The Fifth Gospel; The Mission of Folk Souls* (CW 121); *Occult History* (CW 126); the evolving development of etheric cognitive capacities. Rudolf Steiner continues his Gospel research with *The Gospel of St Matthew* (CW 123). In January, his father dies. In April, he takes a month-long trip to Italy, including Rome, Monte Cassino, and Sicily. He also visits Scandinavia again. July–August, he writes the first Mystery Drama, *The Portal of Initiation* (CW 14). In November, he gives 'psychosophy' lectures. In December, he submits 'On the

1911:

Psychological Foundations and Epistemological Framework of Theosophy' to the International Philosophical Congress in Bologna. The crisis in the Theosophical Society deepens. In January, 'The Order of the Rising Sun,' which will soon become 'The Order of the Star in the East,' is founded for the coming world teacher, Krishnamurti. At the same time, Marie von Sivers, Rudolf Steiner's co-worker, falls ill. Fewer lectures are given, but important new ground is broken. In Prague, in March, Steiner meets Franz Kafka (1883–1924) and Hugo Bergmann (1883–1975). In April, he delivers his paper to the Philosophical Congress. He writes the second Mystery Drama, *The Soul's Probation* (CW 14). Also, while Marie von Sivers is convalescing, Rudolf Steiner begins work on *Calendar 1912/1913*, which will contain the 'Calendar of the Soul' meditations. On March 19, Anna (Eunike) Steiner dies. In September, Rudolf Steiner visits Einsiedeln, birthplace of Paracelsus. In December, Friedrich Rittelmeyer, future founder of The Christian Community, meets Rudolf Steiner. The *Johannes-Bauverein,* the 'building committee,' which would lead to the first Goetheanum (first planned for Munich), is also founded, and a preliminary committee for the founding of an independent association is created that, in the following year, will become the Anthroposophical Society. Important lecture cycles include *Occult Physiology* (CW 128); *Wonders of the World* (CW 129); *From Jesus to Christ* (CW 131). Other themes: esoteric Christianity; Christian Rosenkreutz; the spiritual guidance of humanity; the sense world and the world of the spirit.

1912:

Despite the ongoing, now increasing crisis in the Theosophical Society, much is accomplished: *Calendar 1912/1913* is published; eurythmy is created; both the third Mystery Drama, *The Guardian of the Threshold* (CW 14) and *A Way of Self-Knowledge* (CW 16) are written. New (or renewed) themes included life between death and rebirth and karma and reincarnation. Other lecture cycles: *Spiritual Beings in the Heavenly Bodies and in the Kingdoms of Nature* (CW 136); *The Human Being in the Light of Occultism, Theosophy, and Philosophy* (CW 137); *The Gospel of St Mark* (CW 139); and *The Bhagavad Gita and the Epistles of Paul* (CW 142). On May 8, Rudolf Steiner celebrates White Lotus Day, H.P. Blavatsky's death day, which he had faithfully observed for the past decade, for the last time. In August, Rudolf Steiner suggests the 'independent association' be called the 'Anthroposophical Society.' In September, the first eurythmy course takes place. In October, Rudolf Steiner declines recognition of a Theosophical Society lodge dedicated to the Star of the East and decides to expel all Theosophical Society members belonging to the order.

Also, with Marie von Sivers, he first visits Dornach, near Basel, Switzerland, and they stand on the hill where the Goetheanum will be built. In November, a Theosophical Society lodge is opened by direct mandate from Adyar (Annie Besant). In December, a meeting of the German section occurs at which it is decided that belonging to the Order of the Star of the East is incompatible with membership in the Theosophical Society. December 28: informal founding of the Anthroposophical Society in Berlin.

1913: Expulsion of the German section from the Theosophical Society. February 2–3: Foundation meeting of the Anthroposophical Society. Board members include: Marie von Sivers, Michael Bauer, and Carl Unger. September 20: Laying of the foundation stone for the *Johannes Bau* (Goetheanum) in Dornach. Building begins immediately. The fourth Mystery Drama, *The Soul's Awakening* (CW 14), is completed. Also: *The Threshold of the Spiritual World* (CW 147). Lecture cycles include: *The Bhagavad Gita and the Epistles of Paul* and *The Esoteric Meaning of the Bhagavad Gita* (CW 146), which the Russian philosopher Nikolai Berdyaev attends; *The Mysteries of the East and of Christianity* (CW 144); *The Effects of Esoteric Development* (CW 145); and *The Fifth Gospel* (CW 148). In May, Rudolf Steiner is in London and Paris, where anthroposophical work continues.

1914: Building continues on the *Johannes Bau* (Goetheanum) in Dornach, with artists and co-workers from seventeen nations. The general assembly of the Anthroposophical Society takes place. In May, Rudolf Steiner visits Paris, as well as Chartres Cathedral. June 28: assassination in Sarajevo ('Now the catastrophe has happened!'). August 1: War is declared. Rudolf Steiner returns to Germany from Dornach—he will travel back and forth. He writes the last chapter of *The Riddles of Philosophy*. Lecture cycles include: *Human and Cosmic Thought* (CW 151); *Inner Being of Humanity between Death and a New Birth* (CW 153); *Occult Reading and Occult Hearing* (CW 156). December 24: marriage of Rudolf Steiner and Marie von Sivers.

1915: Building continues. Life after death becomes a major theme, also art. Writes: *Thoughts during a Time of War* (CW 24). Lectures include: *The Secret of Death* (CW 159); *The Uniting of Humanity through the Christ Impulse* (CW 165).

1916: Rudolf Steiner begins work with Edith Maryon (1872–1924) on the sculpture 'The Representative of Humanity' ('The Group'— Christ, Lucifer, and Ahriman). He also works with the alchemist Alexander von Bernus on the quarterly *Das Reich*. He writes *The Riddle of Humanity* (CW 20). Lectures include: *Necessity and Freedom in World History and Human Action* (CW 166); *Past and Present in the*

Human Spirit (CW 167); *The Karma of Vocation* (CW 172); *The Karma of Untruthfulness* (CW 173).

1917:   Russian Revolution. The U.S. enters the war. Building continues. Rudolf Steiner delineates the idea of the 'threefold nature of the human being' (in a public lecture March 15) and the 'threefold nature of the social organism' (hammered out in May–June with the help of Otto von Lerchenfeld and Ludwig Polzer-Hoditz in the form of two documents titled *Memoranda,* which were distributed in high places). August–September: Rudolf Steiner writes *The Riddles of the Soul* (CW 20). Also: commentary on 'The Chymical Wedding of Christian Rosenkreutz' for Alexander Bernus (*Das Reich*). Lectures include: *The Karma of Materialism* (CW 176); *The Spiritual Background of the Outer World: The Fall of the Spirits of Darkness* (CW 177).

1918:   March 18: peace treaty of Brest-Litovsk—'Now everything will truly enter chaos! What is needed is cultural renewal.' June: Rudolf Steiner visits Karlstein (Grail) Castle outside Prague. Lecture cycle: *From Symptom to Reality in Modern History* (CW 185). In mid-November, Emil Molt, of the Waldorf-Astoria Cigarette Company, has the idea of founding a school for his workers' children.

1919:   Focus on the threefold social organism: tireless travel, countless lectures, meetings, and publications. At the same time, a new public stage of Anthroposophy emerges as cultural renewal begins. The coming years will see initiatives in pedagogy, medicine, pharmacology, and agriculture. January 27: threefold meeting: 'We must first of all, with the money we have, found free schools that can bring people what they need.' February: first public eurythmy performance in Zurich. Also: 'Appeal to the German People' (CW 24), circulated March 6 as a newspaper insert. In April, *Towards Social Renewal* (CW 23) appears—'perhaps the most widely read of all books on politics appearing since the war'. Rudolf Steiner is asked to undertake the 'direction and leadership' of the school founded by the Waldorf-Astoria Company. Rudolf Steiner begins to talk about the 'renewal' of education. May 30: a building is selected and purchased for the future Waldorf School. August–September, Rudolf Steiner gives a lecture course for Waldorf teachers, *The Foundations of Human Experience (Study of Man)* (CW 293). September 7: Opening of the first Waldorf School. December (into January): first science course, the *Light Course* (CW 320).

1920:   The Waldorf School flourishes. New threefold initiatives. Founding of limited companies *Der Kommende Tag* and *Futurum A.G.* to infuse spiritual values into the economic realm. Rudolf Steiner also focuses on the sciences. Lectures: *Introducing Anthroposophical*

Medicine (CW 312); *The Warmth Course* (CW 321); *The Boundaries of Natural Science* (CW 322); *The Redemption of Thinking* (CW 74). February: Johannes Werner Klein—later a co-founder of The Christian Community—asks Rudolf Steiner about the possibility of a 'religious renewal,' a 'Johannine church.' In March, Rudolf Steiner gives the first course for doctors and medical students. In April, a divinity student asks Rudolf Steiner a second time about the possibility of religious renewal. September 27–October 16: anthroposophical 'university course.' December: lectures titled *The Search for the New Isis* (CW 202).

1921:   Rudolf Steiner continues his intensive work on cultural renewal, including the uphill battle for the threefold social order. 'University' arts, scientific, theological, and medical courses include: *The Astronomy Course* (CW 323); *Observation, Mathematics, and Scientific Experiment* (CW 324); the *Second Medical Course* (CW 313); *Colour.* In June and September–October, Rudolf Steiner also gives the first two 'priests' courses' (CW 342 and 343). The 'youth movement' gains momentum. Magazines are founded: *Die Drei* (January), and—under the editorship of Albert Steffen (1884–1963)—the weekly, *Das Goetheanum* (August). In February–March, Rudolf Steiner takes his first trip outside Germany since the war (Holland). On April 7, Steiner receives a letter regarding 'religious renewal,' and May 22–23, he agrees to address the question in a practical way. In June, the Klinical-Therapeutic Institute opens in Arlesheim under the direction of Dr Ita Wegman. In August, the Chemical-Pharmaceutical Laboratory opens in Arlesheim (Oskar Schmiedel and Ita Wegman are directors). The Clinical Therapeutic Institute is inaugurated in Stuttgart (Dr Ludwig Noll is director); also the Research Laboratory in Dornach (Ehrenfried Pfeiffer and Gunther Wachsmuth are directors). In November–December, Rudolf Steiner visits Norway.

1922:   The first half of the year involves very active public lecturing (thousands attend); in the second half, Rudolf Steiner begins to withdraw and turn toward the Society—'The Society is asleep.' It is 'too weak' to do what is asked of it. The businesses—*Der Kommende Tag* and *Futurum A.G.*—fail. In January, with the help of an agent, Steiner undertakes a twelve-city German lecture tour, accompanied by eurythmy performances. In two weeks he speaks to more than 2,000 people. In April, he gives a 'university course' in The Hague. He also visits England. In June, he is in Vienna for the East–West Congress. In August–September, he is back in England for the Oxford Conference on Education. Returning to Dornach, he gives the lectures *Philosophy, Cosmology, and*

Religion (CW 215), and gives the third priests' course (CW 344). On September 16, The Christian Community is founded. In October–November, Steiner is in Holland and England. He also speaks to the youth: *The Youth Course* (CW 217). In December, Steiner gives lectures titled *The Origins of Natural Science* (CW 326), and *Humanity and the World of Stars: The Spiritual Communion of Humanity* (CW 219). December 31: Fire at the Goetheanum, which is destroyed.

1923:
Despite the fire, Rudolf Steiner continues his work unabated. A very hard year. Internal dispersion, dissension, and apathy abound. There is conflict—between old and new visions—within the Society. A wake-up call is needed, and Rudolf Steiner responds with renewed lecturing vitality. His focus: the spiritual context of human life; initiation science; the course of the year; and community building. As a foundation for an artistic school, he creates a series of pastel sketches. Lecture cycles: *The Anthroposophical Movement; Initiation Science* (CW 227) (in Wales at the Penmaenmawr Summer School); *The Four Seasons and the Archangels* (CW 229); *Harmony of the Creative Word* (CW 230); *The Supersensible Human* (CW 231), given in Holland for the founding of the Dutch Society. On November 10, in response to the failed Hitler-Ludendorff putsch in Munich, Steiner closes his Berlin residence and moves the *Philosophisch-Anthroposophisch Verlag* (Press) to Dornach. On December 9, Steiner begins the serialization of his *Autobiography: The Course of My Life* (CW 28) in *Das Goetheanum*. It will continue to appear weekly, without a break, until his death. Late December–early January: Rudolf Steiner re-founds the Anthroposophical Society (about 12,000 members internationally) and takes over its leadership. The new board members are: Marie Steiner, Ita Wegman, Albert Steffen, Elisabeth Vreede, and Gunther Wachsmuth. (See *The Christmas Meeting for the Founding of the General Anthroposophical Society,* CW 260.) Accompanying lectures: *Mystery Knowledge and Mystery Centres* (CW 232); *World History in the Light of Anthroposophy* (CW 233). December 25: the Foundation Stone is laid (in the hearts of members) in the form of the 'Foundation Stone Meditation.'

1924:
January 1: having founded the Anthroposophical Society and taken over its leadership, Rudolf Steiner has the task of 'reforming' it. The process begins with a weekly newssheet ('What's Happening in the Anthroposophical Society') in which Rudolf Steiner's 'Letters to Members' and 'Anthroposophical Leading Thoughts' appear (CW 26). The next step is the creation of a new esoteric class, the 'first class' of the 'University of Spiritual Science' (which was to have been followed, had Rudolf Steiner lived longer, by two more advanced classes). Then comes a new language for

Anthroposophy—practical, phenomenological, and direct; and Rudolf Steiner creates the model for the second Goetheanum. He begins the series of extensive 'karma' lectures (CW 235–40); and finally, responding to needs, he creates two new initiatives: biodynamic agriculture and curative education. After the middle of the year, rumours begin to circulate regarding Steiner's health. Lectures: January–February, *Anthroposophy* (CW 234); February: *Tone Eurythmy* (CW 278); June: *The Agriculture Course* (CW 327); June–July: *Speech Eurythmy* (CW 279); *Curative Education* (CW 317); August: (England, 'Second International Summer School'), *Initiation Consciousness: True and False Paths in Spiritual Investigation* (CW 243); September: *Pastoral Medicine* (CW 318). On September 26, for the first time, Rudolf Steiner cancels a lecture. On September 28, he gives his last lecture. On September 29, he withdraws to his studio in the carpenter's shop; now he is definitively ill. Cared for by Ita Wegman, he continues working, however, and writing the weekly instalments of his *Autobiography* and *Letters to the Members/ Leading Thoughts* (CW 26).

1925:   Rudolf Steiner, while continuing to work, continues to weaken. He finishes *Extending Practical Medicine* (CW 27) with Ita Wegman. On March 30, around ten in the morning, Rudolf Steiner dies.

INDEX

A NOTE FROM RUDOLF STEINER PRESS

We are an independent publisher and registered charity (non-profit organisation) dedicated to making available the work of Rudolf Steiner in English translation. We care a great deal about the content of our books and have hundreds of titles available – as printed books, ebooks and in audio formats.

As a publisher devoted to anthroposophy...

- We continually commission translations of previously unpublished works by Rudolf Steiner and invest in re-translating, editing and improving our editions.

- We are committed to making anthroposophy available to all by publishing introductory books as well as contemporary research.

- Our new print editions and ebooks are carefully checked and proofread for accuracy, and converted into all formats for all platforms.

- Our translations are officially authorised by Rudolf Steiner's estate in Dornach, Switzerland, to whom we pay royalties on sales, thus assisting their critical work.

So, look out for Rudolf Steiner Press as a mark of quality and support us today by buying our books, or contact us should you wish to sponsor specific titles or to support the charity with a gift or legacy.

office@rudolfsteinerpress.com
Join our e-mailing list at www.rudolfsteinerpress.com

RUDOLF STEINER PRESS